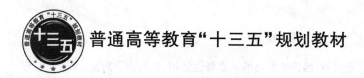

普通高等教育"十三五"规划教材

实用汉英翻译教程

主　编　秦罡引

北京邮电大学出版社
www.buptpress.com

内 容 简 介

《实用汉英翻译教程》共包括12章内容,涵盖了翻译的基本概念知识、汉英语言对比、汉语词汇翻译、汉语成语翻译、汉语句子翻译、汉语篇章翻译及新闻、旅游、科技、商务、法律、文学等各类汉语文本翻译的基本技巧与实例。每一章还提供了相关的译文欣赏和实践练习等内容。附录除提供实践练习参考译文外,还补充了20篇短文翻译练习及参考译文,以及大学英语四级翻译真题及参考译文。本书将为广大读者,特别是在校大学生学习汉英翻译提供帮助。

图书在版编目(CIP)数据

实用汉英翻译教程 / 秦罡引主编. - - 北京:北京邮电大学出版社,2018.9
ISBN 978-7-5635-5070-8

Ⅰ.①实… Ⅱ.①秦… Ⅲ.①英语 – 翻译 – 教材 Ⅳ.①H315.9

中国版本图书馆 CIP 数据核字(2018)第 213238 号

书　　　名:	实用汉英翻译教程
著作责任者:	秦罡引　主编
责任编辑:	徐振华　廖娟
出版发行:	北京邮电大学出版社
社　　　址:	北京市海淀区西土城路10号(邮编:100876)
发　行　部:	电话:010-62282185　传真:010-62283578
E-mail:	publish@bupt.edu.cn
经　　　销:	各地新华书店
印　　　刷:	北京玺诚印务有限公司
开　　　本:	787 mm×1 092 mm　1/16
印　　　张:	10.5
字　　　数:	255 千字
版　　　次:	2018年9月第1版　2018年9月第1次印刷

ISBN 978-7-5635-5070-8　　　　　　　　　　　　　　　　　　定　价:25.00元
・如有印装质量问题,请与北京邮电大学出版社发行部联系・

编委会

主　编　秦罡引
副主编　陆　同　毕海荣
编　委　程　呈　屈璟华　吴银燕
　　　　孙　艾　王佩玉　刘　倩

前　言

　　翻译是外语学习者应当掌握的语言技能之一。近年来，汉英翻译已被列入大学英语四、六级考试内容，旨在考察学生的英语应用能力。翻译涉及两种语言、两种文化，与英语听、说、读、写基本技能相比更为综合。培养学生的翻译能力，特别是汉英翻译能力，已成为各高校大学英语教学的目标之一。翻译作为大学英语课程培养的主要技能受到广泛重视并被列入大学英语后续课程或拓展课程。

　　《实用汉英翻译教程》针对大学英语教学特点，突出实用性、实践性，既对翻译的基本原理、英汉两种语言的对比进行了简要的阐述，也对汉英翻译的技巧方法加以重点介绍，并配以丰富的例证讲解汉英翻译的技巧和方法。重视技巧方法同时，更强调翻译实践能力的培养。

　　《实用汉英翻译教程》在简要介绍翻译的基本概念及对汉英两种语言进行分析对比的基础上，从汉语词汇、成语的翻译入手，逐步探讨汉语句子、篇章的翻译，最后过渡到各类汉语文本的翻译，形成一个层进式的逻辑体系。每一章都包括一个译文欣赏部分，目的是帮助读者逐步提高翻译鉴赏能力，进而达到提高翻译技能的目的。实践练习部分难度、题量适中，以方便学生进行课后练习。

　　《实用汉英翻译教程》附录 1 为每一章的实践练习参考译文，附录 2 的短文翻译练习为学生课外自主训练提供了丰富的资源，附录 3 为大学英语四级历年汉英翻译真题及参考译文，可为学生参加四级考试提供复习参考依据。

　　限于编者水平与经验，书中疏漏与不当之处在所难免，恳请广大读者批评指正。

编者

目 录

第一章 绪论 ……………………………………………………………… 1
一、翻译的基本概念 ……………………………………………………… 1
二、翻译的方法与步骤 …………………………………………………… 2
三、翻译的标准 …………………………………………………………… 4
四、译文欣赏 ……………………………………………………………… 6
五、实践练习 ……………………………………………………………… 6

第二章 汉英语言对比 …………………………………………………… 8
一、汉英词汇对比 ………………………………………………………… 8
二、汉英句法对比 ………………………………………………………… 10
三、汉英篇章对比 ………………………………………………………… 13
四、译文欣赏 ……………………………………………………………… 15
五、实践练习 ……………………………………………………………… 16

第三章 汉语词汇的翻译 ………………………………………………… 17
一、选择词义 ……………………………………………………………… 17
二、词汇翻译的转性译法 ………………………………………………… 20
三、词汇翻译的具体法和抽象法 ………………………………………… 24
四、译文欣赏 ……………………………………………………………… 25
五、实践练习 ……………………………………………………………… 26

第四章 汉语成语的翻译 ………………………………………………… 28
一、套译法 ………………………………………………………………… 28
二、意译法 ………………………………………………………………… 31
三、加注法 ………………………………………………………………… 32
四、译文欣赏 ……………………………………………………………… 33
五、实践练习 ……………………………………………………………… 35

第五章 汉语句子的翻译 ………………………………………………… 36
一、顺序译法 ……………………………………………………………… 36
二、换序译法 ……………………………………………………………… 37
三、断句译法 ……………………………………………………………… 39
四、合句译法 ……………………………………………………………… 41

1

五、译文欣赏 …… 43
　　六、实践练习 …… 46

第六章　汉语篇章的翻译 …… 47
　　一、衔接的翻译 …… 47
　　二、连贯的翻译 …… 50
　　三、风格的翻译 …… 52
　　四、译文欣赏 …… 55
　　五、实践练习 …… 57

第七章　新闻文本的翻译 …… 59
　　一、标题的翻译 …… 59
　　二、新闻报道的翻译 …… 61
　　三、汉英篇章对比 …… 63
　　四、译文欣赏 …… 66
　　五、实践练习 …… 67

第八章　旅游文本的翻译 …… 69
　　一、人名、地名的翻译 …… 69
　　二、景点介绍的翻译 …… 71
　　三、历史典故的翻译 …… 73
　　四、译文欣赏 …… 75
　　五、实践练习 …… 76

第九章　科技文本的翻译 …… 77
　　一、论文摘要的翻译 …… 77
　　二、科技报告的翻译 …… 80
　　三、专利说明书的翻译 …… 82
　　四、译文欣赏 …… 83
　　五、实践练习 …… 84

第十章　商务文本的翻译 …… 86
　　一、商标、品牌的翻译 …… 86
　　二、商务广告的翻译 …… 88
　　三、商务合同的翻译 …… 89
　　四、商品说明书的翻译 …… 91
　　五、译文赏析 …… 93
　　六、实践练习 …… 94

第十一章　法律文本的翻译 …… 96
　　一、协议条约的翻译 …… 96

二、立法文本的翻译 …………………………………………………… 99
　　三、讼诉文书的翻译 …………………………………………………… 101
　　四、译文欣赏 …………………………………………………………… 102
　　五、实践练习 …………………………………………………………… 104
第十二章　文学文本的翻译 …………………………………………… 105
　　一、诗词的翻译 ………………………………………………………… 105
　　二、散文的翻译 ………………………………………………………… 107
　　三、小说的翻译 ………………………………………………………… 110
　　四、译文欣赏 …………………………………………………………… 112
　　五、实践练习 …………………………………………………………… 113
附录1　实践练习参考译文 …………………………………………… 114
附录2　短文翻译练习 ………………………………………………… 123
附录3　大学英语四级翻译历年真题及参考译文 …………………… 134
参考文献 ………………………………………………………………… 155

第一章 绪 论

一、翻译的基本概念

翻译是人们在语言交流过程中用两种或两种以上语言进行沟通的桥梁,它的目的是把一种语言,也称为源语(source language)所表达的信息用另一种语言,也称为目标语(target language)完整地再现出来。

Cambridge Encyclopedia of Languages(《剑桥语言百科全书》)将翻译描述为:It is sometimes said that there is no task more complex than translation — a claim that can be readily believed when all the variables involved are taken into account. Translators not only need to know their source language well; they must also have a thorough understanding of the field of knowledge covered by the source text, and of any social, cultural, or emotional connotations that need to be specified in the target language if the intended effect is to be conveyed. The same special awareness needs to be present for the target language, so that points of special phrasing, local (e.g. regional) expectations, and so on, can all be taken into account.

美国语言学家、翻译家、翻译理论家尤金·A. 奈达(Eugene A. Nida)指出,Translation consists in reproducing in the receptor language the closest natural equivalent of the source language message, first in terms of meaning and secondly in terms of style. 翻译是用最恰当、自然和对等的语言从语义到文体再现源语的信息。奈达有关翻译的定义指明,翻译不仅是词汇意义上的对等,还包括语义、风格和文体的对等,翻译传达的信息既有表层词汇信息,又有深层的文化信息。

英国著名的翻译家和翻译理论家彼得·纽马克(Peter Newmark)对翻译的定义如下:
Translation is first a science, which entails the knowledge and verification of the facts and the language that describe them — here, what is wrong, mistakes of truth, can be identified;

Secondly, it is a skill, which calls for appropriate language and acceptable usage;

Thirdly, an art, which distinguishes good from undistinguished writing and is the creative, the intuitive, sometimes the inspired, level of the translation;

Lastly, a matter of taste, where argument ceases, preference are expressed, and the variety of meritorious translation is the reflection of individual differences.

古今中国的专家学者对翻译的定义也不胜枚举。唐代语言学家贾公彦指出:"译即易,谓换易言语使相解也"。现代著名散文翻译家张培基将翻译定义为:"翻译是运用一种语言把另一种语言所表达的思维内容准确而整体地重新表达出来的语言活动"。当代著名的英美文学翻译家孙致礼指出:"翻译是把一种语言表达的意义用另一种语言传达出来,以达到沟通思想情感、传播文化知识、促进社会文明,特别是推动译语文化兴旺昌盛的目的"。

对于翻译在历史上的地位和意义,不少学者都有过评说。国学大师季羡林曾说:"中华文化之所以能常葆青春,万灵智药就是翻译。翻译之为用大矣哉!"

目前,全世界有3 000多种语言,其中汉语是使用最为广泛的语言之一。中华民族的文化博大精深,是世界优秀文化遗产中一颗璀璨的明珠。在其5000年的历史中,中国文化对人类发展与进步有着不可磨灭的贡献。在经济全球化的今天,弘扬中国优秀的文化与传统,让世界了解中国,是中国学者和翻译工作者的历史使命。

翻译活动在中国由来已久,2000多年前的周朝,翻译的概念就已经出现了。在《礼记》中就有记载:"中国、夷、蛮、戎、狄……五方之民,言语不通,嗜欲不同。达其志,通其欲,东方曰寄,南方曰象,西方曰狄鞮,北方曰译。"东汉末年(公元150年),有人将佛经译为汉语。到了唐朝,丰富的佛经翻译实践造就了一批翻译理论家,如玄奘等。到了清朝,当推著名的翻译家严复,他翻译了赫胥黎的《天演论》(Theory of Evolution)和亚当·斯密的《原富》(The Wealth of Nations)。"五四运动"之后,我国出现了诸如鲁迅、瞿秋白、郭沫若、朱生豪、林语堂、钱钟书等一批伟大的翻译家,此后,翻译经历着发展的高潮。

翻译活动在西方也有2000多年的历史。早在公元前3世纪,学者们就把希伯来语的《圣经》译为希腊语。到了公元5世纪,为了传播基督教,又将《圣经》译为拉丁语。14到16世纪文艺复兴时期,出现了英文版的《圣经钦定本》以及《伊利亚特》《奥德赛》的英译本。第二次世界大战后,随着经济与科技的飞速发展,出现了机器翻译,翻译在西方文明发展中发挥着越来越大的作用。

二、翻译的方法与步骤

(一)翻译的方法

翻译的方法通常包括直译和意译,近年来又出现了归化法和异化法。

直译(Literal Translation):指译文语言条件许可时,在译文中既保持原文内容,又保持原文的形式——特别指原文的比喻、形象和民族、地方色彩等。例如:

浑水摸鱼:fish in troubled water
趁热打铁:strike while the iron is hot
连锁反应:chain reaction
君子协定:gentleman's agreement

酒后吐真言。
[译文]There is truth in wine.
好事不出门,坏事传千里。
[译文]Bad news travels fast.

希特勒在发动第二次世界大战时是武装到牙齿的,可是没过几年,就被彻底击败了。

[译文]Hitler was armed to teeth when he launched the Second World War, but in a few years, he was completely defeated.

在老头子的葬礼上,他们只不过挤了几滴鳄鱼的眼泪,因为在他生前,没人真正喜欢他。

[译文]They were crying crocodile tears at the old man's funeral because nobody had really liked him.

直译不等于死译。如果以词为单位,严格、机械地将译入语的词汇与原文对等,过分拘泥于原文的形式,译文就会生硬晦涩,往往是佶屈聱牙、难以卒读,或根本无法理解。

意译(Liberal/Free Translation):指既忠实原文内容,又不拘泥原文结构形式与修辞手法的翻译方法。

由于英汉两种语言所涉及的地域文化、思维方式有很大的差异,简单地用直译法不仅会使译文晦涩难懂,而且还会出现误译、错译。例如:早恋不能译为 early love,豆腐渣工程不能翻译为 bean-curd project,民族委员会不能译为 national committee。而应按照目标语言对应的表达方式进行翻译,正确的译文应为: puppy love, jerry-built project, ethnic affairs commission。类似的例子还有:

多此一举 carry coal to Newcastle
对牛弹琴 cast pearls before a swine
一贫如洗 as poor as a church mouse
悬梁刺股 be extremely hardworking in one's study

她出生于富贵人家。

[译文]She was born with a silver spoon in her mouth.

直译与意译没有优劣之分,二者相互协调、互相渗透、互为补充、不可分割。它们之间也没有任何排斥关系,好的译作是二者的结合体。

归化法是要把源语本土化,以目标语或译文读者为归宿,采取目标语读者所习惯的表达方式来传达原文的内容。归化翻译要求译者向目的语的读者靠拢,译者必须像本国作者那样说话,原作者要想和读者直接对话,译作必须变成地道的本国语言。归化翻译有助于读者更好地理解译文,增强译文的可读性和欣赏性。

异化法是译者尽可能不去打扰作者,让读者向作者靠拢。在翻译上就是迁就外来文化的语言特点,吸纳外语表达方式,要求译者向作者靠拢,采取相应于作者所使用的源语表达方式,来传达原文的内容,即以目的语文化为归宿。使用异化策略的目的在于考虑民族文化的差异性,保存及反映异域民族特征和语言风格特色,为译文读者保留异国情调。

归化和异化作为两种翻译方法是对立统一、相辅相成的,绝对的归化和绝对的异化都是不存在的。在翻译实践中,译者应根据具体的源语和目的语的语言特点、民族文化等,恰当运用两种翻译方法,以达到具体的、动态的统一。

(二)翻译的步骤

翻译的步骤通常包括理解、表达和校核三个阶段。在翻译实践中,理解是表达的前提,但理解与表达通常是相互联系、相辅相成的统一过程,不能截然分开。译者在理解原文的同时,也在选择表达方式;在表达的同时,又会进一步加深理解。

理解是翻译过程的第一阶段。它既包括对语言现象和文化现象的理解,又包括对逻辑关系的理解,对有可能发生歧义的语句要善于分析,进而做出正确判断。例如:

法官的责任感战胜了父子私情,他还是宣判自己的儿子有罪。

[译文]He allowed the father to be overruled by the judge, and declared his own son guilty.

如果我们试图实施这些轻率而愚蠢的主张,以印度语和其他15种官方承认的各邦语言取代英语的话,印度就会因语言的纷杂而乱成一团。

[译文]If we try to implement these harebrained ideas that English should be replaced by Hindi and the 15 recognized state languages, India will become a Tower of Babel.

表达阶段是译者把自己从原文所理解的内容用目的语重新表达出来的过程。表达是理解的结果,但理解正确并不意味着必然能表达得正确。因此,我们必须学习许多具体的方法和技巧,如直译、意译、直译加意译和直译加注释等。例如:

焚书坑儒

[译文]Burn books and bury scholars. This is a notorious culture-ruining act in Qin dynasty in China. In order to consolidate his rule, the first emperor of the Qin dynasty ordered that all classics be burned and scholars who had not obey the order be buries alive.

谋事在人,成事在天。

[译文]Man proposes, God disposes.

冰冻三尺,非一日之寒。

[译文]Rome is not built in one day.

我觉得那个年轻人不怎么样。

[译文]I have no opinion of that young man.

这对年轻夫妇并不相配,一个西施,一个张飞。

[译文]The couple is not well matched, one is Xi Shi — a famous Chinese beauty, while the other is Zhang Fei — a well-known ill-tempered brute.

校核是把译文与原文进行比较。至少校核两遍:

第一遍,对照原文校对,检查有无疏漏、误译的地方;

第二遍,脱离原文审校,检查有无生硬、拗口的地方。

三、翻译的标准

翻译标准就是指翻译实践时译者所遵循的原则,任何翻译实践总要遵循一定的翻译标准或原则,衡量一篇译文的好坏同样也离不开一定的翻译标准,因此翻译标准的确立对于指导翻译实践有着重要的意义。然而由于人们看待翻译的角度不同,自然有了不同的翻译标准。概括起来,它们大体可分为以下三类。

1. 以作者和读者为取向的翻译原则(the author-and-reader-oriented translation principle)。这一原则考虑作者的同时,又考虑了读者,比较全面。持这一原则的人在西方有18世纪末的英国学者亚历山大·泰特勒(Alexander Fraser Tytler,1747—1814),他在《论翻译的原则》

(*Essay on the Principles of Translation*)一书中提出了著名的翻译三原则:

(1)译文应完全复写出原作的思想。(A translation should give a complete transcript of the ideas of the original work.)

(2)译文的风格和笔调应与原文的性质相同。(The style and manner of writing should be of the same character as that of the original.)

(3)译文应和原作同样流畅。(A translation should have all the ease of the original composition.)

在我国持这一翻译原则的有玄奘、严复和鲁迅等人。玄奘是唐代著名的佛经翻译家,主张翻译"既须求真又须喻俗"(A good translation should be both faithful to the original and intelligible to the public.),意即译文要"忠实通顺"。严复是我国清末时期的名学者,他在《天演论》(译例言)(1898)中提出了"信、达、雅"三字标准(faithfulness, expressiveness and elegance)。"信"是"意义不背本文"。"达"是不拘原文形式,尽译文语音的能事以求原意明显。"信""达"互为照应,不可分割开来。"雅"在今天看来是不可取的,因为这个"雅"是用汉朝以前字法句法,即所谓的上等文言文。鲁迅先生认为:"凡是翻译,必须兼顾两面,一当然力求其易解,一则保存着原作的丰姿。"这就是说,译文既要信,又要顺(both faithful to the source language and smooth in expression)。我国当代翻译理论家张培基等人在其《英汉翻译教程》中所提出的"忠实""通顺"标准也属此类型。

这类翻译标准或原则的共同特点是:翻译既要"忠实",又要"通顺",即译文必须既要考虑到原作者,又要考虑到译文的读者。用张培基等人的话说就是:"所谓忠实,首先指忠实于原作的内容。"译者必须把原作的内容完整而准确地表达出来,不得有任何篡改、歪曲、遗漏阉割或任意增删的现象。

2. 以译出语或译入语为取向的翻译原则(the source-language-oriented or the target-language-oriented translation principle)。以译出语为取向的翻译原则唯原文的形式是举,唯恐译文失真,有违原文作者的原意,因此翻译时完全采取词对词、句对句的直译方法。而以译入语为取向的原则是一味以译文读者的口味为准绳,完全采用归化的译法。如把"诸葛亮"译作Solomon(所罗门,古以色列国国王大卫之子,以智慧著称)。美国当代翻译理论家尤金·奈达(Eugene Nida)早年提出的"以读者的反应对等"的原则基本上也是以读者为取向的。

这两种翻译原则流传到今天就是所谓的"直译"和"意译"说。"直译"和"意译"作为两种具体翻译方法有着自己存在的价值(如直译常用来翻译科技文献等作品,意译常用来翻译广告、影视等文本),但如果将二者当中的任何一个视为指导翻译实践的唯一原则,都显然过于绝对化,难以指导出好的译作。

3. 以美学为取向的翻译原则(the aesthetic-oriented translation principle)。这类翻译原则主要为文学翻译家所提倡。如美国的意象派诗人庞德(Ezra Pound,1885—1975),我国的傅雷、钱钟书和许渊冲。庞德"重诗歌翻译的意象,在某种程度上反映了文学翻译是美感经验再现的特征,"傅雷认为"以效果而论,翻译应当像临画一样,所求的不在形似而在神似"。钱钟书提出:"文学翻译的最高标准是'化'。把作品从一国文字转变成另一国文字,既不能因语文习惯的差异而露出生硬牵强的痕迹,又能完全保存原有的风味,那就算得入于'化境'"。许渊冲提倡文学翻译要做到"意美、音美、形美"(beauty in meaning,

beauty in sound and beauty in form），并在这一理论的指导下译出了举世公认的优秀文学译作。

这一翻译原则的共同特点可以说是译文重神似非形似，语言必须美，即许渊冲先生所主张的"words in best order""best words in best order"。这里必须指出，美学取向的翻译原则多适合于文学翻译，以此指导翻译实践的确产生了不少精彩的文学译作。但是，该原则对于不少人来说显得过于"高深"和"抽象"，同时也不太适合用来指导非文学作品的翻译实践。

四、译文欣赏

看书，可以博览，可以细嚼，没有人会怪你喜新厌旧，也没有人要求你从一而终。你大可以从一本书换到另一本，喜爱的书，不妨一读再读；不耐看的书，又可随手抛下，谁也不会因此而伤心失望。人际关系错综复杂，那"书际关系"呢？只要花点时间去了解，再高深的学问也弄得明白。

[译文]Books can be read cursorily, or chewed and digested. None will ever call you fickle-minded, and none will ever demand that you should be constant in your affection. You can go from one book to another. And you can read your favorite book over and over again. When you lay aside the book you dislike, none will ever feel hurt or disappointed. While interpersonal relations are most complicated, what about your relations with books devote your time to studies, and you will be able to acquire any knowledge no matter how profound it is.

人们普遍认为英语是一种世界语言，经常被许多不以英语为第一语言的国家使用。与其他语言一样，英语也发生了很大的变化。英语的历史可以分为三个主要阶段：古英语，中古英语和现代英语。英语起源于公元5世纪，当时三个日耳曼部落入侵英国，他们对英语语言的形成起了很大的作用。在中世纪和现代社会初期，英语的影响遍及不列颠群岛。从17世纪初，它的影响力开始在世界各地显现。欧洲几百年的探险和殖民过程导致了英语的重大变化。今天，由于美国电影、电视、音乐、贸易和技术、包括互联网的大受欢迎，美国英语的影响力尤其显著。

[译文]English is known as a world language, usually used by many nations whose first language is not English. Like other languages, English has changed greatly. The history of the English language can be divided into three main periods: Old English, Middle English and Modern English. The English language started with the invasion of Britain by three Germanic tribes during the 5th century AD, and they contributed greatly to the formation of the English language. During the medieval and early modern periods, the influence of English spread throughout the British Isles, and from the early 17th century its influence began to be felt throughout the world. The processes of European exploration and colonization for several centuries led to significant change in English. Today, American English is particularly influential, due to the popularity of American cinema, television, music, trade and technology, including the Internet.

五、实践练习

(一) 翻译下列短语。

(1) 学习知识_____
(2) 文化程度_____
(3) 素质教育_____
(4) 社会工作_____
(5) 基本利益_____
(6) 正式声明_____
(7) 大龄青年_____
(8) 恶性循环_____
(9) 人才市场_____
(10) 国际社会_____

(二) 翻译下列句子。

(1) 给你排上队了。
(2) 这本书在图书馆可以找到。
(3) 他们应该听听老师的意见。
(4) 不尝黄连苦,怎知蜂蜜甜。
(5) 越是民族的,越是世界的。
(6) "五四运动"首先在北京发起。
(7) 他考上了大学,父母亲很高兴。
(8) 经常接触英语,就会自然而然地学会。
(9) 我们合作的基础是相互尊重,相互信任。
(10) 贵国人民的友好给我们留下了很深的印象。

第二章　汉英语言对比

为更好地了解和掌握本书第一章中对翻译的界定、方法及标准,本章着手于翻译的本体,即汉语和英语,并对这两种语言进行对比分析。宏观来讲,汉英的区别主要在于前者重语义,而后者重结构。微观来讲,汉英对比又可细化到英汉词汇、句法和篇章等层面的比较和分析。这些层面的分析将分三个小节依次展开。

一、汉英词汇对比

汉英语言中,关于词的定义众多,尤其是在至今仍未有定论的汉语中。本书因以翻译为核心,也为避免困扰读者,采用王力、张培基、丰国钦等人的观点,统一将汉英语言中最小的意义单位称为"词"。以此推理,由单一或多个词组成而又不足以构成句子的集合视为词汇。词汇在汉英对比中可从形态变化和词义变化两个角度解读。

形态变化是指汉英词的形式变化。如词缀(affixation)的变化和表达语法意义的词性变化。由此,形态变化主要存在于英语中,汉语没有严格意义的形态变化。

关于形态变化,首先从词缀(affixation)说起,它包括前缀(prefix)和后缀(suffix)。汉语没有词缀,英语多词缀。英语的词缀灵活多变,一缀多义,规模大,数量多。而汉语没有严格意义上的词形变化。例如:当我们要表达"他行进的速度快得令人惊讶"或"他的快速行进使我们感到惊讶"时,英语可根据词缀的不同变化方式有如下表达:

He moved astonishingly fast.

He moved with astonishing rapidity.

His movements were astonishingly rapid.

His rapid movements astonished us.

His movements astonished us by their rapidity.

The rapidity of his movements astonished us.

He astonished us by moving rapidly.

He astonished us by his rapid movements.

He astonished us by the rapidity of his movements.

(连淑能,2006:02)

除词缀外,汉英词汇在形态变化的不同之处还体现在具有语法意义的词性变化上。例如:

我给他一本书。

［译文］I gave him a book.

他已给我两本书。

［译文］He has given me two books.

他爸爸常常给他一些书。

［译文］His father often gives him books.

汉语中的主格、宾格、所有格和时态(现在、过去和将来)等没有形态上的变化,汉语中"我""他""给"等没有形式变化。而英语中有明显的变化,如"him""gave""have given"等。

不仅形态上汉英语言有很大区别,其在表达意义上也各有千秋。这就涉及汉英语言中的词性的划分。汉英语言中的词都可大致分为实词和虚词。实词是指具有实际意义的词,它组成句子的基本内容,如名词、形容词、副词等。虚词,又称功能词,指在句子中链接实词以表达不同的意思的词,如介词、连词等。

英汉语中既有相似点,又有不同点。相似在于两种语言中的实词有上下义词的特点。上义词是对事物的概括性、抽象性的说明;下义词是事物的具体表现形式或更为具体的说明。这里的上下义关系,也称种属关系,就是指几个单词的词义属于另一个词的词义范畴。以名词 color(颜色)为例,其下义词有:white(白色)、black(黑色)、red(红色)、green(绿色)、yellow(黄色)、blue(蓝色)、brown(棕色)、orange(橘色)、grey(灰色)等。反之,这些具体的颜色的上义词为 color(颜色)。

不同点在于,汉语的谓语也复杂多样,可以是动词、名词、形容词。若是动词,可以有一个动词,也可以有两个动词,还可以没有动词。例如:

他出国留学去了。

［译文］He has gone abroad for further studies.

汉语句中的"出国""留学""去"都是动词,可以连用。英语句中只能有一个实义动词。

除以上汉英实词的区分外,汉英虚词的差异简要归纳如下。总体来说,英语中虚词有冠词、介词、助动词、并列连接词和从属连接词等。汉语的虚词包括介词、助词和连词等。在这两种语言中,虽都有大量的虚词,但各有特点。可分为以下几点。

(1)汉语中没有冠词,而英语特有的却是定冠词和不定冠词。并且在英语中,冠词的用法常有正误之分,因此英译汉时可以省略。但在英语中也有特殊例子,有无冠词,意义天壤之别。如常见的 out of question(毫无疑问)和 out of the question(不可能),这里 the 的有无在翻译成汉语时意义差别极大,需特别关注此类词或词组。同样的例子还有 she was with (a) child 这里冠词 a 的有无很关键,有 a 意为她带着一个孩子,没有则翻译成她怀着孕。

(2)汉语多助词,英语只有助动词。在汉语中助词可分为动态助词(如、者、了、过)、结构助词(如的、地、得)和语气助词(如吗、呢、吧、啊、呀等)。这些助词有一部分相当于上文讲到的英语中形态的变化,有一部分能调整结构,表达丰富的语气色彩。以"啦"为例,她过去很久啦!(确定语气)She has been there a long time! 在本句中"啦"字没有直接对译的英文词汇,则需靠借语气或感叹号来传达。

(3)汉语少介词,英语多介词。严格来说,现代汉语没有真正的介词。汉语中的介词常常是由动词代替的,汉译英时,可借助英语的介词来翻译。例如:

汤姆**支持**特朗普。

［译文］Tom voted **with** Trump.

她是一个**脱离了**低级趣味的人。

[译文]She is a girl **above** vulgar interests.

在这两个例句中,"支持"和"脱离了"作为动词,在英语中可分别用"with"和"above"来代替。

基于汉英中实词和虚词的不同,可以发现汉英在词汇层面上具有不完全对等的特点。针对这种情况,张培基先生提出相应策略,核心主张为尽量使翻译的文本在汉英语言中都可接受,即增加翻译文本的笼统性。如使用上义词,使用中性或表现力较弱的词;文化概念替代法(如向外国人介绍"梁山伯与祝英台",可以说 Chinese Romeo and Juliet);直接使用外来词或外来词加注释;对非核心词汇省略不译。因此在翻译中会有**选词**、**选义**和**转性译法**等。该部分翻译技巧将在本书第三章具体解读。

二、汉英句法对比

句法是研究句子的各个组成部分和它们的排列顺序。就句法而言,汉英差别较大。英语只有五种基本句型(主谓、主谓表、主谓宾、主谓+双宾、主谓宾+宾语补语)。其他各种长短句都由这五种基本句型演变而来,如变式、扩展、组合或倒装。相比而言,汉语的句型就丰富得多。按照表意功能和表达形式划分有:话题句("话题语"+"评论语")、施事句("施事语"+"动作语")、关系句(各种表达关系的复句)、呼叹句(交谈中相互呼唤,应对或感叹的句子)、祈使句(表达要求,命令或请求的句子)以及存现句(表示人或事物存在或消失的句子)。

汉英基本句型如表2.1所示。

表2.1　汉英常用基本句型

汉语常用基本句型	英语五种基本句型
话题句:"话题语"+"评论语" 例如:开车他没有经验。 译文:He is inexperienced in driving.	主语+谓语 例如:The telephone rang.
描写句:"主题语"+"描写语(形容词)" 例如:房间干干净净。 译文:The room is neat and tidy.	主语+谓语+表语 例如:She appeared cheerful.
说明句:"主题语"+"说明语(名词)" 例如:今天星期日。 译文:Today is Sunday.	主语+谓语+宾语 例如:The news surprised me.
呼叹句:交谈中相互呼唤,应对或感叹的句子 例如:是呀,他车开得真好! 译文:Yes, he is an excellent driver!	主语+谓语+间接宾语+直接宾语 例如:She sang us a song.
存现句:表示人或事物存在或消失的句子 例如:黑暗中开来了一部车子。 译文:A car is coming in the dark.	主语+谓语+宾语+宾语补语 例如:He painted the door green.

续表

汉语常用基本句型	英语五种基本句型
有无句:"所有者"+"被所有者" 例如:他有房。 译文:He owns a house.	
施事句:"施事语"+"动作语" 例如:他在学习开车。 译文:He is learning how to drive.	
祈使句:表达要求、命令或请求的句子 例如:请勿酒后驾车。 译文:Please don't drink and drive.	
关系句:各种表达关系的复句 例如:(因为)他天天练习开车,(所以)很快就学会了。 译文:He soon learned how to drive because of his daily practice.	

如表 2.1 所示,汉英基本句型相差较大,但仍有相同点,如都至少会有主谓结构。现以汉英语共有又常见的主谓结构为例进行对比。汉语的主谓结构要比英语复杂得多。在形式上,汉语主语多种多样,且可有可无。只要符合语法规范且不影响句子理解即可。在语义上,它既可以表示施事、受事,也可表示时间、地点等,可用名词、动词,也可用形容词、数量词。而英语中,主语不可或缺,且有严谨的主谓一致限定。通常由名词性短语(NP)和动词性短语(VP)构成。因此,英语句子主次分明,层次清楚,严谨规范。例如:

书读完了。(受事主语)

[译文]The book has been finished.

全校到处在建新楼。(地点主语)

[译文]New buildings are being built all over the campus.

在第一句话中,"书"和"The book"都是主语,且都表示受事。但是汉语句子中的主语"书"如果在有前后语境的情况下可以省略,而英语中主语"the book"则不能省略,只能用代词代替。此外,第二句话中的汉英主语表示的意义也不相同。汉语中的主语"全校"表示地点主语,而英语中的"New buildings"仍表示受事。

除主谓结构的差别外,汉英在句法上还有许多有规律可循的差异,简单概括如下。

(1)汉语多短句,英语多长句。由于汉语是义合语言,重语义。不同的意思往往通过不同的短句表达出来。相比而言,英语是形合语言,重结构。只要结构上没有出现错误,许多意思往往可以放在一个长句中表达。例如:

人们对历史研究方法产生了兴趣,这与其说是因为外部对历史作为一门知识学科的有效性提出了挑战,还不如说是因为历史学家内部发生了争吵。

[译文]Interest in historical methods had arisen less through external challenge to the validity of history as an intellectual discipline and more from internal quarrels among historians themselves.

该英文翻译是个典型的长句,由 27 个词组成,中间无标点符号,靠语法结构 less

through…and more from 传达意思:构成一个复杂的状语修饰动词 arisen。而在中文原句中,"产生兴趣"这一重要内容通过一个独立的句子表达。

(2)汉语多分句,英语多从句。英语句子不仅可以在简单句中使用很长的修饰语使句子变长,同时也可以用从句使句子变复杂,而这些从句往往通过从句引导词与主句或其他从句连接,整个句子尽管表面上看错综复杂,但却是一个整体。汉语本来就喜欢用短句,加上表达结构相对松散,汉语中的分句翻译成英语时,往往变成英语句子中的从句。例如:

总的来说,得出这样一个结论是有一定程度把握的,但是必须具备两个条件:能够假定这个孩子对测试的态度和与他相比的另一个孩子的态度相同;他也没有因缺乏别的孩子已掌握的有关知识而被扣分。

[译文]On the whole such a conclusion can be drawn with a certain degree of confidence but only if the child can be assumed to have had the same attitude towards the test as the other with whom he is compared, and only if he was not punished by lack of relevant information which they possessed.

原文中整句话的逻辑关系十分清楚:……能够得出结论……但是只要……而且只要……。英语中两个 only if 引导的从句使整个句子变得有层次感。

(3)汉语多动词,英语多代词。在句子的主语,宾语等名词成分中,汉语多用动词,英语多用名词和代词。英语不仅有 we, you, he, they 等人称代词,而且还有 that, which 之类的关系代词,在长而复杂的句子,为了使句子结构正确、语义清楚,同时避免表达上的重复,英语常使用很多代词。汉语虽然也有代词,但由于结构相对松散、句子相对较短,不能使用太多的代词,这样语义会更加清楚。例如:

届时,将出现由机器人主持的电视访谈节目及装有污染监测器的汽车,一旦这些汽车污染超标(或违规),监测器就会使其停驶。

[译文]There will be television chat shows hosted by robots, and cars with pollution monitors that will disable them when they offend.

(4)汉语多主动,英语多被动。英语比较喜欢用被动语态,科技英语尤其如此。汉语虽然也有"被""由"之类的词表示动作是被动的,但这种表达远没有英语的被动语态那么常见,因此,汉语中的主动在英译中往往成了被动。下面我们先看一组常用的英译:

必须指出……	It must be pointed out that…
必须承认……	It must be admitted that…
人们认为……	It is imagined that…
不可否认……	It cannot be denied that…
由此可知……	It will be seen from this that…
必须认识到……	It should be realized that…
人们(总是)强调……	It is (always) stressed that…
可以毫不夸张地说……	It may be said without fear of exaggeration that…

鉴于以上例证,我们可以观察到英语中的被动语态较多。但需注意的是,并不是所有情况都应该或倾向于使用被动语态。主被动的使用也是基于语境的。当我们在汇报前人研究时,使用被动语态的概率就大于主动语态,因为这里的被动多显所阐述事物的客观性。而在自我介绍时,多使用主动语态,提升自我意识,多显陈述者的自信。

汉英在句法上的区别虽在翻译时有规律,但是翻译理解的不仅是句子和词典义,而也应了解它们的延伸义。为此,需要引入非语言知识和智力,即语篇。

三、汉英篇章对比

语篇的定义,和词汇、句法的定义一样也有争议。胡壮麟先生(1994)认为语篇指"不完全受句子语法约束的在一定语境下表示完整语义的自然语言",他认为语篇可以是一个词,一个短语或词组,可以是一个小句,也可以是一副对联,一首小诗,一篇散文。基于此,张德禄先生将语篇概括为具有意义的一个单位。为方便读者理解,本书取以上两位学者的定义,将词、词组、小句到多个句子组成的具有意义的单位统称为语篇。所有语言的篇章都有一个共同的目的,即传达作者的思想,不同的是如何传达。汉英语篇也不例外。本小节在汉英句法对比的基础上,对汉英篇章的构建进行对比,发现汉英语篇的不同点在词汇、句法和多个句子构成的不同层次的语篇上均有些规律可循。

(一)汉英语在词汇层面的语篇差异

(1)汉语多重复,英语多变化。这里的重复和变化是指构成段落的词汇。在词汇上,为避免语言乏味,凸显交流多样化,英语在表达相同的意思时往往变换表达方式。如第一句说"我认为"可以用"I think",第二句可能要换成"I believe"或"I reckon"之类的表达。相比之下,汉语对变换表达方式的要求没有英语那么高。

(2)汉语多推理,英语多引申。英语有两句俗话:一是 you know a word by the company it keeps(要知义如何,关键看词伙),二是 words do not have meaning, but people have meaning for them(词本无义,义随人生)。这说明词典对词的定义和解释是死的,而实际运用中的语言是活的。从原文角度来说,这种活用是词义和用法的引申,翻译的时候要准确理解这种引申,译者就需要进行引申。例如:

尽管关于历史的定义几乎和历史学家一样多,现代实践最符合这样一种定义,即把历史看作是对过去重大历史事件的**再现**和解释。

[译文]While there are almost as many definitions of history as there are historians, modern practice most closely conforms to one that sees history as the attempt to **recreate** and explain the significant events of the past。

从逻辑上来讲,"过去的重大历史事件"是不能"重新创造"的,作者显然对 recreate 一词的词义进行了引申,

译者经常会有这样一种感受:某个词明明认识,可就是不知道该怎样表达。这其实就是词的引申在起作用。再如:

我上周买了一支笔,**红芯的**。

[译文]I bought a pen last week and **it is** red.

英译时,it is 是本来没有的,在汉语中属冗余。但在英语中(仅以例中表达方式为准)必须要有,用来回指前面提到的 a pen。这里的回指也是在讲英语中的引申。

(二)汉英语在句法层面的语篇差异

汉语多后重心,英语多前重心。在表达多逻辑思维时,汉语由于社会文化的影响,构建语篇时常先论证再表达观点。由原因到结果、由假设到推论、由事实到结论,即重心在后。英语往往是先表达观点后论证。判断或结论等在前,事实或描写等在后,即重心或主要信息在前,次要信息在后。例如:

由于贵国政府的提议,才得以这样快地重新实现访问。这使我感到特别高兴。

[译文]I was all the more delighted when, as a result of the initiative of your Government, it proved possible to reinstate the visit so quickly.

上述例句中,汉英语句在陈述因果关系。我们可以明显看出,汉语先因后果,而英语先果后因。前者把重要信息放后面讲的就是汉语多后重心,而后者把重要信息放前面则体现英语多前重心的观点。

从汉译英中,不难看出,英语和汉语的重心在句中的位置有时是不一样的,翻译的时候如果不进行调整,势必给表达造成很大困难。只有了解这些区别,才能对汉译英有正确的认识,才能在翻译中抓住重点,找到解决问题的办法。

(三)汉英语在多个句子合成层面的语篇差异

汉语在由多个小句组成的语篇中,更多地注意衔接和连贯。一般情况下,衔接和连贯的表现也多在于句中一些小词的用法上。主要有以下规律可循。

(1)汉语的指示词在数量和用法上比英语多。指示词是指由代词、副词等构成的前后文指代的关系。代词有"这,那"(this, that),副词有"这里,那里,现在"(here, there, now)。虽然汉英都有这层指示意义,但是汉语在数量和复杂程度上都多于英语。如指代人或物,汉语用这(些),那(些);指代处所,汉语用这(儿),那(儿);指代性质,汉语有这(样),那(样)等,而英语中则只有单复数的区别。

(2)汉语多例证,英语多论证。例证和论证是指在证明作者观点时,汉语通过多种例子强调作者观点。在汉语论证中,例子起举足轻重的作用。英语正好相反,在证明作者观点时,通常通过演绎或归纳推理来论证,例子起解释说明或辅助作用,个数一般在一个左右。如当我们证明读书很重要时,汉语的语篇构建一般是先阐明观点,然后通过一系列的伟人、名人因努力学习而成功的例子。这样的例子最常见于高考作文。英语语篇大多数较理性,一般围绕读书是什么、为什么和怎样读三个角度论证。如培根的《论读书》一文,作者首先讲明为什么读书,说读书足以怡情、足以博彩、足以长才。然后谈如何读书,说书有可浅尝者,有可吞食者,少数则须咀嚼消化。

需要注意的是,以上规律不是覆盖性地适用于所有的文体。这里的文体指独立成篇的文本体裁(或样式、体制),是文本构成的规格和模式,是某种历史内容长期积淀的产物。它反映了文本从内容到形式的整体特点,属于形式范畴,如新闻、旅游、科技、商务、法律和文学等文体。鉴于此,在翻译时我们首先要了解文章的文体,做出相应的调整,再进行翻译。为方便读者进一步了解这些文体及其翻译,本书在后六章对常见的文体均有详细解读。

四、译文欣赏

不论是英年早逝,还是老年故去,都没有比虚度年华更令人遗憾。一个人活了十八岁可能比另一个人活了八十年活得更加充实。对于生活,我们认为并不是要去不顾一切地积累大量的他以为有价值的经验,而是应该过好每天的时光。也就是说,他总是把每一天当作那是他生命中唯一的一天来过。这意思是说,人应当要寻求平和感和力量感去对付生活中的失意和痛苦。坚持不懈地努力去发现能更接近生活的办法,增加并维持生活的乐趣和价值。

[译文]It would be more regretful to idle your life out than you die young or die old. It is quite possible that a person who dies at his eighteenth would live more fruitfully than a person who dies at eighty. We do believe that it would be better for him to pass each passing day worthfully than to accumulate lots of valuable experience regardless of the consequences. That is to say, he should try to pass each day of his life as if it would be the only day in his life. It means that he should try his best to cope with all the depressions and pains in his life peacefully and forcefully. He should try his utmost to find means to get access to life and increase and keep the interest and value of life.

人类历史上鲜为人知的最大奥秘之一就是我们居于其中的现代世界是中国和西方多种成分的独特综合。很可能现代世界所赖以建立的一半以上的主要发明和发现都是来源于中国,而这是鲜为人知的。为什么我们中国人没有认识到这种巨大的真理呢?主要的原因是中国自鸦片战争一百多年来的衰败使中国人失去了自尊感,因而看不到这一点。如果这些发现发明的创始人自己就不再坚持自己的首创权利了,甚至他们自己对这些创造的记忆都淡薄了,为什么他们的继承者还要煞费苦心地把这些失去的首创权利物归原主呢?直到现在很多西方人是否愿意知道事实真相依然是个问题。自我满足地认为是西方人自己孤立无助地达到了他们今天的地位,总比把这些发明创造的功劳归于别人更舒服些。

[译文]One of the biggest mysteries in human history of the modern world in which we live is the unique integration of many elements of China and the West. It is highly probable that over the half of the dominant inventions and discoveries have their origin from China, which is hardly known to the outside world. Why didn't we Chinese realize such an important truth? The main reason is that the declining and corruption of China in recent 100 years since the Opium War deface the Chinese people and make them lose their self-respect, thus failing to see this point. If the inventors and discoverers didn't persist in their own rights for originality and even lost the memory of such rights, why would the successors of these inventions and discoveries like to worry about returning such rights to the real originators? So it is a real problem that the westerners are still reluctant to admit this fact until now. It would be comfortable to lie on the glory of the laurel to credit themselves with the claim that they attained such a height in science independently without any help of others.

我是在一个小镇上长大的,从镇上的小学校到我家,只需步行10分钟。离当前不算太太久远的那个时代,小学生可以回家吃午饭,而他们的母亲,则会老早在家等候着。这一切对如今的孩子来说,无疑是一种奢望了,可是那时的我,却并不以为然。我觉得做母亲的给她的孩子制作三明治,鉴赏手指画,检查他们的家庭作业,都是理所当然的事。我从来没有想过:像我母亲这样一个颇有抱负又很聪明的女人,在我降生之前,她有一份工作,而且后来她又谋了份差事,可是,在我上小学那几年,她却几乎天天陪着我吃午饭,一同打发午餐时的每一分钟。只记得,每当午时铃声一响,我就一口气地往家里跑。母亲总是站在门前台阶的最高层,笑盈盈地望着我,那神情分明表示:我便是母亲心目中唯一最重要的东西了。为此,我一辈子都要感谢我的母亲。

[译文]I grew up in a small town where the elementary school was a ten-minute walk from my house and in an age, not so long ago, when children could go home for lunch and find their mothers waiting. At the time, I did not consider this a luxury, although today it certainly would be. I took it for granted that mothers were the sandwich-makers, the finger-painting appreciators and the homework monitors. I never questioned that this ambitious, intelligent woman, who had had a career before I was born and would eventually return to a career, would spend almost every lunch hour throughout my elementary school years just with me. I only knew that when the noon bell rang, I would race breathlessly home. My mother would be standing at the top of the stairs, smiling down at me with a look that suggested I was the only important thing she had on her mind. For this, I am forever grateful.

五、实践练习

翻译下列句子。

(1) 我建议他立刻戒烟。
(2) 我既不喝酒,也不抽烟。
(3) 这个小学生文章写得不错。
(4) 他既有藏书癖,又爱好书法。
(5) 这些乡下小姑娘唱歌唱得很好。
(6) 政府号召建立更多的技术学校。
(7) 我是个业余演员,他演得比我好。
(8) 越南战争不断地消耗美国的资源。
(9) 每天早上,她都要到湖区去散步。
(10) 他反对的理由是:这个计划不现实。

第三章　汉语词汇的翻译

词汇,又称语汇,是一种语言里所有的(或特定范围的)词和固定短语的总和。词汇是语言的基本单位,是句子或篇章的基本组成部分。英语和汉语都具有非常丰富的词汇量,一词多义、一词多类现象在英汉两种语言中都十分普遍。越是常用的词,越是具有繁多的词义和词类,这就为准确翻译带来了很大困难。在翻译过程中,如何正确选择词义是准确翻译词汇的关键所在。

一、选择词义

汉英翻译中的选择词义,就是在正确理解汉语原文的基础上,选择恰当的英语词汇表达汉语原文的意思。正确选择词义是保证译文质量的重要条件,选择词义主要通过以下途径来实现。

(一)根据语境来选择词义

语境(Context),也叫上下文,是指词、短语、语句或篇章所处的前后语言环境。一词多义现象在英语和汉语中都非常普遍,同一个词语在不同的语境下的含义往往大相径庭,正如英国著名语言学家弗斯(Firth)所说:"Each word when used in a new context is a new word."(每一个词用在新的语境中就是一个新词)。在翻译中选择词义时,语境分析的作用非常重要。语境分析可以使词汇的意义单一化和具体化,有助于正确理解原文和选择词义。

例1:"意见"的不同译法

(1)用户对贵公司的产品意见很大。

[译文] The customers have a lot of complaints about your products.

[分析] 在原句的语境中,"意见"的意思是"抱怨""投诉",因此译成 complaint。

(2)我觉得这是个好主意,你的意见呢?

[译文] I think it's a good idea. What's your opinion?

[分析] 在原句的语境中,"意见"的意思是"看法",因此译成 opinion。

(3)他太自私了,大家对他有意见。

[译文] He is selfish, so we are angry with him / we dislike him.

[分析] 在原句的语境中,"意见"的意思是"对他有看法""对他很反感、很生气",可以用 angry 和 dislike 来翻译。

(4)你应该听从医生的意见。

[译文] You should follow the doctor's advice.

[分析]在原句的语境中,"意见"等同于"建议",因此译成 advice。

(5)他们在会上闹起了意见。

They had a dispute at the meeting.

[分析]在原句的语境中,"闹意见"等同于"起争执",因此译成 have a dispute。

(6)两位领导人就双边关系及共同关心的问题交换了意见。

The two leaders exchanged views on bilateral relations and issues of common concern.

[分析]在原句的语境中,"意见"等同于"看法",是个比较正式的词,因此译成 view。

例2:"头"的不同译法

(1)他的头靠在我的肩上。

[译文] His head rested on my shoulder.

[分析]原句语境里的"头"是指人体的器官,是该词的本义,因此译成 head。

(2)玛丽正在梳头。

[译文] Mary was combing her hair.

[分析]汉语"梳头"的真正意思是梳理头发,因此要译成 comb one's hair。

(3)他是我们班的头儿。

[译文] He is the head / monitor of our class.

[分析]汉语语境中"头儿"的意思是"领导""首领",因此译成 head 或 monitor。

(4)她站在桥西头。

[译文] She stood at the west end of the bridge.

[分析]"桥头"是指桥的一端,在英语中是用 end。

(5)孩子们正在山头上玩耍。

[译文] Children are playing on the top of the hill.

[分析]"山头"就是"山顶",因此要译成 top 而不是 head。

(6)我们从头开始吧。

[译文] Let's start from scratch / from the very beginning.

[分析]原句语境中的"头"指最初的状态,习语 start from scratch 表示"从头做起""白手起家"。

(7)这是我头一次来北京。

[译文] This is the first time I came to Beijing.

[分析]"头一次"就是"第一次",和英语中的 head 没有任何关系。

(8)事情不能只顾一头。

[译文] We mustn't pay attention to only one aspect of the matter.

[分析]原句语境中的"头"是指事情的一个方面,因此译成 aspect。

(9)他们是一头的。

[译文] They are on the same side.

[分析]"是一头的"表示"是一伙儿的""是站在一边儿的",因此译成 on the same side。

(10) 他头天上午就来了。

［译文］He came here the previous morning / yesterday morning.

［分析］"头天上午"指"前一天上午"，因此译成 the previous morning 或 yesterday morning。

(二)根据词的搭配关系来选择词义

在汉语长期的使用过程中,形成了很多固定搭配。一个词与不同的词搭配,往往会有不同的含义。在翻译这些固定搭配时,对于其中共同的词语,往往需要译成不同的英语单词。

例 1:"浓"字在不同搭配中的译法

浓茶:strong tea

浓墨:thick (or dark) ink

浓烟:dense / thick smoke

浓眉:heavy / thick / bushy eyebrows

兴趣很浓:take a great interest in sth.

玫瑰花香味很浓:The rose has a heavy fragrance.

这幅画颜色太浓:The painting is too heavily colored.

例 2:"接"字在不同的搭配的译法

接到一封信:receive a letter

接电话:answer the phone

接风:give a dinner for sb. from afar

接济:give material / financial assistance to sb.

接班:take over from / take one's turn on duty / succeed

接球:catch a ball

接吻:kiss

接新生:meet the freshmen

例 3:"学习"字在不同的搭配的译法

学习文化:learn to read and write

学习先进经验:learn from others' advanced experiences

学习外语:learn a foreign language

学习成绩:academic records, school records, model oneself on Lei Feng

学习年限:period of schooling

互相学习:learn from each other

以雷锋为学习的榜样:follow the example of Lei Feng

(三)根据词的感情色彩来选择词义

词汇按照感情色彩可以分为褒义、贬义和中性。在翻译时,必须根据上下文考虑词的感情色彩,再根据词的褒贬选择合适的译词,这样才能体现出原文的精神。

1. 她父亲是一位有名的外科医生。

［译文］Her father is a famous surgeon.

黄金荣是旧上海有名的大流氓。

［译文］Huang Jinrong was a notorious rogue in Shanghai in the old times.

［分析］第一句中的"有名"是褒义词，而第二句中的是贬义词，因此两句译文中使用了不同的表示"有名"的英文词。

2. 他们讲唯心论，我们讲唯物论。

［译文］They preach idealism, whereas we advocate materialism.

［分析］对于相同的"讲"字，前半句用了贬义词 preach（鼓吹、说教），后半句用了褒义词 advocate（倡导），一褒一贬，贴切地反映了原文的意义。

3. 诗人应该具有丰富的想象力。

［译文］A poet should have rich imagination.

真遗憾，你的想象力太丰富了。

［译文］What a pity! You've got into wild flights of fancy.

［分析］第一句中的"想象力"是褒义词，因此译成了 imagination。第二句中的"想象力"是个贬义词，暗含"幻想"之意，因此译成了 fancy。

4. 我们应该从这里得出一条经验，就是不要被假象所迷惑。

［译文］We should draw a lesson here. Don't be misled by false appearances.

［分析］一提到"经验"，很容易想到 experience，但句中的"经验"其实是从错误或失败中得出的教训，因此要译成 lesson。

5. 她追求的是真理，而他追求的是荣华富贵。

［译文］What she seeks is truth, and what he hankers after is nothing but high position and great wealth.

［分析］第一个"追求"是褒义词，译成褒义词 seek。第二个"追求"是贬义词，因此译成含有贬义的 hanker。

二、词汇翻译的转性译法

所谓转性译法（Conversion），是指在翻译过程中，把原语中某个词的词性在译入语中转换成另一种词性，这被称为词类转换。英语和汉语的词类大部分是重合的，但是在翻译过程中，某个词的词性不一定要拘泥于原句所用的词性，需要根据译入语的习惯进行灵活处理，译成其他词性。例如，把汉语动词转变词性译为英语名词，把汉语名词转变词性译为英语动词。

（一）汉语动词的转性译法

汉语词汇的一大特点是频繁使用动词，在一个句子中常常出现几个动词连用的情况；而一个英语句子一般只有一个动词作谓语。在汉英翻译过程中，汉语动词常常转性译成英语名词、介词、介词短语、形容词、副词和非谓语动词。

1. 汉语动词转译成英语名词

在英语句子中，名词结构占绝对优势，所以汉译英时，汉语动词通常译成英语名词。

例① 人口在不断地增加。

[译文] There is a steady increase in population.

[分析] 汉语中的"增加"是动词,在英语中转译成了名词 increase。

例② 现在辞职就是承认失败。

[译文] To resign now would be an admission of failure.

[分析] 汉语中的"承认失败"是个动词短语,在英语中转译成了名词短语 an admission of failure。

例③ 她教书教得好。

[译文] She is a good teacher.

[分析] 汉语中的"教书教得好"是动词结构,在英语中转译成了名词短语 a good teacher。

例④ 他对他们越来越憎恨。

[译文] Her hatred for them grew more.

[分析] 汉语中的"憎恨"是个动词,在英语中转译成了名词 hatred。

2. 汉语动词转译成介词或介词短语

例① 政府支持这个项目。

[译文] The government is behind this project.

[分析] 汉语中的"支持"是动词,在英语中转译成了介词 behind。

例② 我感觉到冰冷的枪口顶住了我的头。

[译文] I felt the gun, cold, against my head.

[分析] 汉语中的"顶住"是动词,在英语中转译成了介词 against。

例③ 警察在抓罪犯。

[译文] The police is in pursuit of the criminal.

[分析] 汉语中的"抓"是动词,在英语中转译成了介词短语 in pursuit of。

例④ 他的智力超过常人。

[译文] He has intelligence beyond the ordinary.

[分析] 汉语中的"超过"是动词,在英语中转译成了介词 beyond。

3. 汉语动词转译成形容词或副词

例① 他不停地来回走着,激动得说不出话来。

[译文] He kept on walking back and forth, being too excited to say a single word.

[分析] 汉语中的"激动"是动词,在英语中转译成了形容词 excited。

例② 他非常清楚自己的缺点。

[译文] He is quite aware of his shortcomings.

[分析] 汉语中的"清楚"是动词,在英语中转译成了形容词 aware。

例③ 我打开窗子,让新鲜空气进来。

[译文] I opened the window to let fresh air in.

[分析] 汉语中的"进来"是动词,在英语中转译成了副词 in。

例④ "放我出去!"房间里的孩子叫道。

[译文] "Let me out!", the child in the room cried.

[分析] 汉语中的"出去"是动词,在英语中转译成了副词 out。

4. 汉语动词转译成非谓语动词

例① 我看不起他,他酗酒、好赌、言语粗俗。

[译文]What I despise about him was his drinking, gambling and cursing.

[分析]汉语中的"酗酒""好赌""言语粗俗"都是动词结构,在英语中转译成了非谓语动词drinking, gambling和cursing。

例② 又要教书,又要照顾家庭,我是在忙不过来了。

[译文]My teaching and my family are proving more than enough to fill my time.

[分析]汉语中的"教书"是动词,在英语中转译成了非谓语动词teaching。

例③ 她转过身,看见一辆救护车开了过来。

[译文]Turning around, she saw an ambulance driving up.

[分析]汉语中的"转过身"是动词,在英语中转译成了非谓语动词turning around。

(二)汉语名词的转性译法

在汉英翻译中,汉语名词可以转性译成英语动词、形容词和副词。

1. 汉语名词转译成英语动词

例① 他的态度极其镇静。

[译文]He behaved with great composure.

[分析]汉语中的"态度"是名词,在英语中转译成了动词behave。

例② 他的呼吸有股大蒜味道。

[译文]His breaths smells of garlic.

[分析]汉语中的"味道"是名词,在英语中转译成了动词smell。

例③ 他这次旅行所见所闻给他留下了深刻的印象。

[译文]What he saw and heard on his trip impressed him deeply.

[分析]汉语中的"印象"是名词,在英语中转译成了动词impress。

例④ 中国科学研究发展的特点是理论联系实际。

[译文]The development of scientific research in China is characterized by integration of theory with practice.

[分析]汉语中的"特点"是名词,在英语中转译成了动词be characterized。

2. 汉语名词转译成英语形容词或副词

例① 计算机的灵活性比较大,因此能做很多不同的工作。

[译文]Computers are more flexible, and can do a greater variety of jobs.

[分析]汉语中的"灵活性"是名词,在英语中转译成了形容词flexible。

例② 楼下有人找你。

[译文]There is a man downstairs who wants to see you.

[分析]汉语中的"楼下"是名词,在英语中转译成了副词downstairs。

(三)汉语形容词和副词的转性译法

1. 汉语形容词和副词转译成英语名词

例① 我们感到解决这个复杂的问题是困难的。

[译文] We found difficulty in solving this complicated problem.
[分析] 汉语中的"困难的"是形容词,在英语中转译成了名词 difficulty。

例② 独立思考是学习所绝对必要的。
[译文] Independent thinking is an absolute necessity in study.
[分析] 汉语中的"必要的"是形容词,在英语中转译成了名词 necessity。

例③ 代表们表示坚决反对原子武器。
[译文] The delegation expressed their determination to oppose atomic weapons.
[分析] 汉语中的"坚决"是副词,在英语中转译成了名词 determination。

例④ 只要一发现有可能反对他的人,他就本能地用他的魅力和风趣将这人争取过来。
[译文] When he catches a glimpse of a potential antagonist, his instinct is to win him over with charm and humor.
[分析] 汉语中的"本能地"是副词,在英语中转译成了名词 instinct。

2. 形容词和副词的相互转译

例① 我想男孩子的思维方式和女孩子是不一样的。
[译文] I suppose boys think differently from girls.
[分析] 汉语中的"不一样的"是形容词,在英语中转译成了副词 differently。

例② 总裁为这次出访做了极为周密的准备。
[译文] The president had prepared meticulously for his journey.
[分析] 汉语中的"周密的"是形容词,在英语中转译成了副词 meticulously。

例③ 他们热忱地欢迎他。
[译文] They gave him a hearty welcome.
[分析] 汉语中的"热忱地"是副词,在英语中转译成了形容词 hearty。

例④ 我们必须充分利用现有技术设备。
[译文] We must make full use of existing technical equipment.
[分析] 汉语中的"充分地"是副词,在英语中转译成了形容词 full。

例⑤ 他每年去北京一次,使他接触到许多国内有名的作家。
[译文] His annual visits to Beijing brought him into contact with many well-known writers of our country.
[分析] 汉语中的"每年"是副词,在英语中转译成了形容词 annual。

3. 形容词和副词转译成介词或介词短语

例① 阳光普照大地。
[译文] The sun shines over the earth.
[分析] 汉语中的"普"是副词,表示"全、广、遍"之意,在英语中转译成了介词 over。

例② 他在城里到处乞讨。
[译文] He went begging about the town.
[分析] 汉语中的"到处"是副词,在英语中转译成了介词 about。

例③ 厨房又脏又乱。
[译文] The kitchen was in a mess.
[分析] 汉语中的"脏"和"乱"是形容词,在英语中转译成了介词短语 in a mess。

例④ 我们的教育方针,应该使受教育者在德育、智育、体育方面都得到发展,成为有社会主义觉悟、有文化的劳动者。

[译文] Our educational policy must enable everyone who receives an education to develop morally, intellectually and physically and become a worker with both socialist consciousness and culture.

[分析] 汉语中的"有社会主义觉悟的"和"有文化的"都是形容词,在英语中转译成了介词短语 with both socialist consciousness and culture。此外,"德育""智育""体育"三个名词转译成了副词,名词短语"得到发展"转译成了动词 develop。

三、词汇翻译的具体法和抽象法

具体法是将原文中意义比较抽象和模糊的单词、词组、成语或句子翻译成译入语中比较具体和明确的单词、词组、成语或句子,使译文形象、生动和明确。抽象法就是将原文中比较具体和明确的单词、词组、成语或句子翻译成译入语中比较抽象和模糊的单词、词组、成语或句子,从而使译文变得一般化和概括化。具体法和抽象法可以消除或降低语言差异给翻译带来的损失,从而使译文产生与原文同样的效果。

(一) 具体法

例① 我们决不能姑息坏人。

[译文] We should never warm snakes in our bosoms.

[分析] 译文借用英语习语 to warm snakes in one's bosoms 来翻译"姑息坏人",非常形象、具体。

例② 他每天要处理许多棘手的问题。

[译文] He has many hot potatoes to handle every day.

[分析] 汉语中的"棘手"可以译成 difficult,但不如习语 hot potato(烫手的山芋)生动具体。

例③ 你应该把好坏分清楚

[译文] You should separate the sheep from the goats.

[分析] 英语习语 to separate the sheep from the goats 表示"分清好坏、明辨是非",用它来翻译"把好坏分清楚"显得非常具体而明确。

例④ 你不要过早乐观,真正的困难还在后头呢。

[译文] Don't count your chickens before they are hatched. The real difficulties still lay ahead.

[分析] 如果把"不要过早乐观"直译成 don't be optimistic early,不如借用英语谚语 Don't count your chickens before they are hatched 形象、具体。

例⑤ 他们根本不知道什么是时尚,只不过是在盲从而已。

[译文] They actually know nothing about what fashion is. They are only following others like sheep.

[分析] 汉语中的"盲从",如果译成 follow blindly 则显得比较抽象,但不如译成习语 follow like sheep 更生动具体。

(二) 抽象法

大量使用抽象名词是英语的一大特点。在翻译一些具体而形象的汉语名词时,可以用英语中同义的抽象名词来翻译。

例① 黑暗中一个黑影吓得他魂飞魄散。

[译文] He was half dead with a black figure in the darkness.

[分析] 汉语中的"魂飞魄散"形象生动,但英语中没有对应的说法,无法借译,只好译成抽象的 half dead。

例② 他拜倒在了她的石榴裙下。

[译文] He worshipped her on his knees.

[分析] "拜倒在石榴裙下"是汉语中特有的说法,表示男人对女性崇拜倾倒的意思。此句采用抽象法译成 He worshipped her on his knees。

例③ 我不贪图下海挣大钱,只想毕业后在中学里找个铁饭碗。

[译文] I don't want to earn good money by engaging myself in trade, I just want to find upon graduation a secured job in a middle school.

[分析] "铁饭碗"也是汉语特有的说法,采用抽象法译成 a secured job,虽然不如汉语具体而形象,但也符合汉语说法的实质。

例④ 他万万没有想到在他前进的道路上竟会出现那么多的拦路虎。

[译文] He had never expected that so many obstacles would stand in his way.

[分析] "拦路虎"表示"困难、障碍"之意,英语中没有类似的比喻说法,只好放弃原文形象,只译出其喻义 obstacles。

例⑤ 真正的好朋友应该是雪中送炭。

[译文] A real good friend should be offering timely help.

[分析] "雪中送炭"也是汉语特有的成语,抽象译成 offer timely help,保留汉语的喻义。

四、译文欣赏

甲:这一点小意思,请务必收下。
乙:你这人真是有意思,怎么也来这一套?
甲:哎,只是意思意思。
乙:啊,真是不好意思。

[译文]
A: This is a little gift as a token of my appreciation. Please take it.
B: Oh, aren't you a bit too polite? You shouldn't do that.
A: Well, it just conveys my gratitude.
B: Ah, thank you then, though I really don't deserve it.

于是——洗手的时候,日子从水盆里过去;吃饭的时候,日子从饭碗里过去;默默时,便从凝然的双眼前过去。

[译文]Thus, the day flows away through the sink when I wash my hands, wears away in the bowl when I eat my meal, passes away before my day-dreaming gaze as I reflect silence.

总而言之,我们应拿出更多的财力加强基础设施建设,加强高新技术建设,加强现有企业技术改造。

[译文]In a word, we should pool more money to strengthen construction in infrastructure, speed up the development of high and new technologies, quicken the technological renovation in the enterprises.

这本书一问世立即受到人们,特别是大学生的青睐,并多次再版。无须解释人们为什么这么喜爱这本书,因为只要稍加浏览,就可以看到书里反映了文明社会中对于友谊的看法。

[译文]This book enjoyed an immediate acceptance, especially among college students, and was reprinted many times. Its popularity needs no explanation, for a browse through it shows that it reflects the notions of civilized friendship.

五、实践练习

1. 翻译下列短语,注意"上"字与不同词语搭配时的译法。
(1) 上车＿＿＿＿＿＿＿＿＿
(2) 上山＿＿＿＿＿＿＿＿＿
(3) 上班＿＿＿＿＿＿＿＿＿
(4) 上当＿＿＿＿＿＿＿＿＿
(5) 上火＿＿＿＿＿＿＿＿＿
(6) 上进＿＿＿＿＿＿＿＿＿
(7) 上冻＿＿＿＿＿＿＿＿＿
(8) 上马＿＿＿＿＿＿＿＿＿
(9) 上演＿＿＿＿＿＿＿＿＿
(10) 上任＿＿＿＿＿＿＿＿＿
(11) 上课＿＿＿＿＿＿＿＿＿
(12) 上瘾＿＿＿＿＿＿＿＿＿
(13) 上访＿＿＿＿＿＿＿＿＿
(14) 上门＿＿＿＿＿＿＿＿＿
(15) 上飞机＿＿＿＿＿＿＿＿＿

2. 翻译下列句子,注意用转性译法翻译画线的词语。
(1) 他不爱多说话,但常常微笑;那微笑是自然的、温暖的。
(2) 屈原怀着悲痛的心情,抱了一块石头,投汨罗江自杀了。
(3) 他们不应该以怨报德。
(4) 这是独处的妙处;我且受用这无边的荷香月色好了。
(5) 汉语的特点之一是动词占优势。
(6) 一切爱好和平的人们都要求禁止原子武器。
(7) 那艘新建轮船的处女航是成功的。
(8) 林则徐认为,要成功地制止鸦片买卖,就得首先把鸦片销毁。

3. 用具体法翻译下列句子中的画线部分。
(1) 他这个人只管自己的事。
(2) 你真是说话不看对象。
(3) 少时所学,到老不忘。
(4) 我不想依靠父母过日子。
(5) 他知道不论境遇如何,都可以把家庭作为靠山。

4. 用抽象法翻译下列句子中的画线部分。
(1) 这是他们自己的事情,你去插一脚干嘛?
(2) 别人家里鸡毛蒜皮的事情你都知道得这么全,真是个顺风耳啊!
(3) 王冕一路风餐露宿,九十里大站,七十里小站,一径来到山东济南府。
(4) 敌军闹得全村鸡犬不宁。
(5) 只要你嫁给我,鸡鸭鱼肉,绫罗绸缎,一辈子享受不尽。

第四章 汉语成语的翻译

对于成语,《现代汉语词典》是这样定义的:"人们长期以来习用的、形式简洁而意义精辟的、定型的词组与短语。"成语结构严整,对仗工整,言简意赅,形象生动,是汉语文化的精华,具有浓厚的中华文化特色。由于汉语和英语在语言和文化方面存在巨大差异,因此汉语成语的中国文化特色很难全部在英语译文中得以再现。翻译时,译者应当准确、全面地理解每一个成语的本意和引申义,不能只从字面意义上来翻译。在汉语成语翻译方面,通常会采用以下三种方法:套译法、意译法和加注法。

一、套译法

套译法(Loan Translation; Corresponding Translation; Borrowing Translation)是借助或套用英语中的习语来翻译汉语成语,也称为借用翻译法。套译法实际上是一种直译法,属于归化译法。

(一)形式和内涵完全对等的套译

有些汉语成语和英语中的习语在内容和形式上都完全符合或基本符合,双方具有相同或类似的意义和修辞格。翻译这类汉语成语时,可以直接完全套用英语同义的习语,这样能最大限度地保留汉语成语的比喻、形象和民族色彩,可以给外国读者新鲜、生动和耳目一新的感觉。例如:

火上浇油:add fuel to the fire / pour oil on fire
如履薄冰:to be on thin ice
井底之蛙:to be like a frog at the bottom of a well
赴汤蹈火:go through fire and water
三三两两:in / by twos and threes
君子协定:gentlemen's agreement / an agreement of gentlemen
隔墙有耳:Wall has ears.
浑水摸鱼:fish in troubled waters
趁热打铁:strike while the iron is hot
不可救药:beyond cure / hopeless
充耳不闻:turn a deaf ear
时时刻刻:every now and then

彻夜不眠：stay up the whole night
一语道破；一语中的：hit the mark with a single comment
一针见血：hit the nail on the head
眼不见，心不烦：out of sight, out of mind
随波逐流：go with the tide
牢不可破：so strongly built as to be indestructible
史无前例：without precedent in history
攻其不备：strike somebody when he is unprepared
和风细雨：as mild as a drizzle and as gentle as a breeze
槁木死灰：withered wood or cold ashes
外强中干：outwardly strong but inwardly weak
礼尚往来：courtesy requires reciprocity
刻骨铭心：to be engraved on one's heart and bones
重见天日：see the daylight again
百川归海：all rivers flow to the sea
画饼充饥：draw cakes to allay hunger
口蜜腹剑：to be honey-mouthed and dagger-hearted

从上述例子可以看出，形式和内涵完全对等的套译既能保持原文的形式，又能保持原文的特色内容。在这类套译里，汉英成语具有完全相同的形象和比喻。形式和内涵完全对等的套译是一种形神兼顾的翻译，能使英语读者一目了然，产生相同或类似的联想，能充分传递汉语成语包含的信息，并使读者欣然接受。

对于像"牢不可破""史无前例""口蜜腹剑"这些英语中没有现成习语可以套用，且字面形式和比喻形象都能为英语读者所接受的汉语成语，则完全直译，即把成语中的每个部分都直译出来。

（二）形式和内涵不完全对等的套译

尤金·A.奈达（1964）曾指出："两种语言之间，在词组与句子方面相等（equivalence）的不是没有，但比较少，比较多的相当（corresponding），而绝大部分既不相等又不相当。"汉语成语和英语习语之间的关系也是如此。正是由于汉英两种语言的不完全对应，在套用英语习语翻译汉语成语时，就会出现形式和内涵不完全对等的套译：内容相同，但形式有差异。这种差异主要体现在以下三个方面。

1. 在英语译文中改变成语的字面形式或比喻形象。

例如，"艳如桃李"一词的翻译可以直接套用英语中的习语 as red as a rose。按照英语习惯，形容女人脸色的"红润""绯红"要用"玫瑰"来类比，如果在译文中硬把"玫瑰"换成"桃李"，反而不符合英语的习惯，令英美人费解。

2. 英语译文完全采用与汉语成语不同的语言形式和设喻方式，但喻义相同，也就是说，二者只是神似。

例如，"山穷水尽"可以套用英语习语 at the end of one's rope，但它们的区别十分明显：汉语是两个动宾短语，而英语是一个介词短语；汉语是用"山路已尽"和"水到尽头"来比喻陷入绝境、无路可走,而英语是用"(像动物一样被拴)在绳子的尽头"来比喻"束手无策、毫无选择"。虽然二者的语言形式和设喻方式完全不同,但表达的含义基本相同。

3. 在英语译文中省略部分汉语成语的内容。

例如,对于"破釜沉舟"一词,可以套用英语习语 burn one's boats,但英语译文只体现了汉语"沉舟"的意思,省略了"破釜"的意思。虽然形式和内容上有些缺失,但 burn one's boats 这个习语已经足以显示"不留后路、誓死一搏"的含义了。又如,"同心同德"可以套用英语短语 with one mind,省略了对"同德"的翻译,因为 with one mind 包含了"同德"的含义。

下面是这三种不完全对等套译的更多例子。

沧海一粟:a drop in the ocean
挥金如土:spend money like water
害群之马:a black sheep
笑掉大牙:laugh off one's head
掌上明珠:the apple of the eye
原形毕露:show one's colors
骨瘦如柴:as lean as a rail
本末倒置:put the cart before the horse
贪得无厌:as greedy as a wolf
洞若观火:as clear as daylight
爱屋及乌:love me, love my dog
弱不禁风:as weak as water
怒不可遏:make one's blood boil
半斤八两:six of one and half a dozen of the other
杀鸡取卵:kill the goose that lays golden eggs
面如土色:as pale / white as ashes / sheet / death
过河拆桥:kick down the ladder
滴水穿石:constant dripping wears the stone
逃之夭夭:show a clean pair of heels / take to one's heels
了如指掌:know something like the palm / back of one's hand
得寸进尺:give him an inch and he'll take an ell / a mile /a yard
无风不起浪:there is no smoke without fire
老虎屁股摸不得:don't beard the lion
谋事在人,成事在天:Man proposes, God disposes.
不入虎穴,焉得虎子:Go to the sea, if you would fish well.
山中无老虎,猴子称霸王:When the cats are away the mice will play.
棋逢对手,将遇良才:Diamonds cut Diamonds.
宁为鸡首,不为牛后:Better be the head of a dog than the tail of a lion.
倾盆大雨:rain cats and dogs
小题大做 make a mountain out of a molehill
枉费心机:go on a wild goose chase

开门见山:Come straight to the point.
直言不讳;实话实说:call a spade a spade
拐弯抹角;旁敲侧击:to beat about (around) the bush
酒后吐真言:There is truth in wine; In wine there is truth.
另有企图;别有企图;别有用心:have other fish to fry; have an axe to grind
两袖清风:clean hands
昙花一现:a flash in the pan / wok
风烛残年:have one foot in the grave
猫哭老鼠:shed crocodile tears
轻举妄动:a leap in the dark
否极泰来:The darkest hour comes before the dawn.
少年老成:have an old head on young shoulders
心有余而力不足:The spirit is willing but the flesh is weak.
物以类聚,人以群分:Birds of a feather flock together.
江山易改,本性难移:The leopard cannot change his spots.
好事不出门,坏事传千里:Bad news travels fast. ("好事不出门"没有翻译,省略了)
自吹自擂:blow one's own trumpets("自擂"省略了)
能工巧匠:skilled craftsman
称兄道弟:call each other brothers
赤手空拳:to be bare-handed
心慈手软:soft-hearted
自给自足:self-sufficient
天长地久:eternal like skies
无影无踪:vanish without any trace
安家落户:make one's home

二、意译法

　　套用英语习语来翻译汉语成语,既保留了原文的风格和喻体,又便于英语读者理解和接受,真正做到了译文的"信、达、雅"。但是,由于英汉两种语言在语言结构、民族色彩和思维习惯等方面的差异,大多数的汉语成语在英译时都难以套用英语习语,甚至都不能直译,只能采用意译的方法。例如,成语"初露锋芒"如果直译成 show primarily one's blade,则容易让英语读者不解:为什么要露出刀刃？露出刀刃想干什么？其实,成语中的"锋芒"并不是指刀刃,只是代指一个人的才能或力量,因此该成语最好意译成 show primarily one's talent,这样就不会让人产生误解了。
　　一些汉语成语具有独特的民族文化特色,几乎不可能通过直译法在译入语中得以重现,而通过意译法则能有效地传递其含义。虽然意译法难以保全汉语成语的文化特色和具体形象,但是却能简洁迅速地传递成语的喻义。例如,"灯红酒绿"是指一种奢靡的生活方式,可以意译成 dissipated and luxurious,如果直译成 red lantern and green wine,则容易给人一种是在描述某个场景的印象,传递不出该成语的含义。

下面是成语意译的更多例子。

快马加鞭:speed up

五光十色:multicolored

万紫千红:a riot / blaze of colour

单枪匹马:all by oneself

眉飞色舞:beam with joy

落花流水:be shattered into pieces

迎刃而解:be readily solved

前赴后继:advance wave by wave

孤注一掷:at all hazards

趾高气扬:carry one's head high

一帆风顺:plain sailing

有条不紊:in perfect order

倾城倾国:to be extremely beautiful

四分五裂:fall apart / be all split up / disintegrate

罄竹难书:(of crimes) too numerous to mention

锱铢必较:to haggle over every penny

忍无可忍:have exhausted one's patience

噤若寒蝉:keep silent out of fear

抛头露面:to make one's own appearance

虚怀若谷:to be modest and extremely open-minded

东施效颦:crude imitation with ludicrous effect

南柯一梦:a fond dream or illusory joy

初出茅庐:at the beginning of one's career

毛遂自荐:volunteer one's service

暗送秋波:make secret overture to sb.

悬梁刺股:be extremely hard-working in one's study

怨声载道:Complains are heard everywhere.

在成语意译的过程中,可以借用英语中的常用短语。例如,可以将"债台高筑"翻译成 be up to one's ears in debt。译文中的 be up to one's ears in sth. 是个常用短语,表示"在……上忙得不可开交"。

需要注意的是,不少成语既可以直译,也可以意译,各有特色。例如,对于"引狼入室",可以直译为 to bring the wolves into the house / fold(羊圈),也可以意译为 to invite disasters。

三、加注法

汉语中的许多典故成语都蕴含丰富的文化信息和鲜明的民族特色,如"班门弄斧""守株待兔""东施效颦""杞人忧天"等。如果采用直译法翻译这类成语,往往会给英语读者带来理解障碍；而采用意译法则可能丢失汉语成语独特的文化内涵和形象特色，因此，对于这类成语，比较合适的翻译方法就是采用加注法，即在直译的基础上增加注释。通过加注法，在译文中添加英语读者理解成语所需的文化背景知识，既能保留汉语成语的文化特色，又能确保译文为英语读者理解和接受。例如，成语"班门弄斧"可以加注译成 Show off one's proficiency with the axe before Lu Ban, the master carpenter. 如果翻译时不在 Lu Ban 后面加上同位语 the master carpenter 作为注释，那么绝大部分英语读者都会产生疑惑：为什么在 Lu Ban 面前耍斧子？Lu Ban 是干什么的？加上注释之后，自然就会化解人们的这一理解障碍。

又如，"守株待兔"可以直译为 watching the stump and waiting for a hare，然后另加注释：From the story of a pleasant who, seeing a hare run headlong against a tree-stump and break its neck, abandoned his piough and waited by the stump in the hope that another hare would do the same thing. 很明显，这个加注翻译法太长了，比较啰唆。其实，这个成语使用意译法更简单易懂：wait for gains without pains / wait for windfalls.

以下是加注法的更多例子。

木已成舟：The wood is already made into a boat — what's done is done.

杞人忧天：like the man of Chi who was haunted by the fear that the sky might fall — unnecessary anxiety.

东施效颦：Dong shi imitates Xi shi (Xi shi was a famous beauty in the ancient kingdom of Yue. Dong shi was an ugly.)

刻舟求剑：carve a mark on gunwale in moving boat where a sword was lost — disregarding the changing circumstances.

画龙点睛：bring the painted dragon to life by putting in the pupils of its eyes — bring out the crucial point

三顾茅庐：have visited the cottage thrice in succession — to call on sb. repeatedly

宁为玉碎，不为瓦全：I'd rather be a broken piece of jade（翡翠）than a whole tile（瓷砖，瓦片）— It's better to die in glory than live in dishonor.

三个臭皮匠，赛过诸葛亮：Three cobblers（修鞋匠）with their wits combined surpass Zhuge Liang, the mastermind — two heads are better than one.

四、译文欣赏

她曾经是一位百万富翁，对人对事从来都不吹毛求疵。正因如此，她的家里总是门庭若市，那些喜欢攀龙附凤的人，总是欢天喜地来聚会。但是现在，这里却门可罗雀，鲜有人来，因为她的事业正危如累卵。攀龙附凤者想攀高枝儿，不愿和她一起破釜沉舟，共渡难关。所以，当她寻求帮助时，这些肮脏的势利小人都视而不见。她最终明白了这些所谓的"朋友"是靠不住的。虽然有些伤心，但对于那些与势利小人的毫无价值的友谊，她并没有大呼小叫。她决定破釜沉舟，卖掉公司。

［译文］She used to be a millionaire and never found fault with others. Her house used to be a much visited house, and people who are social climbers often came here with great joys. But now it is a deserted island, completely absent of callers, because her career is hazardous in the extreme. Social climbers want to worship the rising sun, not to burn their bridge behind. So these nasty little snobs turn a blind eye to her calling for help. She finally comes to realize that she cannot count on those so-called "friends". A little heart-broken, but she doesn't make a big fuss about the worthless friendship with these snobbish people. She decided to go down with the ship and sell her company.

互助(小小说)

　　L君跻身文坛,盖有年矣,但总是红不起来,颇感寂寞。于是,他找到了各种关系,以盛宴重礼把著名的评论家J君招待了一次。J君有感于其情之盛,慨然允诺说:"现在他们对你太冷落了,就是不公平!我一定要写一篇推荐你的作品的文章,登到大报上,你的作品的优点是……"

　　L君不等J君说完,慌忙摆手摇头,他说:"千万不必!千万不必!我只乞求您写一篇义正词严的文章把我批一个狗血淋头!积数十年之经验,我深知凡被您批了的,都可以风行全国,名震寰球!而您也可以获得另一方面的美誉和利益,那才叫相反相成,相得益彰。"

——王蒙

[译文]

Version 1: Mutual Help ——冯庆华《实用翻译教程》

　　It had been several years since Mr. L. had climbed up in the literary world, but he was still not very popular. Through various connections, he managed to meet the famous critic Mr. J. and invite him to a sumptuous banquet.

　　"They neglect you unfairly," said Mr. J., moved by L's hospitality. "I will write a laudatory essay and publish it in an influential newspaper. Your work is characterized by…"

　　But before Mr. J. could finish, Mr. L. shook his head and said, "please do not compliment my work; I implore you to write an article denouncing me. According to my observations over the past ten years, the works that you criticize become popular both at home and abroad. You, in turn, build your reputation and earn a nice income. That's what we call mutual help."

Version 2: Help Each Other ——夏乙琥

　　Mr. L. had been a member of the literary circles for years without attracting any public attention. He felt deserted, but he managed through various personal connections to invite Mr. J. a famous literary critic, to an elaborate dinner. Mr. J. was quite moved by Mr. L.'s hospitality and promised right away, "it's not fair that you have been so ignored! I must write an article for a key newspaper to recommend your works. The merits of your works are…"

　　Mr. L. cut in, shaking his head and waving his hands, "No! No! I only beg you to write a very severe criticism against me. From my years of experience, I have come to the conclusion that all work criticized by you will become popular not only in our country but also in the world. Meanwhile, you win greater fame through your criticism. This is indeed mutual help and profit!"

　　中国外交人员要立场坚定、目光远大、头脑敏捷、业务熟练、才华出众、风格高尚。

[译文] A Chinese diplomat should be firm in stand, broad in vision, swift in wit, qualified in profession, outstanding in talent, noble in character.

纵目眺望,我饱览了一片无限娇艳的风光:万紫千红,郁郁葱葱,鸟语悦耳,花香袭人,涟漪荡漾,瀑布飞流,层峦起伏,阡陌纵横。真可谓生机勃勃,气象万千。

[译文] As far as sight could reach, I feasted my eyes on a vastness of infinite charm, which presents itself in a profusion of color, in verdant luxuriance, in dulcet warbling, in pervading perfume, in rippling undulation, in cataract sprays, in hilly waves, in field crisscross and verily in vitality and variety.

五、实践练习

(一) 用两种方法翻译下列成语。

(1) 调虎离山_____
(2) 狗仗人势_____
(3) 声东击西_____
(4) 刻骨铭心_____
(5) 涸泽而渔_____
(6) 雪中送炭_____
(7) 家徒四壁_____
(8) 对牛弹琴_____
(9) 画蛇添足_____
(10) 福无双至,祸不单行_____

(二) 翻译下列句子。

(1) 她四面望望空洞的屋子,茫然地笑笑:"真是家徒四壁啊!"
(2) 这个问题搞得他晕头转向。
(3) 贾母听了,如火上浇油一般,便骂:"是谁做了棺椁?"
(4) 多数人兴高采烈之日,却是少数人伤心失意之时。
(5) 他坐在那儿注视着,觉得眼前的景象,既是始终如一,又是变化多端;既是光彩夺目,又是朦胧黑暗;既是庄严肃穆,又是轻松愉快。
(6) 他马马虎虎地看了看那张便条就走了。
(7) "……是些什么人呢? 干这引狼入室的勾当!"
(8) 不要动声色,不要打草惊蛇,我们不妨看看他们如何活动。
(9) 这里山花古松遮掩着悬崖峭壁,鸟语花香,生意盎然,一派秀丽景色。
(10) 他待人处事,八面玲珑。

第五章　汉语句子的翻译

一、顺序译法

在一些场合,汉英句子的叙述层次可相互匹配,这时可以基本依照汉语语句的表达顺序进行英语语句的翻译。这种按照原文顺序,把句子从前往后翻译的方法叫顺序译法,顺序译法不会改变原文表达语序,不会影响对原文内容的理解。例如:

他是一位中国当代优秀作家。

[译文]He is an outstanding contemporary Chinese writer.

如果你不来,我们就会取消此次会议。

[译文]If you don't come, we will cancel the meeting.

领头的是一位40岁的蒙古人,他的妻子是位藏族人。

[译文]The leader is a 40-year-old Mongolian, whose wife is a Tibetan.

顺序译法多用于单一主语的长句,在译文中要分清句中的信息重心。例如:

他还说,不坚持社会主义,不改革开放,不发展中国的经济,不改善人民的生活水平只有死路一条。

[译文]He also said, if we don't stick to socialism, if we don't carry out the reform and opening up to the out side world, if we don't develop China's economy and if we don't improve the living standards of the Chinese people, we will find ourselves in a blind alley.

英语句子很注重信息的主次之分,主要信息放在突出位置,次要信息作为辅助性的描写或叙述手段。所以汉译英时,应该把汉语隐性主次关系发掘出来,译成英语的主次表达方式。例如:

我们喝茶时,我不停地打量着她,看她那纤纤玉手,典雅的举止,亮晶晶的黑眼睛,清秀而没有表情的面庞。

[译文]When we had tea, I could not take my eyes from her small, delicate hands, the graceful way she moved, her bright, black eyes, and expressionless clear face.

这个汉语句子的主干是"我打量她",后面都是我所看到的细节描写。

其中有一半是近5年才来到温哥华地区的,这使温哥华成为亚洲以外最大的中国人聚居地。(1999年TEM8)

[译文]Half of them have come to Vancouver area the past five years only, making it the largest Chinese settlement outside Asia.

汉语原文中"这使……聚居地"是华人移民的结果,故而被译为现在分词短语的形式。

即使在我们关掉床头灯甜甜地进入梦乡时,电仍然为我们工作:开动电冰箱,把水加热,或使室内空调机继续运转。

[译文] Even when we turn off the bedside lamp and are fast asleep, electricity is still working for us, driving our refrigerators, heating our water, or keeping our rooms air-conditioned.

该句子前半部分是一个让步状语从句,后半句的"开动""加热""使……运转"都是"电在为我们工作"的具体内容,因而这三个并行动作被译为现在分词短语的形式,补充说明working 的内容。

罗斯福总统目光炯炯,含笑倾听,一言未发,然后同其他人一样,报以热烈的掌声。

[译文] President Roosevelt listened with bright-eyed smiling attention, saying nothing, and applauding heartily with the rest.

语义表述顺序一致,故顺译。

我给那些因为在近旁而极响的爆竹声惊醒,看见豆一般大的黄色的灯火光,接着又听得毕毕剥剥的鞭炮,是四叔家正在"祝福"了;知道已是五更将近时候。

[译文] I was woken up by the noisy explosion of crackers close at hand and, from the faint glow shed by the yellow oil lamps and the bangs of fireworks as my uncle's household celebrated the sacrifice, I knew that it must be nearly dawn.

原文的句子脉络是:我被爆竹声惊醒、看见灯光、听见鞭炮声、知道"祝福了"、推算时间等,几层意思按照事情发生的先后顺序展开,译文按照此顺序译出,实现形式与内容的吻合,在分句间添加适当的关联词,使译文逻辑关系更清楚。

二、换序译法

换序译法,又称顺序调整法,是将原句中的某一部分(词、词组、短句、从句)进行位置变动,使之更符合译句目标语的语言习惯,最大程度上做到译句语言通顺。

汉民族在思维上历来注重"悟性""直觉",强调"先发生的事先说,后发生的事后说",从整体上汉语表现为意合的语义型语言,语义通过语序表达出来。英美人偏重理性思维,其语言表现为形合的分析型语言,其语义通过逻辑关系体现出来。例如:

世界各国的医学专家们多年来一直致力于构建一整套科学的有关人体健康的标准体系。

[译文] For years, medical experts from different countries have committed themselves to establishing a set of scientific standard system for human health.

句子的主干是:多年来……专家们……构建……体系。而句中的其他部分则多数充当了定语、状语等。

一直在一旁观看的小学生们开始鼓起掌来。

[译文] The pupils that had been watching started to applaud.

句子的主干是:……小学生们开始鼓掌。英语中,当定语较长时,往往后置,译文属典型的定语后置。

我支持你。

[译文] I give you a support.

句子谓语动词"支持"在译文中变成了宾语,放在句末。

这三个县经历了那场中国20世纪70年代第四次较为严重的遍及数省的自然灾害。

[译文] The three counties underwent the fourth rather serious natural disaster that plagued several provinces in China in the 1970's.

句子的主干是:这三个县经历了……自然灾害,其余的定语在译文中分别被前置和后置。

在那场战争中,这道城墙开始出现许多裂痕。

[译文] Many cracks began to appear on the city wall during that war.

句子的主干是:"城墙……开始出现裂痕。"译文中宾语被翻译成了主语,而主语则充当了状语。

她每个周六学画画。

[译文] She learns painting every Saturday.

句子的主干是:她学画画,其余为时间状语,译文中,被后置。

中国乒乓球大奖赛的最后一天,刘国梁在男子单打比赛中一举夺魁后,干脆利落地夺得大奖赛的4项冠军。

[译文] Liu Guoliang completed a clean sweep of four titles after winning the men's singles championship on the final day of the Chinese Table-Tennis Grand Prix.

句子的主干是:刘国梁……夺得冠军。其余的成分为时间状语,在译文中,被后置。

我在山坡上的小屋里,悄悄掀起窗帘,窥见园中大千世界,一片喧闹。

[译文] Without been noticed, I lifted the curtain in my small room, only to spy the bustle of a kaleidoscopic world down in the garden.

句子的主干是:我……掀起窗帘,窥见……世界。时间状语"在山坡上的小屋里"、方式状语"悄悄"在译文中分别被前置和后置;而从句中的谓语"一片喧闹"在译文中,则成为了前置定语,定语"园中"被后置。

对知识与信息的开发、获取、扩散和利用程度的高低将直接决定一个国家的整体经济实力和文化发展水平。

[译文] The keys to the strong economic and cultural growth of a nation's future are successful generation, acquisition, diffusion, and exploitation of knowledge.

句子主干是:……高低……决定……实力和……水平。定语"对知识与信息的开发、获取、扩散和利用程度"在译文中被后置,充当表语;谓语动词"决定"被转化为名词"The keys",与其后的宾语组合成一个名词化短语作句子的主语。译文通过名词化重组语句重心,突出强调谓语所包含的信息。

只要1996到2010年粮食单产年均递增1%,2011到2030年年均递增0.7%,就可以达到预期的粮食总产量目标。

[译文] The predicted total output target of grain can be reached, if the annual average increase rate of per unit area yield of grain is 1% from 1996 to 2010 and 0.7% from 2011 to 2030.

句子中的状语因为太长,译文中,被放在了句末。

中国的海洋资源十分丰富。

[译文] China is rich in marine resource.

句子主语较长。

发生了这样的事不是你的错。

[译文] It's not your fault that this has happened.

句子主语"发生了这样的事"属陈述事实,而"不是你的错"属评论性的语言,英语通常先评论,再事实,故而译文中句子主语放到了后边。

她,一个瘦弱多病的女孩子,以她坚强的毅力写出了一部部催人奋进的小说。

[译文] A thin and weak girl susceptible to diseases, she wrote one inspiring novel after another with her strong will.

译文中,同位语前置,方式状语后置。

三、断句译法

断句,也叫分译或拆句,就是对原文进行层次划分,分别译成两句或更多的句子。其一般原则是:首先透彻理解原文,分析句子与句子之间以及每个句子内各部分之间的关系,弄清这种关系是平行关系还是主辅关系,然后根据英语的表达习惯重新断句、拆句或并句。一句话必要时可断成几句来译,才能使意思清晰,结构合理,合乎英语的表达习惯。

对于长句,可对其进行语法分析,先找出句子的主语、谓语和宾语,然后找出修饰主、宾的定语与定语从句,以及各个成分的修饰语。

1. 一句话中包含两个或多个层次的意思,只有一个主语,通常在第一层意思处断句,之后的另一个或几个层次另为一句,且第二句的主语用代词即可。例如:

一般说来,典型的金属能导热导电,// 表面有光泽,具有延展性和可锻性。

[译文] General speaking, the typical metal conducts electricity and heat. // It shows lustrous surface, usually with white, or so-called metallic luster. It is ductile and malleable.

这个句子只有一个主语:在第一层意思处断句,之后的另外两个层次另为一句,从第二句开始,主语用代词。

在软木塞上钻一个小孔,// 将一根玻璃管插入软木塞的孔中。

[译文] Make a hole through the cork. // Push a tube through the hole in the cork.

这是一个汉语祈使句,主语省略,译文断为两句。

小马儿也就是十三岁,脸上很瘦,身上可是穿得很圆,鼻子冻得通红,挂着两条白鼻涕,耳朵上戴着一对破耳帽儿。(《骆驼祥子》)

[译文] Little horse was no more than thirteen. His face was very thin. But his clothes were bulky. His nose, red with cold, was running. On his ears, he wore a pair of tattered earmuffs.

这是一个流水句,包含了四个不同话题的分句,各分句之间无关联词语来表明它们之间的关系。翻译时,按各分句不同的话题拆分:年龄、脸与身子形成的对比、鼻子、耳朵,我们将整个句子译成相应的四个句子,层次清楚,很好地保持了各层次的相对独立性。

2. 一句话中包含两个或多个层次的意思,不同短句中出现不同主语,不同主语的短句通常另立一句。例如:

不一会,北风小了,路上浮尘早已刮净,剩下一条洁白的大道来,车夫也跑得更快了。

[译文]Presently the wind dropped a little. By now the loose dust had all been blown away, leaving the road way clean, and the rickshaw man quickened his pace. (《一件小事》)

水蒸气接触到冷瓶子时,就冷却为水,// 瓶子就湿了。

[译文]When the steam touches the cold bottle, it cools and changes into water again. // The bottle becomes wet.

原子核由质子,或带正电荷的粒子和中子,不带电荷的粒子的结合体组成,// 各种元素内的质子和中子数量可以不等,但只有一些结合体是稳定的。

[译文]Atomic nuclei consist of combinations of protons, or positively-charged particles, and neutrons, or uncharged particles. // The number of protons and neutrons in each element can vary, but only certain combinations are stable.

耳朵是用来听声音的器官,// 鼻子用来嗅气味,// 舌头用来尝滋味。

[译文]The ear is the organ which is used for hearing. // The nose is used for smelling. // The tongue is used for tasting.

3. 一句话中包含两个或多个层次的意思,如果是定语较多的句子,主干部分成一句,其他补充或说明部分另立一句,而且补充或说明部分含并列或多重意思的可进一步拆分。例如:

因此,关于阀的开启有效行程应当是指气包压力开始下降(即气箱压力明显上升)的 A 点到气包压力开始趋于平稳的 B 点阀所经历的行程。

[译文]Therefore, the effective stroke of the valve during opening should be the distance the valve travels from point A to point B. // At point A the pressure in the air tank begins to fall (that is, the pressure in the clearance of the upper part of the flask begins to rise obviously). At point B the pressure in the air tank begins to be steady.

4. 如果汉语是采用"先总说、后分述"或"先分述、后总说"结构或因果关系的长句,英译时通常总说为一句、分述为一句,或原因为一句、结果为一句。

对于先总后分的句子,一般在句子开头总分之间部分断开。例如:

但他性情不同,// 既不求官爵,又不交纳朋友,// 终日闭户读书。

[译文]He was, however, eccentric. He did not look for an official post, and did not even have any friends. All day he studied behind closed doors.

人的觉悟是不容易的,// 要去掉人民头脑中的错误意识,需要我们做很多切切实实的工作。

[译文]The political awakening of the people is not easy. // It requires much earnest effort on our part to rid their minds off wrong ideas.

以上两个句子都是原句有三层意思,先总说,后分述时意思发生转折,断开翻译使译文意思更加清晰。

总之,微波只能以射线方式传播,// 没有一系列的转播塔,它们就不能越过漫长的距离,把消息传递到遥远的地方。

[译文] In short, microwaves can only travel in straight line. // Without a series of rely towers, it is impossible for them to send messages over long distances to remote places.

对于先分后总的句子,可先在句子的结尾处断开。例如:

灾难深重的中华民族,一百年来,其优秀人物奋斗牺牲,前赴后继,摸索救国救民的真理,// 是可歌可泣的。

[译文] For a hundred years, the finest sons and daughters of the disaster-ridden Chinese nation fought and scarified their lives, one stepping into the breach as another fell, inquest of the truth that would save the country and the people. This moved us to songs and tears.

原句先分后总,对前面的内容作一概括,或者说是一种评论。翻译时在结尾处断开,将最后的判断部分单独译成一个独立的简单句,使译文顺畅,不显累赘。

四、合句译法

合句译法,指的是根据逻辑关系和语言习惯,翻译时把原文中内容关系密切的两个或多个句子合成一个句子。合句译法中有"单句+单句""单句+复句""复句+复句"等类型。合句译法是句法翻译中十分重要的方法之一。在使用得当的情况下,合句译法能有效调整句子长度,使译文词句简练、逻辑关系清晰、语气连贯、一气呵成。因此,合句译法对于汉译英而言意义非凡。

另外,汉语习惯采用短句,而英语惯用长句(特别是科技英语),因此汉译英更常使用合句译法,将意思相近,或意思连贯,或逻辑关系紧密的若干短句合并成较长的复杂句。

(一)合译为简单句

例如:

为了使在破碎机上从事检查与维修的工作人员在适当高度上工作,应安装工作平台。工作平台上应装有扶手、踏板。

[译文] Platform, with handrail and tread, should be built to ensure staffs inspect and maintain the crusher at a proper height.

排料室既可用金属也可用木头制作。排料室应留有检查门,供人员进入排料室内部清扫和检查用。

[译文] It (discharge chamber) can be made of metal or food, with an inspection panel set for workers to do some cleaning and inspection work inside the crusher.

以上两个例子均是借助于 with 引导的介词短语,把两个句子合译为一个简单句,既简化了句式,又如实地传达了原文的意思。

由于西藏地处"世界屋脊",自然条件恶劣,也由于几百年落后的封建农奴制社会形成的各种社会历史条件的限制,西藏在全国还属于不发达地区。

[译文]Tibet, located on the "Roof of the World", is still an underdeveloped area in China because of its harsh natural conditions and various social and historical restrictions formed by centuries of backward feudal serfdom.

虽然汉语句子包含了两个表示原因的"由于……",在译文中,被处理成了由"because of"引出原因的简单句。

(二)合译为并列句

例如:

笛声止了。远远地起了拍掌声和欢笑声。(巴金:《家》)

[译文]The flute stopped, and in the distance there was applause and laughter.

袭人之母也早迎了出来。袭人拉了宝玉进去。(曹雪芹:《红楼梦》,第十九回)

[译文]By now Xiren's mother had come out to greet him too, and Xiren led Baoyu in.

新航线和公交公司不断涌现。竞争降低了旅游成本。

[译文]New airlines and bus companies have emerged, and competition has cut the cost of travel.

油箱内部要彻底清洗。油管在安装之前应认真检查确无异物后再安装。

[译文]Internal oil tank needs cleaning thoroughly and oil pipes should be inspected carefully to get rid of any impurities before installation.

夜幕降临。她还没有回家。

[译文]Night began to fall, but she hadn't come back.

她病了。然而她照旧去上班,并且尽力集中精神工作。

[译文]She was ill, however she still went to work and tried to concentrate.

(三)合译为复合句

两个或两个以上有着逻辑而又语义相关的汉语句子译成英文,如果无法译成一个英语中的简单句或并列句,则可以译为复合句。根据具体情况,主句可以带一个从句,或是带多个从句。

合译为主句带一个从句:

改革价格体系关系国民经济全局,涉及千家万户。一定要采取十分慎重的态度,有计划、有步骤地进行。

[译文]As the price system reforms affected every household and the national economy, they must be carried out extremely prudently in a planned and systematic way.

汉语原文由两个句子组成。两句间有着因果关系。为什么"一定要采取十分慎重的态度,有计划、有步骤地进行",原因在于"改革价格体系关系国民经济全局,涉及千家万户。"因此,英译时可以将第一句处理成一个"as"引导的原因状语从句,放在第二句的前面。经过这样的处理,原句被合译成一个包含因果关系的主从复合句。

思想动向问题,我们应当抓住。这里当作第一个问题提出来。

[译文] We should keep tabs on ideological trends, which I am taking up here as the first question.

汉语原文由两个句子组成,第二个句子是对第一个句子的进一步说明,译文中被合译成了一个非限制性定语从句。

这贾菌亦系荣国府近派的重孙。// 其母亦少寡,独守着贾菌。(曹雪芹《红楼梦》第九回)

[译文] Jia Jun was a great-great-grand-son of the Duke of Rongguo, and the only son of his mother who had been widowed early.

译文被处理成了一个含有定语从句的复合句。

(四) 合译为主句带多个从句

旧历新年来了。这是一年中的第一件大事。//除了那些负债过多的人以外,大家都热烈地欢迎这个佳节的到来。(巴金:《家》)

[译文] The traditional New Year Holiday was fast approaching, the first big event of the year, and everyone, except those who owed heavy debts which traditionally had to be paid off before the year was enthusiastically looking forward to it.

原文由三个汉语简单句构成,译文中,第二个汉语句子被处理成了一个同位语,第三句话被处理成了一个复合句,包含两个定语从句"那些负债过多的人",而按照中国人的传统债具有一个内涵的意义——在旧历新年之前是一定要还的,这层内涵的意义也被翻译成了一个定语从句,解释了为什么"欢迎这个佳节到来的"人群中,要"除了那些负债过多的人"。

每去一次,我的药量就减少一些。最后医生告诉我说,不必再服药了。

[译文] With each visit, the dose of medicine prescribed to me would be progressively reduced, until the time came when the doctor said that I would no longer need them.

译文被处理成了一个包含 until 引导的时间状语和关系副词引导的定语从句的复合句。

五、译文欣赏

我喜欢你是静静的:
仿佛你消失了一样 你从远处聆听我,
我的声音却无法触及你 好像你的目光已经游离而去,
如同一个吻,封缄了你的嘴。
如同我积满一切的灵魂,
而你从一切中出现,充盈了我的灵魂,
你像我的灵魂,
像一只梦想的蝴蝶 你如同"忧郁"这个词。
我喜欢你是静静的:好像你已远去,

你听起来像在悲叹,
一只如鸽般细语的蝴蝶你从远处聆听我,
我的声音却无法触及你,
让我在你的静谧中安静无声,
并且让我籍着你的沉默与你说话。
你的沉默亮若明灯,简单如环,
你如黑夜,拥有寂静与群星,
你的沉默就是星星的力量,遥远而明亮,
我喜欢你是静静的:仿佛你消失了一样远隔千里,
满怀哀恸,仿佛你已不在人世彼时,
一个字,一个微笑,就已足够。
而我会感到幸福,但那样的幸福却不真实。

[译文]

I like for you to be still:

it is as through you are absent

and you hear me from far away and my voice does not touch you

It seems as through your eyes had flown away

and it seems that a kiss had sealed your mouth

as all things are filled with my soul

your emerge from the things, fill with my soul

you are like my soul, a butterfly of dreams

and you are like the word melancholy

I like for you to be still, and you seem far away

It sounds as though you are lamenting,

a butterfly cooing like a dove

And you hear me from far away,

and my voice does not reach you

Let me come to be still in your silence

And let me talk to you with your silence

That is bright like a lamp, simple as a ring

You are like the night, with its stillness and constellations

Your silence is that of a star, as remount and candid

I like for you to be still: it is as though you are absent

distant and dull of sorrow, as though you had died

One word then, one smile, is enough

And I'm happy, happy that's not true…

回信,固然可畏,不回信,也绝非什么乐事。书架上经常叠着百多封未回之信,"债龄"或长或短,长的甚至一年以上,那样的压力,也绝非一个普通的罪徒所能负担的。一叠未回的信,就像一群不散的阴魂,在我罪孽深重的心底幢幢作祟。理论上说来,这些信当然是要回的。我可以坦然向天发誓,在我清醒的时刻,我绝未存心不回人信。问题出在技术上。给我一整个夏夜的空闲,我该先回一年半前的那封信呢,还是七个月前的这封信?隔了这么久,恐怕连谢罪自谴的有效期也早过了吧。在朋友的心目中,你早已沦为不值得计较的妄人。"莫名其妙!"是你在江湖上一致的评语。

[译文]

Replying a letter does make me flinch; however, unreplied letters allow me no release at all. Dozens of unreplied letters pile up on my bookshelf, like a sum of debt waiting to be paid. Some have been waiting there for over one year, while some have newly arrived. The pressure from paying off that debt is far beyond what a junior debtor can endure. The stack of unreplied letters are, like a group of haunting ghosts, continually pestering my guilt-loaded soul. Conventionally, the letters will certainly be replied. I can even swear by heaven that never do I have the intention not to reply when my mind is clear. The problem is how to reply. Even if I spared myself a whole summer night, I would be wavering on which letter to reply first, the 18-month-old one or the 7-month-old? The reply has been delayed for so long that I'm afraid even a heartfelt apology has already lost its power. In friends' heart, I've been marginalized as a cocky man unworthy of care. "unaccountable"! That is their unanimous comment on me.

其实,即使终于鼓起全部的道德勇气,坐在桌前,准备偿付信债于万一,也不是轻易能如愿的。七零八落的新简旧信,漫无规则地充塞在书架上,抽屉里,有的回过,有的未回,"只在此山中,云深不知处",要找到你决心要回的那一封,耗费的时间和精力,往往数倍于回信本身。再想象朋友接信时的表情,不是喜出望外,而是余怒重炽,你那一点决心就整个崩溃了。你的债,永无清偿之日。不回信,绝不等于忘了朋友,正如世上绝无忘了债主的负债人。在你惶恐的深处,恶魔的尽头,隐隐约约,永远潜伏着这位朋友的怒眉和冷眼,不,你永远忘不了他。你真正忘掉的,而且忘得那么心安理得,是那些已经得到你回信的朋友。

[译文]

In fact, even though I pull myself together and settle down at the desk, ready to pay off the debt, my determination will easily be split up by doubts. Old and new letters, replied or yet-to-be, cram the shelf and the drawer in disorder, which reminds me of two verses: "he's simply in the very mountain. In the depths of clouds, his whereabouts are unknown." (from calling on a hermit in vain by Jia Dao). Picking out the letter I decide to reply from such a mess will cost multiplied time and energy as replying the letter does. Moreover, on visualizing the facial expression of friends when they receive the reply — reburned lingering anger rather than surprised delight — my tiny amount of determination dwindle into naught. Consequently, the date when my debt is paid off extends into eternity. Although I haven't replied the letters, I can never forget my friends, any more than a debtor can forget his creditor. In the depth of my disturbed and apologetic heart looms the indelible angry and icy look of my friends. Never can I forget them. Friends who really fall into oblivion, from which guilt is totally absent, are those who have received my reply.

六、实践练习

翻译下列句子。

(1) 京剧是中国流行最广、影响最大的一个剧种。

(2) 隋末唐初时,发明了雕版印刷术(block printing),提高了印刷的速度。

(3) 周恩来的房门开了。他们看到了一个身材修长的人,比普通人高,目光炯炯,面貌引人注目,称得上美男子。

(4) 去年八月那场使七个国家遭受了极大损失的来势凶猛的龙卷风已经引起全球科学家的高度重视。

(5) 即使是最好的厨师,有时也会做出不好的菜来。

(6) 门前放着一堆雨伞,少数也有十几把,五颜六色,大小不一。

(7) 芬芳的气味,比如玫瑰或杏仁的香气,可以减轻人的痛苦,不过这似乎只对女人有效。

(8) 据我所知,今天有许多嘉宾要致辞祝贺。这真是令人期待。

(9) 旅游的间接效益更大,估计创造了1 840亿美元的经济活动,以及5 400万个就业岗位。

(10) 无论你的兴趣是什么,你都可以在北京找到符合你爱好的博物馆。农业、建筑、自然、地质、太空……随便什么。

第六章 汉语篇章的翻译

语篇是交流过程中的一系列连续的语段或句子所构成的语言整体。在结构上,语篇是超出句子的语言单位;在实际应用中,单个词也可以构成一个语篇。语篇的各成分之间,在形式上是衔接的,在语义上是连贯的。

在汉英翻译中,要首先注意到汉英语言形式上的差异,如语篇衔接上的差异,才能译出流利的文字,才能使两种语言达到真正的等值。所以,在翻译过程中,必须解决好衔接和连贯的问题。

一、衔接的翻译

"衔接"(Cohesion)这一概念最早由韩礼德(1961,1962)提出。中国的学者们在研究语篇的衔接手段时,主要是借鉴了韩礼德与哈桑的研究成果,从照应、替代、省略、连接词、词汇衔接、已知信息与新信息等几个方面入手。无论是通过何种手段,衔接都要使篇章连贯,但衔接手段本身可以是显性或隐性的。

(一)照应

在语篇中,如果对于一个词语的解释,不能从词语本身获得,而必须从该词语所指代的对象中寻求答案,这就产生了照应关系(Halliday & Hason, 1976:23)。根据照应对象的差别,人们将其分为人称照应、指示照应与对比照应。照应在英语中的使用大大多于汉语。所以在翻译时要注意增补出在汉语中被隐去的照应手段。例如:

每年农历十二月二十以后,海岛上的居民便开始进入过年倒计时。先搞卫生,掸去一年尘土。接着准备食品,做年糕、炒倭豆、炒番薯片、打米花糖。廿五、廿六起,家家户户开始"谢年":祀祖先。

[译文](1) Every year after the 20th of the lunar 12th month, inhabitants on the island would start their countdown to the Spring Festival. (2) They would sweep their houses clean, flickering every bit of dust off the furniture. (3) After that they begin to prepare various foods: steamed New Year cakes, fried beans, fried sweet potato chips, and baked rice cookies. (4) On the 25th and 26th of the month, households start their "New Year Thanks-giving" rites to pay homage to their ancestors.

原文的第二句话没有出现主语,但根据上下文,可知主语就是第一句话的主语,译文中增补了第二句话的主语"They"、两个按照英语习惯表示所属的物主代词"their"、说明时间

顺序的"After"和指示指称"that",增强篇章的连贯性。再如:

听说,杭州西湖上的雷峰塔倒掉了,听说而已,我没有亲见。(鲁迅《论雷峰塔的倒掉》)

[译文] I hear Leifeng Pagoda by the West Lake in Hangzhou has collapsed. This is here say only, not something I have seen for myself.

译文用了作为中心词的指示代词"this"来回指上文提到的事。

(二) 替代

替代也是语法衔接的重要组成部分,指用"one""do""so"这些替代词去取代上下文出现的成分(黄国文 2001:115)。英语语篇中大多为了避免赘述,使用替代的方式创建连贯。所以在汉译英时,应考虑到英语习惯,在适当的地方将汉语中重复的语词处理成替代。例如:

一切都要从这个实际出发,根据这个实际来制订规划。

[译文] In everything we do we must proceed from this reality, and all planning must be consistent with it.

译文用 it 替代 reality,避免赘述,属于典型的代词替代。

你们到农村去看了一下吗?我们真正的变化还是在农村,有些变化出乎我们的预料。

[译文] Have you been to our countryside? The real changes have taken place there, and some of them have exceeded our expectations.

为了避免赘述,用 there 和 them 分别替代 countryside 和 changes。

中华文明同古埃及文明、古巴比伦文明、古印度文明、古希腊文明等,是人类文明的发源地。

[译文] The Chinese civilization, together with those of ancient Egypt, Babylonia, India, and Greece, is the source of human civilization.

原文中"文明"出现了六次,为了符合英语的习惯,也为了避免赘述,译文中,用 those 来替代。

(三) 省略

省略的功能与替代基本相同,是在不违反语言习惯和语法功能的前提下,将句子结构中的某个成分去掉,避免繁复,突出主要信息,使句子连贯。例如:

我们历来主张尊重世界文明的多样性,倡导不同文明之间的对话、交流与合作。

[译文] We have always upheld the respect for the diversity of civilizations and the dialogue, exchanges and cooperation among them.

原文前面一句中的"世界文明"和后面一句中的"不同文明"指的是同样的内容,所以用 them 替代了 civilization。此外,因为"主张"和"倡导"的意义也相似,连接两个并列关系的句子,所以省略后面的动词。再如:

工业园区土地使用权转让的成本价目前为每亩16万元人民币,年内,对符合国家产业导向、规模大、科技含量高的外商投资项目,按照每100万美元用10亩土地的比例,给予特殊价格优惠。其中注册资本在100万美元到300万美元的,每亩地价为8万元人民币;300

万美元到 500 万美元的,每亩地价为 7 万元人民币;500 万美元到 1 000 万美元的,每亩地价为 6 万元人民币;1 000 万美元以上的每亩地价为 5 万元人民币。

[译文] Currently, the cost of land use transfer in the Zone is charged at the ratio of 160 thousand yuan per Chinese mu, whereas before the end of this year, the price will be lowered down to 1 million US dollars every 10 mu for those large and technology intensive foreign projects that are run in compliance with the industrial orientation of the country. As regards those conglomerates with a registered capital ranging form 1 million (US dollars) to 3 million US dollars, the price is 80 thousand yuan per mu, (the price is) 70 thousand yuan for those with that from 3 million (US dollars) to 5 million (US dollars), (the price is) 60 thousand for those from 5 to10 million (US dollars) and (US dollars) 50 thousand for those over 10 million (US dollars).

译文中,括号里的内容,如果保留,则既不符合英语语言表达习惯,又使篇章显得冗赘繁杂,不能突出主要信息,只有省略掉,才能使语言交际者将更多的精力放在新信息上。

(四)连接词

语篇中使用连接词可以在上下文之间建立某种语义关系,使上下文的逻辑更加清晰,时间和空间顺序也会更加明了。由于汉语是重意合而不重形式联系的语言,它的篇章中较少使用连接词,其语义关系很多是隐性的;英语是形合的语言,更重视形式上的环环相扣,语句间的逻辑关系多由连接词表达出来。因此在翻译中,应当注意将汉语中的隐性关系转换成英语的显性用语。例如:

留得青山在,不怕没柴烧。

[译文] As long as the green hills last, there will be wood to burn.

原文中"留得青山在"与"不怕没柴烧"之间的逻辑关系是只要"留得青山在",就"不怕没柴烧"。

走到路上,还没"断黑",已经一连串地亮起了街灯。

[译文] When you go out for a walk towards the evening, you'll see street laps lit up one after another though it is not yet quite dark.

原文"走到路上"与"还没'断黑'"的逻辑关系是当"走到路上"的时候,"还没'断黑'";而"还没'断黑'",与"已经一连串地亮起了街灯"之间的逻辑关系是虽然"还没'断黑'",但是"已经一连串地亮起了街灯"。在译成英文时,既用了表示时间节点的 when,又用了表示转折关系的 though,这些连词除了引导分句,在形式上起到连接的作用之外,也把原句中所暗指的逻辑关系清晰地表现了出来。

从以上这些例子可以看出,在汉译英的过程中,因为有了这些连词的加入,汉语中原本内在的、隐含的、模糊的逻辑关系在英语语言中得以清晰再现,也正符合了英语语言主从分明,层次清晰,结构形式齐整,语流严谨的特点。

(五)词汇衔接

词汇衔接指通过词的重复、同义、上下义、反义、互补、同现等词汇间的语义关系来实现

语篇连贯。通过词汇衔接,可以产生很强的粘合力,形成一张"词汇网",赋予语篇连贯性。例如:

我养过鸟,养过狗,现在还养猫。

[译文]I've raised birds and dogs, and now I keep cats.

原文是个排比句,动词"养过"用了三次。如果重复使用同一个词,会使文章显得生硬,所以译文中用了两个词"raise"和"keep",既保持了连贯,句子也没有失去活力。再如:

乡镇工业园区已经成为我市乡镇企业"二次创业"的有效载体,极大地改善了企业的发展环境。目前已有3772家企业进驻园区。

[译文]Township industrial zones provide solid vehicles for the city's enterprises in running new businesses and greatly improve the setting for the development of such entities. So far, 3772 establishments have found home in these quarters.

译文除了添加了连接词"so far"增加语篇的连贯之外,对于原文中的出现了三次的"企业",分别用了"enterprise""entities""establishment",既有效地避免了英语中所忌讳的简单重复,又使得译文衔接紧密。

(六)主述位结构和已知信息——新信息结构

通常情况下,信息发出者会选择已知信息作为起点,然后是新信息。已知信息具有衔接上文和引出新信息的作用。因此,从信息结构的视角翻译句子,首要的是把已知信息安排在句首,把新信息置于句尾。信息焦点是信息发出者着意强调的,在译语中应以恰当的方式再现出来,同时要保证目的语的流畅。

(1)我想,其实谁都有一个小小花园,这便是我们的内心世界。(2)人的智力需要开发,人的内心世界也是需要开发的。(2008年英语专业八级考题)

[译文1]I think everybody in fact has a small garden our inner world. One's intelligence needs to be developed. So does the inner world.

译文1尽管避免了重复,但却忽略了英语语句信息的基本布局模式。句(1)的新信息"内心世界"是句(2)的已知信息,因而英译时应将句(2)中的"内心世界"调至句首,这样可以增强与句(1)的语义衔接。

[译文2]I think that everyone of us, as a matter of fact, owns a small garden, namely, our inner world, which needs cultivation as well as our intelligence.(唐文丽,2010)

二、连贯的翻译

对于衔接与连贯之间的关系,比较一致的观点是:衔接是语篇连贯的重要条件,衔接手段的使用可以促成语篇的内在连贯;而连贯是语篇的一种内在状态。具体来看,"衔接"是一种表层结构,通过语法手段和词汇手段来实现一个语篇在结构上的连接;"连贯"是一个深层结构,是一个语篇在逻辑上和语义上的连接。因此,有人说,衔接是语篇的有形网络,而连贯则是语篇的无形网络。连贯是文字成为语篇的原因,是语篇的基本特征。

连贯的手段可以是有形的,也可以是无形的。无形的靠逻辑,属隐性连贯;有形的靠大量的外显。一般认为,英语注重"形合",倾向于采用显性的衔接手段;而汉语注重"意合",较多地采用隐性的衔接方式。汉语常用原词复现和省略,而英语则多用照应和替代。如果在汉译英时能认识到这种差异,合理使用各种衔接手段,译文就会更加连贯。

语篇连贯体现在文体、语法、语义、认知等方面。同时,语篇连贯是翻译的重要基础。因此,译者要充分理解源语语篇,要注意找出其语义、认知连贯以及原文信息和读者的认知环境之间的深层连贯,选择适当的语篇形式,重构译文,采用注释性翻译等技巧补译相应的原文内涵,使译语语篇在译语读者中达到与源语读者相似的反应。

关于语法连贯,语法连贯主要通过衔接手段的应用来实现。通过照应、替代、省略等语法衔接手段,达到语篇的连贯。这一点在衔接的翻译部分已经讲过,这里不再赘述。文体的连贯属于语域部分,我们放在风格部分再讲。

(一) 语义连贯

从语义方面,语篇连贯性在局部表现为语篇中前后相连的句子之间的语义联系,在总体则表现为句子意义与语篇的宏观结构,即语篇主题之间的联系。由于语言所反映的文化差异性,译文语言形式的暗示作用和联想作用不可能和原文语言形式一样。为了体现原文的语义连贯,译者必须要在目的语中做适当的变通与调整。例如:

他走了几步,回头看见我说,"进去吧,里边没人。"(朱自清《背影》)

[译文]Upon walking a few steps, he looked back at me and said, " Go back to your seat, as you leave alone your things in the train."

原文的"进去吧,里边没人"被译成了"Go back to your seat, as you leave alone your things in the train."乍一看,"进去吧"与"里边没人"之间没有关联,但放在当时的场景中,爸爸给我买的橘子和行李都在车上,如果我不早一点进去,这些东西就有可能遗失。所以,"进去吧"与"里边没人"存在着因果关系,所以译文中加了表示因果关系的"as","里边没人"直接解释成了"你把东西放在车上"。

先说我的遗传。(冰心《我的童年》)

[译文]Let me begin with my family background.

原文作者要讲述的是自己的童年,后面的文字介绍了自己的父亲与祖父二人,所以这里的"遗传"并不是字面意思,而是"家庭背景"。

"可不是么……"聪明人也代为高兴似的回答他。(鲁迅《聪明人和傻子和奴才》)

" Oh, Yeah…"

原句中聪明人的话是说话人对前卫事物的肯定,而且很明显这个句子是口语体的形式,所以译者用了"Oh, Yeah"。

好像走进了另一个草木青青的桃花源。

[译文]We often felt as if we had entered a fairyland with lush greenery — a real Shangri-la.

原文中的"桃花源"指的是"与世隔绝的美好地方",与英语中表示"hidden paradise"的"Shangri-la"意思相近。用这个词,使译文更加传神。

中国有一种流行的谦约箴,常说:"钱财不可用罄,福分不可享尽。"独断过甚或利用个人之地位过甚,俗称为"锋芒太露",此常被视为鄙俗之行为而为颠覆之预兆。

[译文]The Chinese counsel for moderation says:"When fortune comes, do not enjoy all of it; when advantage comes, do not take all of it." To be over-assertive and to take full advantage of one's position is called "showing too much edge," a mark of vulgarity and an omen of downfall.

汉语句多主述位结构,在"钱财不可用罄"中,"钱财"和"不可用罄"是主位和述位关系,转换成英语时要用S-V-O结构,才符合英语句特点,故在英译文中,"do not enjoy all of it"的逻辑主语是"you",从上下文看,"钱财、福分"不会让人永远拥有,汉语典故没有体现,但中国读者明白其中隐含的意思,这是汉语句意合的特点决定的,在译文中补充"When…"从句,点明隐含意,体现出英语形合的特点。"锋芒太露"中,"锋芒"作主语,英译文"showing too much edge","edge"作宾语,视角改换,符合英语语言习惯和西方人的审美特点。语言形式的合理转换,是英译文具有审美功能的前提,是对西方读者认知心理的充分考虑。

(二)认知连贯

从认知方面,语篇连贯性涉及语篇接收者在语篇理解过程中的心理运算和认知推理。在翻译时,如果目标语文化中没有这种认知信息,则需要增加文化背景解释或文化内涵注释。例如:

……可是直到近三十岁,才知道孟姜女哭夫哭倒了万里长城的故事。

[译文]…but I did not know until I was about thirty that when Mengchiangnǜ cried over the bones of her husband who had died building the Great Wall in conscript labor, the torrent of her tears washed away a section of the Great Wall.

"孟姜女哭长城"的典故在中国妇孺皆知,属主谓结构的简单句;译文却是一个复杂句,字数大约是原句的三倍,信息容量也明显增大,原因是:在译文读者的认知语境中,没有该典故的文化信息预设,故必须补偿,原文是由三个小句构成的流水句,转换成英语复杂句增添了必要的钩挂成分,如介词、关系词、量词、连词,补充了相关的背景信息,如"who had died building the Great Wall"(修长城),"conscriptlabor"(征夫),"bones"(尸骨)等。从译文的内容、语言形式的变化,可以看出汉语强语境的语言特点,转化为弱语境语言时必须符合目标语读者的语言习惯及审美情趣。

……推动直接"三通"……

[译文]…push for the resumption of direct links of mail, transport and trade…

"三通"指通邮、通航、通商,是中国政府在1981年提出的加强两岸往来的一项政治主张,如果直译为"three direct links",没有相应的文化内涵注释,译文受者将无法理解中国政府对促进两岸和平统一的心愿。

三、风格的翻译

什么是风格?风格是否可译?风格如何翻译?学者们对风格的定义众说纷纭。从广义上理解,风格主要指作品的文学价值和美学价值;从狭义上理解,风格主要涉及语言层面具体的遣词造句。刘宓庆先生(1990)认为,风格不是什么"虚无缥缈"的素质,是可以见诸于"形",表现为风格的符号体系。在风格的符号体系中,风格具体化为形式标记和非形式标记。其形式标记表现在音系标记、语域标记、句法标记、词语标记、章法标记、修辞标记方面;非形式标记表现在表现法、作品的内在素质、作家的精神气质、接受者因素方面。通过利用这些标记,原作中文学的、语言学的风格都可以在译作中得以充分体现。在这里,我们选取其中一个角度——从语域标记的角度来探讨一下风格的翻译。

语域是在特定场合使用的特定语言,包括语场、语旨和语式三个变量。三个变量共同决定了交际中具体语言的使用,即语域。

(一)语场(field)对等

语场指实际发生的事,包括语言发生环境、谈话话题以及参与讲话者的整个活动,语场的范围很广。根据语场,翻译活动涉及政治、文学、法律、宗教、新闻、科技、广告等语篇的翻译。这些语篇各有其不同特征。政治、法律题材的文章语言庄重规范严谨,逻辑性强,采用规范的文体;科技英语客观、准确,逻辑严密,名词化现象较多,广泛使用被动语态和长句;新闻英语文字简洁;广告英语通俗易懂,富有表现力。针对不同的语场,要采用不同的翻译策略。例如:

为了保护和改善鄱阳湖生态经济区环境,发挥鄱阳湖调洪蓄水、调节水资源、降解污染、保护生物多样性等多种生态功能,促进环境保护与经济社会的协调发展,根据《中华人民共和国环境保护法》等有关法律、行政法规的规定,结合本省实际,制定本条例。

[译文]In accordance with the law of the People's Republic of China on Environment Protection, relevant administrative laws and regulations, and the realities of Jiangxi Province, these regulations are enacted with a view to protect and improve the environment of Poyang Lake Eco-economic Zone, play the role in flood storage, regulating water resources, degrading pollution, protecting of multiple ecological functions of biodiversity, and promote coordination between environmental protection and economic and social protection.

因为是法律语言,应该正式严肃,所以,原文中的"为了""根据""制定"分别被翻译成了"with a view to""in accordance with""enact",而通常这三个词在英语中人们会用"in order to""according to"和"formulate"。再如:

两位领导人声明:两国将在互相尊重主权和领土完整、互不侵犯、互不干涉内政、平等互利与和平共处的基础上发展睦邻友好关系。

[译文]The two leaders stated that both countries would develop good neighborly and friendly relations on the basis of mutual respect for sovereignty and territorial integrity, nonaggression, noninterference in each other's internal affairs, equality and mutual benefit and peaceful coexistence.

在翻译正式体的新闻报道,如时事政治、法律新闻时,译者的自由度很小。无论译者是否同意,他都要忠实地再现其思想观点,并可以使用较长的定语和状语来提供背景材料和相关信息。

(二)语旨(tenor)对等

语旨就是发话者要与受话者建立一种什么样的交际关系的意图的具体体现。每个交际者都要根据具体的情景、交流双发的社会地位、相互关系等来组织自己的语言,寻求恰当的语句,用最恰当的词汇和语句来表达感情。例如:

咫尺天涯,竟成海天之遥。南京匆匆一晤,瞬逾三十六载。幼时同袍,苏京把晤,往事历历在目,惟长年未通音讯,此诚憾事。近闻政躬违和,深为悬念。人过七旬,多有病痛,只盼善自珍摄。

[译文] No one ever expect that a strip of water should have become so vast a distance. It is now 36 years since our brief rendezvous in Nanjing. From our childhood friendship to our chats in the Soviet capital, everything in the past is still alive in my memory. But it's unfortunate that we haven't heard from each other for so many years. Recently I was told that you are somewhat indisposed and still has caused much concern. Men in their seventies are often afflicted with illness. I sincerely hope that you will take good care of yourself. (张培基,1999:462)

原文是廖承志1982年至蒋经国先生一封信中开头的几句话,原文古雅、高洁。译文也是选用了典雅的词语和完整的句子,再现了原文优美的文风和高雅的文情。就这段话的语旨而言,通信的双方有着深厚的友情,书信中充满了对对方的深切关怀,显示了他们之间的亲密关系。

(三)语式(mode)对等

语式指语言交际的渠道或媒介,包括修辞方式,主要分为书面和口头、正式体和非正式体。语式体现了语篇功能,不同的语式也要求译者采用不同的翻译策略。在翻译中,要力求再现原文的语式,口语不可翻译成书面语,正式语言不可翻译成非正式体。例如:

宁波大学是一所包括文、经、法、理、工、农、师范等多学科的综合性大学,受国家教委和省、市政府的共同领导。邓小平为学校亲笔题写了校名,江泽民为学校题了辞。在创建和发展过程中得到爱国侨胞的大量捐助和广泛支持。

[译文] Ningbo University is a comprehensive university offering academic courses in liberal art, economics, law, science, agronomy and education. It is under the co-leadership of the State Education Commission and the provincial and municipal governments. Ningbo University has its name celebrated by DengXiaoping's autograph and JiangZeming's inscription. Throughout its establishment and development, the University has been upheld by considerable donations and general support from patriotic overseas Chinese.

原文是一段说明性的文字,使用的语言很正式。考虑到这点,译文运用书面语,采用正式文体,在文中再现原文语式,从而使译文更加趋于完美。

刘姥姥又说到:"这里的鸡儿也俊,下的蛋也巧,怪俊的,我也俞一个。"(曹雪芹,1974:511)

[译文] Even your hens here are refined, she remarked, "laying such tiny, dainty eggs as these. Well, let me fuck one of them."(杨宪益,1999:558)

译者用非正式和口语的语气再现了原文中刘姥姥粗俗但幽默的语域特征。

语域理论给文本分析提供了一个理论框架,而译者对源语语篇文本的理解,显然受到源语语篇语场、语旨、语式的影响。同样,译者在生成目的语语篇时,也受到以上因素的制约。只有对这三个变量进行正确分析和转化,才能忠实地再现原文的内容和风格。

四、译文欣赏

谈结婚
——郁达夫

前些日子,林语堂先生似乎曾说过女子的唯一事业,是在结婚。现在一位法国大文豪来沪,对去访问他的新闻记者的谈话之中,又似乎说,男子欲成事业,应该不要结婚。

华盛顿·欧文是一个独身的男子,但《见闻短记》里的一篇歌颂妻子的文章,却写得那么的优美可爱。同样查而斯·兰姆也是个独身的男子,而爱丽娅《独身者的不平》一篇,又冷嘲热讽,将结婚的男女和婚后必然的果子——小孩们——等,俏皮到了那一步田地。

究竟是结婚的好呢,还是不结婚的好?这问题似乎同先有鸡呢还是先有鸡蛋一样,常常有人提起,而也常常没有人解决过的问题。照大体看来,想租房子的时候,是无眷莫问的,想做官的时候,又是朝里无裙莫做官的,想写文章的时候,是独身者不能写我的妻的,凡此种种似乎都是结婚的好。可是要想结婚,第一要有钱,第二要有闲,第三要有职,这潘驴……的五个条件,却也很不容易办到。更何况结婚之后,"儿子自己要来",在这世界人口过剩,经济恐慌,教育破产,世风不古的时候,万一不慎,同兰姆所说的一样,儿子们去上了断头台,那真是连祖宗三代的楣都要倒尽,那里还有什么"官人请! 娘子请!"的唱随之乐可说呢? 左思右想,总觉得结婚也不好的,不结婚也是不好的。

[译文]

A Chat about Marriage
Yu Dafu

Translated by Zhang Peiji

The other day, Mr Lin Yutang said something to the effect that women's only carrier lies in matrimony. Now, an eminent French Writer declared at a press interview after arriving in Shanghai that men should stay bachelor if they want to achieve success in life.

Washington Irving was a confirmed bachelor, but in his Sketch Book there is an article extolling the wife as a graceful and lovely life-long partner. Charles Lamb, also a single man, in A Bachelor's Complaint of the Behaviour of Married People, one of his essays signed "Elia", speaks mockingly of married people with their inevitable postnuptial fruits — the children.

Marriage or no marriage, which is more desirable? That sounds like the chicken-and-egg question, which, though often discussed, remains a perpetual puzzle. Generally speaking, one who has no family dependants is not supposed to rent a house, one who has no petticoat influence in the government should refrain from becoming an official, an unmarried male writer is in no position to writer about "my wife". All these seem to hint at the advantages of marriage. But, to get married, you need to have five prerequisites, namely, money, leisure, employment, good looks and potentness, of which all are not always available. What is more, after your marriage, your offspring will come to this world of themselves. And in a world with overpopulation, economic crisis, educational bankruptcy and deteriorating public morals, they may, just as Charles Lamb says, through their own acts of indiscretion, be sent to the gallows. With such a terrible misfortune befalling your family, how could you still have wedded bliss to speak of?

Thinking the matter over and over again, I cannot but come to the conclusion that neither matrimony nor bachelorship has anything to recommend itself.

文学翻译:周作人的《美文》之英译

外国文学里有一种所谓论文,其中大约可以分作两类。一批评的,是学术性的。二记述的,是艺术性的,又称作美文。这里边又可以分出叙事与抒情,但也很多两者夹杂的。这种美文似乎在英语国民里最为发达,如中国所熟知的爱迭生,阚姆,欧文,霍桑诸人都做有很好的美文,近时高尔斯威西,吉欣,契斯透顿也是美文的好手。读好的论文,如读散文诗,因为他实在是诗与散文中间的桥。中国古文里的序,记与说等,也可以说是美文的一类。但在现代的国语文学里,还不曾见有这类文章,治新文学的人为什么不去试试呢? 我以为文章的外形与内容,的确有点关系,有许多思想,既不能作为小说,又不适于做诗,(此只就体裁上说,若论性质则美文也是小说,小说也就是诗,《新青年》上库普林作的《晚间的来客》,可为一例,)便可以用论文式去表他。他的条件,同一切文学作品一样,只是真实简明便好。

我们可以看了外国的模范做去,但是须用自己的文句与思想,不可去模仿他们。《晨报》上的浪漫谈,以前有几篇倒有点相近,但是后来(恕我直说)落了窠臼,用上多少自然现象的字面,衰弱的感伤的口气,不大有生命力。我希望大家卷土重来,给新文学开辟出一块新的土地来,岂不好么?

The Aesthetic Essay

In foreign literature there is the so-called lunwen (treatises), which is roughly divided into two groups: the reflecting ones, piping (critical), are scientific articles. The others are jishu (descriptive) and yishuxing (artistic), they are also called meiwen (aesthetic essay). Within these texts, one can distinguish between xushi (narrative) and shuqing (lyric). But there are also many mixed texts. It seems to me, that in the field of the aesthetic essay, English literature has achieved the greatest success. For example, Joseph Addison, Charles Lamb, Robert Owen, and Nathaniel Hawthorne are all well known for their aesthetic essays. In addition, the younger generation including John Gabsworthy, George Robert Gissing, and Gilbert Keith Chesterton is elegant in writing aesthetic essays.

Reading a good treatise is just as enjoyable as reading a sanwenshi (prose-poem), because the latter accurately acts as a bridge between poetry and prose. In the three genres of pre-modern literature xu (foreword), ji (record), and shuo (explanations) one can also see forms of the aesthetic essay. But in modern literature so far aesthetical wenzhang (essay) have yet to appear. Why don't the people that shape the New Literature try to write it? In my opinion, there is a relationship between an essay's form and its content. Many ideas, that cannot be expressed in either a poem or story, can still be expressed in a treatise. Here, the word "treatise" refers to its literary form. Because of its essence, the aesthetic essay belongs to the story, and the story is nothing else but a poem. An example for this is "The guest in the evening" by Alexander Kiprin, which appeared in the New Youth. As in other works of literature, truth, simplicity and clarity are the prerequisites. We can imitate the foreign form of aesthetic essays, but we can never copy them, because we have to express our own thoughts in our own sentences. Articles similar to these were published in the rubric "On romanticism" of the Morning Post some time ago. But later (please excuse my openness) they returned to the restrictions of the old norms again. However natural they might have appeared upon a first glance, they did not show any strong vitality with their weakened, sad and sentimental styles. I hope that the aesthetical essay is encouraged to come back, and will open up a new field for the New Literature. Wouldn't that be wonderful?

五、实践练习

翻译下列短文。

(1)《"诺诺"误国,"谔谔"兴邦》

"诺诺"者,唯命是从,凡事好好好,是是是,逢人点头哈腰,遇事不辨青红皂白,正所谓"唯唯诺诺"。

"谔",指正直的言论。"谔谔",表示勇于讲真话,有分歧时也敢于据理力争。

先秦时期有过"千人之诺诺,不如一人之谔谔"的说教。说明当时很敬重直言争辩,哪怕争辩者只是一人孤军奋战。待到后来,谔谔之士则成了"珍稀动物",许多人邀欢尚且不暇,哪里还有直言的心思!《论语》中说:"君子坦荡荡,小人长戚戚",有些读书人把"坦荡荡"没挂在心上,"戚戚之态"倒是如影相随,辜负了老夫子的语重心长。

近几年的"两会",一改若干年前召开"没有杂音"的团结大会的传统,竟开成在某些问题上"有些争论"的大会,一些代表、委员直言不讳论国事,有的代表、委员还发表了与个别政府部门"大政方针"不同的声音;也有些代表、委员之间展开了辩论,有的人甚至向某些部委叫板"发难"。真可谓各抒己见,议论纷纷。

其实议论纷纷很好。有文章说,简写的开会"会"字,拆开来就是"人云",开会的人议论纷纷才像个会议,也说明我们的政治生活很正常,民主空气高涨,凡事能够集思广益,群策群力。

是啊,如果像有些基层把"两会"开成每年一次的"例行公事",与会人员见面时"握握手",开会时"拍拍手",表决时"举举手",散会时"挥挥手",这类兴师动众、劳民伤财的会议,开与不开能有多大区别?

有个别领导同志一时还不大习惯与会者"七嘴八舌",尤其反对"唇枪舌剑"地辩论。他们不明白,所谓"民主协商""兼听则明",都少不得"七嘴八舌"。君子和而不同。从不尽一致走向一致,那是真正的和谐共识。相反,不论多么重要、多么复杂的问题,举国上下,从无异议,从无杂音,那就有点假了。上古之人,不重"千人之诺诺",而重"一士之谔谔",是心胸开阔与襟怀坦荡的表现。一千人说顺从与阿谀奉承的话,不如一个人直言不讳更有意义与价值。

(2)生命的三分之一

一个人的生命究竟有多大的意义,这有什么标准可以衡量吗?提出一个绝对的标准当然很困难;但是,大体上看一个人对待生命的态度是否严肃认真,看他对待劳动、工作等的态度如何,也就不难对这个人的存在意义做出适当的估计了。

古来一切有成就的人,都很严肃的对待自己的生命,当他活着一天,总要尽量多劳动、多工作、多学习,不肯虚度年华,不让时间白白浪费掉。我国历代的劳动人民以及大政治家、大思想家等都莫不如此。

班固写的《汉书·食货志》上有下面的记载:"冬,民既入;妇人同巷相从夜绩,女工一月得四十五日。"这几句读起来很奇怪,怎么一月能有四十五天呢?再看原文底下颜师古做了注解,他说:"一月之中,又得夜半为十五日,共四十五日。"

这就很清楚了。原来我国的古人不但比西方各国的人更早地懂得科学地、合理地计算劳动日;而且我们的古人老早就知道对于日班和夜班的计算方法。

一个月本来只有三十天,古人把每个夜晚的时间算作半天,就多了十五天。从这个意义上说来,夜晚的时间实际上不就等于生命的三分之一吗?

对于这三分之一的生命,不但历代的劳动者如此重视,而且有许多大政治家也十分重视。班固在《汉书·刑法志》里还写道:"秦始皇躬操文墨,昼断狱,夜理书。"

有的人一听说秦始皇就不喜欢他,其实秦始皇毕竟是中国历史上的一个伟大的人物,班固对他也还有一些公平的评价。这里写的是秦始皇在夜间看书学习的情形。据刘向的《说苑》所载,春秋战国时有许多国君都很注意学习。

为什么古人对于夜晚的时间都这样重视,不肯轻易放过呢?我认为这就是他们对待自己生命的三分之一的严肃认真的态度,这正是我们所应该学习的。

第七章　新闻文本的翻译

新闻有其独特的文体特征。新闻报道要遵循及时、客观、准确(timely, objective and accurate)的原则。新闻报道的翻译，除遵循一般的翻译原则外，还应遵循新闻翻译的基本规律。

一、标题的翻译

在信息化时代，新闻是人们生活不可缺少的一部分。新闻标题是新闻内容的高度浓缩，也是吸引读者视线的关键所在，在国际报道中，新闻占了相当大的比重，而英语新闻更是重中之重，标题被当作英语新闻报道全文的精炼概括，为了吸引读者关注，往往采用各种手法来提升新闻标题的吸引力。同时给新闻标题的翻译带来不少挑战。新闻标题是新闻的重要部分，做好新闻标题的翻译极为重要。

(一)中英文标题对比

新闻标题是新闻的眼睛，也是新闻的重要组成部分。新闻标题是新闻文本对新闻内容加以概括或评价的简短文字。其字号大于正文，作用是划分、组织、揭示、评价新闻内容、吸引读者阅读。按不同的分类标准可以分不同的种类。

中英文标题都是新闻的重要组成部分，是对全部新闻内容的浓缩和提炼，使读者能在短时间内选择新闻、阅读新闻和理解新闻。新闻报道讲究客观公正，但是新闻标题具有明显的政治倾向，媒体编辑往往利用制作标题的机会借题发挥，在概括或浓缩新闻内容的同时，巧妙地融入自己的政治倾向，借以体现媒体的政治方针，宣传自己的政治主张，便于引导舆论。中英文标题在写作方面，都十分精练，含义深邃。

英语新闻相对较长，占字空间较大，所以标题必须十分简单。为了节省空间，英语新闻标题采用各种省略方法，一些动词、连接词和冠词会被省略。

(二)英语新闻标题的特点

1. 措辞简短

首先，英文标题力求用有限的文字来表达清楚的新闻内容，因此偏爱用字母较少的词，为节省墨水和空间，句子中的虚词被省去，结果剩下的都是实词，特别是名词。名词具有很强的表意功能，信息量大，同时又具有广泛的语法兼容性。它可以充当多种词类角色，如动词、形容词、副词等,也可以简约明了的形式和结构表达完整的句法概念。

其次,英语新闻标题中还多使用"时髦词"(Vogue Words)。"新"是新闻的生命,同时也是新闻语言的生命。这是由新闻的本质决定的。新闻报道要放开眼界、与时俱进,将一切新事物、新现象、新思想、新潮流通过各种新闻媒介传播给广大受众。

再次,英语新闻标题为追求简洁经常使用缩略语和数字,英语新闻标题中常见的有很多缩写,可分为三种:组织机构专有名词;常见事物的名称及表示人们的职业、职务或者职称的名词。

例如:澳大利亚国内生产总值稳定增长(Australia's GDP Growth Outlook Improves)其中的 GDP(Gross Domestic Product)即国内生产总值,常采用缩写形式。

2. 时态的选择

在英语新闻中现在时被广泛使用,为给读者以新鲜出炉、形象生动、跃然纸上的感觉。英语标题中一般不采用过去时态,而是采用现在时态,使读者在阅读时如置身于新闻事件的发生现场,这叫"新闻现在时(Journalistic Present tense)"。

例如:法国文化颓然不振(French Culture Is In the Doldrums)中的"is"采用现在时态。

3. 修辞

为追求形式的新奇以吸引读者,英语新闻标题还经常使用修辞手法。

(1)比喻。例如:"Children Under Parents' Wing"标题形象地用翅膀来比喻父母的保护,用到了比喻的修辞手法。

(2)转喻:这是一种生动活泼而富有幽默形象的修辞手法,它凭借联想用一种事物名称来代替另一种事物。例如:"Big brother"中用"老大哥"来代替"国家监管的监视后端"读来相映成趣,发人深省,同时也增加了严肃话题的可读性。

(3)对比:对比注重的是内容。在标题中,对比是利用词义间的相反或者相对来突出文章的内容。例如:"New Blood, Ancient Wounds"中"New"和"Ancient"造成词义上的对比,增强语言的表现力。

(4)双关语:双关是文字游戏,用一个词或短语把两个毫不相关的东西联系在一起,其特殊性就在于两种事物之间的联系,表面上是一个意思,而暗喻中又有另一个意思。例如:"Microsoft opens a new window."中"window"既有窗户的意思,又指微软的新产品。

(三)英语新闻标题的翻译技巧

在阅读英语报刊时,不仅要看懂新闻的标题,还要能恰当地翻译新闻标题,这样才能正确地理解英语新闻标题的特点,从而正确判断新闻标题的寓意。翻译英语新闻标题时应注意三个方面:一要准确理解把握特点;二要翻译得当,增强可读性;三要注意读者的接受能力。这要求新闻翻译工作者多注意日积月累,对英语国家的国家历史、文化典故、时代背景有相当程度地了解和认识。在翻译时,能将原新闻标题的妙笔生花,画龙点睛之笔用同样精炼的汉语表达出来,让读者感受到异曲同工之效。在对英语新闻标题进行翻译时,应该充分考虑英语和汉语的差异性,并且能兼顾汉语的表达习惯。

很多情况下,新闻标题因其独特的选词、句型结构和语法特点,理解和翻译并不容易,它不仅要求译者对中西方国家的文化、历史及事件发生的背景有全面地了解,还要熟知中西方的历史及语言的修辞特点,并掌握特定的翻译技巧。只有这样,才能更好地传达作者的原意,达到翻译"信、达、雅"的效果。

1. 直译或者基本直译

如果新闻标题的含义很明白清楚,英语的表达方式与汉语完全或基本相同,直接翻译后中国读者不至于产生理解上的困难时,可以采用直译或基本直译。但直译不能影响准确达意,不能破坏标题的风格。

例如:武昌部分路段路灯"失明"(Some Street Lamps in Wuchang *Blinded*)中"失明"一词直接译为"blinded",表示路灯不亮了,同时也采用了拟人的修辞手法,读者可以清楚地理解此标题的含义。

2. 意译

如果原新闻标题采用直译的方法不能准确概括新闻的内容,或不能如实体现作者意图,或者不合英语的表达习惯时,可根据情况适当采用意译。许多新闻标题不仅以其简洁精炼引人注意,同时也通过运用各种修辞既有效地传递一些微妙的隐含信息,又使读者在义、音、形象等方面得到完美的享受。

例如:公交站牌"说胡话"(Pubic Transport Signpost *Gives Wrong Directions*)中"说胡话"即指错路,采用了意译的翻译方法。

3. 采用翻译权衡手法

有时一些新闻标题因修辞手法,或因文化及语言差异,在英语中难以表达其微妙意义时,不妨根据原新闻标题的字面意思结合新闻内容翻译出合适的标题,可采用如下方法。

(1) 增词使意义完整

英语新闻标题用词一般不多和英语标题倾向于对某一内容作"重点化"处理不求面面俱到这两点决定了其一般比较精炼简短。而汉语新闻标题追求"全面性"和汉语一词一意,使得汉语标题用词相对较多。所以,在英译标题时,可以结合英语和汉语新闻标题的特点,适当增减一些词语,使标题形式更合理,意义更趋完整,例如"人愈老,智愈高,心愈平","Older, Wiser, Calmer"这条新闻聚焦于当今老龄化社会,尤其是老人们退休以后在处理各种问题时表现出来的睿智和冷静。翻译成"Older, Wiser, Calmer"使得"人""智""心"三字意义更加明确,句式更加整齐,更加符合读者的阅读习惯。

(2) 减词

在新闻标题翻译中减词是最为常见的方式,尽可能地减去原来标题中只具有语法功能的冠词、感叹词、关系词、连词、代词等以求语言的简练。同时省略标题中的次要信息以突出主要信息。

例如:"西部大开发""(Grand) Western Development"中的"大(Grand)"一词无需译出,读者即可明白其意。

正如好的新闻标题能够永远地留在人们心间一样,好的英译新闻标题也能使读者耳目一新,给人留下深刻的印象。新闻翻译者假如能够把握英语新闻标题的特点并把握相关翻译技巧,能以最简明扼要的形式向读者揭示新闻的主要内容,使读者更好地了解世界。

二、新闻报道的翻译

新闻报道一般包括标题(headline)、导语(lead)和正文(body)三部分。本节主要讨论新闻报道正文的编译(adapted translation)和解释性翻译(interpretative translation)问题。

(一)编译(Adapted Translation)

新闻报道的翻译,往往采用非逐字对译法。新闻报道之所以能引起读者的兴趣,是由于新闻价值在起作用。所谓新闻价值(news value),即指衡量新闻事实的客观标准。"读者兴趣"是新闻价值特殊要素之一。对外新闻报道,一要考虑本国国情,二要考虑外国受众的要求和兴趣,对新闻内容进行选择,做到正确无误,"有的放矢"。因此,有时在国内报道中占相当篇幅的新闻,在对外报道中则被编译成简讯、图片新闻等。请对比下面的新闻报道,注意领会英文报道是怎样择要而编的。还应注意句子结构变化、语态变化等。例如:

从容上阵枪响世惊　李对红喜摘射击金牌　以687.9环创下新的奥运纪录

我国女子运动员李对红今天在女子运动手枪决赛中,以687.9环战胜所有对手,并创造新的奥运记录。她为中国射击队在本届奥运会上夺得了第一块金牌,也使中国代表团夺得的金牌数上升为6枚。

(《光明日报》1996年7月2日)

Li Shoots Nation's 6th Gold

China's Li Duihong won the women's 25-meter sport pistol Olympic gold with a total of 687.9 points early this morning Beijing time.

(China Daily, July 27, 1996)

两辆公交车在行驶中猛然相撞,造成客车严重毁损,97名乘客和司售人员不同程度受伤,其中37人因脑外伤、脾破裂、骨折、肝挫伤、脑震荡等被医院收治。这一罕见的重大交通事故发生在昨天清晨闸北公园南首的共和新路干道上。

(《文汇报》1992年4月8日)

A total of 97 people were injured, 37 seriously, when two buses collided in Shanghai's Gonghe Xinlu Monday morning. Traffic on the roads was restored two hours later after the two damaged buses were removed, the local Wen Hui Bao reported.

(China Daily, April 11, 1992)

(二)解释性翻译(Interpretative Translation)

新闻讲求清晰易懂。同英语新闻一样,汉语新闻报道词语求新,创新意识强,"行话""套话""历史典故"等丰富多样,变化多端。要想清晰易懂地把它们翻译出来,介绍给国外受众,常常需要使用解释性翻译的方法。解释性翻译能使报道更趋客观,清晰明了,有助于增强传播效果。

在汉语新闻报道的翻译中,常常对有关历史事件、地理名称、我国独有的机构、节日、习俗、"行话""套话"、历史典故等采用解释性方法。譬如"巴金""老舍"译作"Chinese writers Ba Jin and Lao She","北京""上海"分别译作"the capital city of Beijing"和"the largest industrial city of Shanghai","山东"译作"Shandong in east China",以便让外国读者了解以上这些地方的地理位置及特点。再如：

澳门回归祖国，再次印证了邓小平"一国两制"伟大构想的胜利。

［译文］Macao's historic return to its motherland proves again the victory of the great concept of "One Country, two systems" put forward by former paramount Chinese leader Deng Xiaoping.

译文中增加了评介性注释词语 historic 和 former paramount Chinese leader，从而达到了准确、生动、内涵丰富的目的。

新年伊始，沙尘暴袭击了甘肃省和内蒙古自治区。大风裹着尘土进入北京。

［译文］On the first day of the new year, sandstorms hit northwestern China's Gansu Province and north China's Inner Mongolia Autonomous Region. Strong dust-laden winds also swept across Beijing.

译文中增加了两个表示方位的词语 northwestern China's 和 north China's，帮助读者了解沙尘暴的具体位置和走向，从而体现了新闻报道的准确性原则。

三、汉英篇章对比

从信息内容上看，无论汉语还是英语信息都很注重报道的新闻价值（news value）。新闻价值是事实本身所具有的足以构成新闻的特殊素质的总和，是选择和衡量新闻事实的客观标准。一篇报道所引发的"读者兴趣"（reader's interest）是新闻价值的重要体现。此外，汉英新闻报道都十分强调内容的准确性。撰稿者应以忠实地报道客观事实为宗旨，力求真实、简洁、生动，不可误导读者。

在文体色彩方面，汉英新闻文本存在着较大的差异。西方传媒将读者奉为上帝，十分注重新闻的社会效应。英语新闻具有很强的商业性，新闻撰写者总是不遗余力地调动各种语言手段以吸引读者的注意力。因此，在英语新闻中常常有许多标新立异、别具一格的词句，报道的语气和口吻也比较亲切随和。相比较而言，汉语新闻的商业化程度较低，作者在撰稿时较少考虑到稿件的商业价值和轰动效应，而是注重实事求是地向读者讲清事实，说明观点。因此，汉语新闻的语气一般比较客观冷静、实事求是。另外，英语新闻写作向来奉行"the simpler, the better"的原则，文风力求简洁晓畅，力戒冗余拖沓。由于受中国思维方式和审美习惯的影响，汉语新闻中往往有不少冗余信息，译者须结合实际情况对其进行灵活处理，对其加以简化、修改甚至删除。

汉英新闻报道在语句表达、句子衔接、论证手段和语篇发展模式层面存在异同。

（一）语句表达

从内容上来看，英语与汉语的意义重心是不同的。英语一般是前重心，把主要信息放在主句中或句子的开头；而汉语则与之相反，一般是后重心，把次要的部分放在句首。例如：

据法新社最新报道，伊朗一架客机 15 日在西部加兹温省坠毁，据说机上 168 人全部遇难。（搜狐新闻，09/7/15）

［译文］A passenger aircraft crashed in northwestern Iran on Wednesday and up to 169 people on board were feared killed, ISNA news agency reported. (New York Times, 09/7/15)

(二)句子衔接

为了取得语篇连贯,汉语经常使用重复,同时较多使用省略,涉及各种句子成分。例如:

据伊朗国家电视台15日报道,伊朗一架客机当天在该国西北部加兹温附近坠毁,机上153名乘客和15名机组人员全部遇难。这架坠毁的图——154客机隶属于里海航空公司。客机于当地时间11时33分(北京时间15时03分)从伊首都德黑兰的霍梅尼国际机场起飞,准备飞往亚美尼亚首都埃里温,但在起飞后16分钟坠毁。霍梅尼国际机场的工作人员已经向新华社记者证实,坠毁的客机上没有中国乘客。(搜狐新闻,09/7/16)

英语中则词汇关联用得最多,包括同义词、近义词、反义词、上下义关系和语义场等。在替代方面,汉语和英语中通过名词和动词之间的转换来实现替代的表现最为活跃。同时,英语中的词语替代和短句替代均多于汉语。例如:

The Chinese authorities have detained or questioned at least seven Chinese steel industry executives in a broadening corruption investigation connected to the detentions last week of four employees of the mining giant Rio Tinto, state-controlled news media reported Monday. The investigation, which began with accusations that the four Rio Tinto workers had conspired to steal state secrets, has rapidly widened, according to accounts on government Web sites and in Chinese news media. It now includes accusations of widespread bribery in business dealings, as well as allegations that the four workers paid for detailed government trade and manufacturing data to give Rio Tinto executives an edge in iron ore negotiations with Chinese state-controlled steelmakers. (New York Times, 09/7/13)

文中使用了多组关联词,如同义词"detained"和"questioned"及"accusations"和"allegations";也用到了多个连接词,如"which""that""as well as"等,构成定语从句、同位语从句等句法关系。

另外,汉语语篇多有名词省略的情况,而动词和短句省略却很罕见。英语中名词省略的情况较少。在关联层面,汉语篇章多通过自身内容的发展来体现句子之间的关联,连接词用得很少。而英语多通过关联词的使用来明确句子之间的关联度和发展关系。这是因为汉语可以不使用任何衔接手段,省略名词主语,构成一个不影响段落连贯的"话题链"。而英语是主语突出性语言,即使整个段落谈论同一主题,也必须保证外显的联系,不能省略句子主语。

语义衔接上的这些差别跟汉语和英语各自的词法、句法特点有比较密切的关系。英语是以形合为主的语言,语法关系较为严谨,讲究句子结构完整,经常充当句子主语的名词很难被省略。这是由于英语篇章需要用语言手段给每个事件定义和定位,使各个事件的相互关系明确,层次分明。而汉语则是重语境,意合性的语言,汉语文章"有时并不需要用一定的语法手段或其他语言手段来表现,而是靠层次内容之间的自然衔接"。换句话说,汉语段落间的连贯更多是依靠语义和事件的内在联系和逻辑来实现的。

(三)论证手段

在新闻报道中,数据和引用是最常见的,但汉语新闻较多引用官员和相关负责人,有时还会引经据典;而英语新闻则较多引用专家和普通人。而且,英语中的数据使用频率也明显高于汉语新闻。这可能是因为西方机构和民间组织的调查统计数据涉及的范围更广,公开度更大。汉语新闻报道更偏向于权威性;而英语新闻报道更多用事实和数据来说话,更符合新闻报道真实性和科学性的特点。例如:

然而,参加今年军演的美军数量从2016年的2.5万人降至1.75万人,美国国防部长詹姆斯·马蒂斯(James Mattis)否认此举可被解读为迎合朝鲜。

[译文]However, the number of US troops involved in this year's war games has been cut to 17 500 from 25 000 in 2016, a move that James Mattis, US defence secretary, denied could be interpreted as pandering to Pyongyang.

这段文字使用了具体的数据,也引用了美国国防部长詹姆斯·马蒂斯的观点,使本则新闻报道更具真实性、权威性和科学性。

(四) 语篇发展模式

新闻报道的语篇发展模式实际上就是新闻诸要素的展开形式。东方语言的语篇发展模式是不断扩展的螺旋形,弧线围绕着主题,却不直接触及主题,而是从各个角度间接地表述和论说,往往到最后才点明主题。英语语篇则呈直线形式发展,多以主题句开始,主题句提出本段的中心内容,后接辅助句逐步展开,说明主题句的具体内容,其间不附加其他与主题没有直接关系的内容。这种方式有助于读者快速领会新闻重点,比较迎合受众的接受心理。其基本格式是:先在导语中描写一个新闻事件中最有新闻价值的部分。然后,在报道主体中按照事件各个要素的重要程度,依次递减进行描述。通常一个段落只描述一个事件要素。

很多汉语新闻报道也是采用这种倒金字塔形,但也有同样比例的正金字塔形发展模式。这种方式刚好与倒金字塔形相反,是以时间顺序作为行文结构的发展模式,依序分别是引言、过程、结果,采用渐入高潮的方式,将新闻重点摆在文末,一般多用于特写。

汉语新闻报道以往一般是遵循时间顺序,但是这种"讲故事"的写法已经不适合受众的阅读习惯,所以折中形在吸收中外新闻报道之长的情况下诞生了。其基本格式是:先把事件中最重要的部分在导语中简明地体现出来。然后,进一步具体阐述导语中的这个重要部分,形成支持,不至于使受众在接受时形成心理落差。因而,这一部分实际上是一个过渡性段落。再次,按照事件发展的时间顺序把"故事"陈述完。

此外,还有在汉英翻译中出现频率最少的平铺直叙型。这种发展方式就是注重行文的起、承、转、合,力求文字的流畅和精准。

最近还有一种"华尔街日报体"的模式。其主要特点就是在文首特写新闻事件中的一个"镜头",一般是一个人的言行或一个特定事件,从而引出整个新闻报道,如以下有关能源短缺报道的开头段:

From the outside, there is nothing unusual about the stylish new gray and orange row houses in the Kranichstein District, with wreaths on the doors and Christmas lights twinkling through a freezing drizzle. But these houses are part of a revolution in building design: There are no drafts, no cold tile floors, no snuggling under blankets until the furnace kicks in. There is, in fact, no furnace. (New York Times, 09/7/13)

汉语的语篇发展模式在整体上的确异于英语,没那么直接,迂回处明显要多些。这种情况跟汉语的句式组织结构特点有一定关系。汉语的复句就常采用迂回的编码方式,即暂时偏离基本意图,待原因、时间、方式、条件、让步等提供之后,再转到基本意图上。在句式结构上,汉英两种语言的差异主要可归纳为:英语族人倾向于形式分析,抽象思维,从小到大,从未知到已知,突出主观作用,以主体为中心,主客体界限分明;汉语族人倾向于整体思维,情感思维,从大到小,从已知到未知,从实际出发,注重主客体融合。

四、译文欣赏

中国已于本月15日起开始执行联合国安理会在朝鲜多次试射导弹后一致通过的制裁决议。中国当时表示,政策缓冲期为3周,之后将不再为进口自朝鲜的煤、铁矿石、水海产品办理进口手续。这轮制裁旨在将朝鲜30亿美元年度出口额削减1/3。如果制裁得到全面执行,可能会对朝鲜经济造成强烈影响。在投票支持新的强硬制裁措施后不久,中国外交部长王毅表示:"鉴于中国同朝鲜的传统经济联系,执行决议、付出代价的主要是中方。"他补充称:"为了维护国际核不扩散体系,为了维护地区的和平稳定,中方将一如继往全面、严格执行好有关决议的所有内容。"

[译文]

China this month moved to implement the sanctions on North Korea passed unanimously by the UN Security Council following Pyongyang's repeated missile tests. Beijing said it will cut off imports of North Korean coal, iron ore and seafood in three weeks. The sanctions aim to cut North Korea's $3 billion in annual exports by a third. If universally implemented, they could have massive repercussions for the country's economy. Shortly after voting in favour of the new hard-hitting measures, Wang Yi, China's foreign minister, said: "Given China's traditional economic ties with North Korea, China more than anyone will pay a price for implementing the resolution." He added: "In order to maintain the international nuclear non-proliferation system and regional peace and stability, China will, as always, enforce the full content of relevant resolutions in a comprehensive and strict manner."

一项调查指出,北京超过14%的流动人口已经在这座城市购房。调查中的流动人口覆盖了一直居住在北京、但没有北京户口的人群。根据北京市社会科学院及社会科学文献出版社发布的《北京蓝皮书:北京社会发展报告(2016—2017)》,北京流动人口拥有的房产总数估计超过120万套。这一结果是基于一项样本约为8 000人、分散在13个区的流动人口的调查,这13个区中不包括延庆、密云以及平谷。报告发现,购买住房的流动人口年龄为30至44岁,拥有本科以上学历。他们通常是某一行业的专业技术人才,月收入4 000元以上,多为已婚人士。该报告称,在外企、国企和事业单位就职的流动人口购房的比例较高。

[译文]

More than 14% of the floating population in Beijing has purchased houses in the city, according to a survey. The floating population in the survey covers people without Beijing hukou, or permanent household registration, though they permanently live in Beijing. The total number of flats owned by migrants in Beijing is estimated to exceed 1.2 million, according to *Beijing*

Bluebook: *Report on Beijing's Social Development* (2016—2017), released by the Beijing Academy of Social Sciences and Social Sciences Academic Press. The findings are based upon a survey sample of some 8 000 migrants scattered in Beijing's 13 districts, which do not include Yanqing, Miyun and Pinggu districts. The report finds that these flat owners are 30 to 44 years old and hold at least a college degree. They usually have expertise in a certain industry and their monthly income is over 4 000 yuan. Most are married. A higher percentage of flat owners are seen among those employed with foreign companies and State-owned enterprises and institutions, according to the report.

自2012年中国共产党第十八次全国代表大会以来,得益于中央政府改善教育事业的努力,我国教育事业总体发展水平已经超越世界上许多国家。其中,九年义务教育净入学率达到99.9%,高于高收入国家。而学前教育毛入学率达77.4%,高于中高收入国家69.2%的平均水平。高中阶段教育和高等教育毛入学率则分别达到87%和42.7%,均高于中高收入国家平均水平。为了保证没有学生因贫困辍学,我国教育支出占国内生产总值(GDP)的比例连续五年在4%以上。今年年初,我国发布教育事业发展"十三五"规划,重申教育支出占GDP的比例将不低于4%。

[译文]

Since the 18th National Congress of the Communist Party of China in 2012, China's overall education development has outpaced many countries around the world, thanks to the central government's efforts to improve the sector. The retention ratio of nine-year compulsory education reached 99.9%, higher than the upper-income countries. The gross enrollment ratio for China's preschool education came to 77.4%, higher than the average of upper-middle-income countries of 69.2%. The gross enrollment ratio for senior secondary education and higher education reached 87% and 42.7%, respectively, both of which are higher than the average of upper-middle-income countries. To make sure that no student drops out of school due to poverty, China has spent over 4% of GDP on education for five straight years. At the beginning of 2017, the country released the 13th Five-Year Plan on Education, reiterating that spending on education will account for no less than 4% of the country's GDP.

五、实践练习

翻译下列短文。

(1)最近的一份报告指出,国内日益普及的共享单车服务已经帮助缓解了大城市的交通拥堵。由国内地图和导航提供商高德地图、交通运输部科学研究院和清华大学戴姆勒可持续交通研究中心发布的这项报告指出,今年第二季度,全国最大的100个城市中,近8成城市的交通状况有所改善。这是2014年高德推出全国各地"拥堵指数"以来,该指数首次出现下行迹象。报告指出,人们的出行方式发生了很大变化,随着共享单车服务在许多城市快速发展,交通拥堵得到缓解。共享单车企业 ofo 表示,在其共享单车投放量最大的前20座城市中,有19座城市的交通状况有所改善。高德地图称,北京超半数主要地铁站,高峰期的拥堵程度同比下降了4.1%。

(2) 一份有关中国留守儿童的最新报告称,近三成农村学生处于完全留守(父母均外出)状态。近日,为留守儿童提供经济和心理帮助的非政府组织"上学路上"发布了《中国留守儿童心灵状况白皮书》。白皮书显示,一半以上的农村完全留守儿童与父母一年见面少于2次。根据报告,在对国内17个省级地区14 868人的抽样调查中,58.1%的农村学生处于留守状态,其中处于完全留守状态的农村学生占26.1%。该报告估计处于完全留守状态的农村学生可能多达1 000万。据《新京报》报道,一名民政部官员表示,一项目标是在2017年底前将所有农村留守儿童纳入监护范围的专项行动正在进行。民政部表示,无人监护且联系不上外出务工父母的留守儿童,将被送至其他亲属或寄养机构临时照料。

第八章 旅游文本的翻译

一、人名、地名的翻译

(一) 人名的翻译

(1) 国际标准

中国有一套中文姓名英译的国际标准——以汉语拼音作为英译规则。中文姓名翻译成英文时,按照汉语拼音来写,姓氏和名的首字母要大写,名字拼音要写在一起。如"李雷"和"韩梅梅"翻译为英文分别是"Li Lei"和"Han Meimei"。

(2) 名人的固定英文译名

一些中国科学家、学者等知名人士,则使用其固定的英文译名,如"孙中山"和"蒋介石"英译名称分别是"Sun Yat-sen"和"Chiang Kai-shek"。

(3) 广东与香港人名译法规则

由于广东和香港地区较早与海外进行商务交流,因此广东和香港地区的人名英译是采用粤语发音来进行音译,如"董建华"英译为"Tung Chee Hwa"。

(4) 起英文名+姓

很多演艺圈、经济圈、文化圈等的名人,会给自己起一个英文名,再加上自己的姓氏音译如 Jack Chan(成龙)、Leehom Wang(王力宏)。

(二) 地名的翻译

地名的英译较为复杂。用汉语拼音字母拼写中国地名,不仅是中国的统一标准,而且是国际标准,全世界都要遵照使用。

1. 专名是单音节的英译法

专名是单音节,通名也是单音节,这时通名应视作专名的组成部分,先音译并与专名连写,后重复意译,分写。例如:

恒山 Hengshan Mountain(山西)

淮河 the Huaihe River(河南、安徽、江苏)

渤海 the Bohai Sea(辽宁、山东)

2. 通名专名化的英译法

通名专名化主要指单音节的通名,如山、河、江、湖、海、港、峡、关、岛等,按专名处理,与

专名连写,构成专名整体。例如:

都江堰市 Dujiangyan City

绥芬河市 Suifenhe City

白水江自然保护区 Baishuijiang Nature Reserve

3. 通名是同一个汉字的多种英译法

通名是单音节的同一个汉字,根据意义有多种不同英译法,在大多数情况下,这些英译词不能互相代换。例如:

(1) mount:峨眉山 Mount Emei(四川峨眉)

(2) mountain:五台山 Wutai Mountain(山西)

(3) hill:象鼻山 the Elephant Hill(广西桂林)

(4) port:牛尾海 Port Shelter(香港)

(5) forest:蜀南竹海 the Bamboo Forest in Southern Sichuan(四川长岭)

在某些情况下,根据通名意义,不同的汉字可英译为同一个单词。例如:"江、河、川、水、溪"英译为 river。例如:

嘉陵江 the Jialing River(四川)

永定河 the Yongding River(河北、北京、天津)

古田溪 the Gutian River(福建)

4. 专名是同一个汉字的不同英译法

专名中同一个汉字有不同的读音和拼写,地名中这样的汉字有七八十个之多,每个字在地名中的读音和拼写是固定的,英译者不能一见汉字就按语言词典的读音和拼写翻译,而只能按中国地名词典的读音和拼写进行翻译。例如:

陕西省 Shanxi Province

陕县 Shanxian County(河南)

洞庭湖 the Dongting Lake(湖南)

洪洞县 Hongtong County(山西)

六合县 Luhe County(江苏)

六盘水市 Liupanshui City(贵州)

5. 以人名命名的地名英译法

以人名命名的地名英译,人名的姓和名连写,人名必须前置,通名后置,不加定冠词。这种译法多用于自然地理实全地名,但有例外。例如:

张广才岭 Zhangguangcai Mountain(吉林、黑龙江)

郑和群礁 Zhenghe Reefs(海南南沙群岛)

如果以人名命名的非自然地理实体地名,姓和名分写,人名前置或后置按习惯用法,大致有以下三种译法:

(1) 人名 + 通名

黄继光纪念馆 Huang Jiguang Memorial(四川中江县)

(2) 人名's + 通名

中山陵墓 Sun Yat-sen's Mausoleum(江苏南京市)

(3) the + 通名 + of 人名
昭君墓 the Tomb of Wang Zhaojun(内蒙古呼和浩特市)

6. 地名中的符号不能省略
地名中的符号如果省略就会造成读音甚至语义错误。地名中有两种符号不能省略。
(1) a,o,e 开头的音节连接在其他音节后面的时候,如果音节的界限会混淆,用隔音符号,地名中的隔音符号不能省略。例如:
(陕西)西安市 Xi'an City(如果省略隔音符号,就成为 Xian,可以读成仙、先、现、限、鲜、险、县等)
(广西)兴安县 Xing'an County(如果省略隔音符号,就成为 Xingan County 新干县,在江西吉安地区)
(2) 汉语拼音 ü 行的韵母跟声母 n、l 拼的时候,ü 上面的两点不能省略。如果省略,就会造成误解。例如:
(山西)闾河 the Lühe River(如果省略 ü 上面的两点,就变成 the Luhe River 芦河、在江西)
(台湾)绿岛 Lüdao Island(如果省略 ü 上面的两点,就变成 Ludao Island 鹭岛,在黑龙江海林)
但是也有例外。例如:
绿春县 Luchun County(云南红河)
绿曲县 Luqu County(甘肃甘南)

二、景点介绍的翻译

随着国家开放程度的日益扩大,中国的旅游业得到了极大的发展,入境旅游人数急剧增多,相应的对服务行业的要求也增加了,旅游英语成为热门。中文旅游景点介绍具有语言华丽、引经据典、富于文采、古香古色等特点,关于旅游景点介绍的英译日益重要。

(一)中文旅游景点介绍的翻译

精良的旅游英语翻译能够迎合旅游者的文化品位,也能突出中国旅游业的特色与吸引力。在英译旅游景点介绍资料时,需要注意以下问题。

1. 不同语言习俗对旅游资料翻译的影响
对比中英旅游景点介绍文字材料可以发现:汉语多写实得意,英语常写意传情。
如:"三潭映月、湖心亭、阮公墩三个小岛鼎立湖中。"
译者将它译为:The three islands named "Three Pools Mirroring the Moon", "the Midlake Pavilion" and "the Ruangong Mound" stand in the Lake, adding much charm to the scene.
中文资料中"鼎立"一词看似写实,实则写意,因为三个小岛的位置不一定像青铜器里的鼎一样,只是从中国人的审美眼光来看,"三足鼎立"是一种美感,而译文并没有刻板地直译,而是用分词短语 adding much charm to the scene 传达了原文隐含的信息,从而达到写意传情的目的。

2. 不同语言特点在翻译中的处理与应用

汉英是两种不同的语言,二者既有共性又有区别,因此在翻译时要充分注意两种语言的特点。

(1)深刻理解语言材料。

例如下面介绍杭州天气的句子:"杭州的春天,浓妆艳抹,无不相宜;夏日荷香阵阵,沁人心脾……"译文:"Sunny or rainy, Hangzhou looks its best in spring. In summer, lotus flowers bloom." 其中"浓妆艳抹"译成"Sunny or rainy",显然出自苏轼的诗:"水光潋滟晴方好,山色空蒙雨亦奇,欲把西湖比西子,淡妆浓抹总相宜。"这就是所谓的"互文意义"。如果不熟悉这首诗,自然不能领会"淡妆浓抹"的意味,在翻译时免不了会闹笑话。

(2)注重译文的"可接受性"。

有时候译文准确无误,但是外国游客由于不了解相关文化背景,所以造成理解障碍,导致译文可接受性不强。

例如,在介绍绍兴的文字中有这么一句话:"绍兴是越瓷的产地",按照字面理解,译成 Shaoxing is the home of Yue porcelain 即可,但是外国人不懂什么是越瓷,读了这句话无法产生预期的共鸣。因此,有必要添加解释性句子,译成"Shaoxing is the home of Yue porcelain. Yue is a state name used to refer to the Shaoxing region in ancient China." 这样一来,外国游客对中国历史多了几分了解,自然理解上容易了些。

又如:"刘备章武三年病死于白帝城永安宫,五月运回成都,八月葬于惠陵"。"章武三年"到底是公元多少年,对于中国人都不太熟悉,何况对中国文化不了解的外国游客。因此,译者将它译为:"Liu Bei died of illness in 223 at present day Fengjie county, Sichuan Province, and was buried here in the same year." 直接换算成公元纪年,扫除交流障碍,方便外国游客,增强了译文的可接受性。

(3)注意文化差异

语言是文化的外化,语言的差异很大程度上是由文化的差异引起的。因此,在旅游景点介绍资料的翻译中,要充分考虑跨文化的交际规则,避免不必要的文化冲突。例如,中国人重直觉与具象而西方人重理性与逻辑,这种文化的差异在语言上表现为汉语的形象性和英语的功能性。

汉语介绍景点时,常用"天下第一"的字眼,往往并不是真的说该处风景是天下第一,而是一种夸张的表达,言其超凡脱俗、引人入胜。这种说法如果译成英语,就要注意不能译成 No.1,因为外国读者由于重理性与逻辑,往往会较真。如位于缙云县的鼎湖峰号称"天下第一峰",就不能译成"No.1 peak in the world",否则很可能招到外国游客的质疑。

(二)中文旅游景点介绍的翻译技巧

1. 增添法

由于中外文化差异很大,各自历史发展进程不一,外国游客往往对中国老百姓人人皆知的情况不一定很了解,旅游翻译资料有必要做一些解释,提供一些人文历史、风土人情等方面的背景知识,帮助读者理解其意,唤起读者的兴趣。

例如,在介绍桂林风土人情的文章中,把"三月三节"翻译成"San Yue San Festival"还不够,因为外国游客对此一无所知,不能唤起他们的兴趣和共鸣,所以应加上适当的解释,比如译成：

The festival usually takes place on the third day of the lunar third month, when minority people, especially the young get together for folk song contests to make friends with each other.

外国人对景点名称不一定感兴趣，但想了解取名的由来。所以有些译名适当加上一些解释，可以引起游客的注意和兴趣。

例如，"骆驼山""Luo Tuo Hill"可做些解释："It shapes like a camel, hence the Camel Hill.""象鼻山"译为"Xiangbi Hill or the Elephant Hill (The hill bears resemblance to an elephant dipping its trunk into the river. Hence the name."

2. 删节法

在介绍资料的翻译中，要考虑到外国游客的口味。中文景点介绍往往在介绍景点之后会有感而发地引用古诗词，使文章富于文采和历史感，能引起中国人的游兴，但是对于缺乏中国传统知识的外国人而言，这种引用并不能唤起共鸣，所以有时候可以将之删去不翻译。

例如："这些山峰，连同山上绿竹翠柳，岸边的村民农舍，时而化入水中，时而化入天际，真是'果然佳胜在兴平'"。这段描写漓江的文字，先是写景，最后引用古诗感叹，算是一种总结，但译者并没有将它译出："These hills and the green bamboo and willows and farm houses merge with their reflections in the river and lead visitors to a dreamy world."对于景物的描写自然能传出一种美感，勾起游客的游兴，如果译成"Really Xingping has sceneries."可能读者的反应不大，不如不译。

3. 改写法

汉语描写景色的词汇丰富，多用对偶、排比，翻译起来很困难，多采用意译。勉强逐字逐句照译，可能反而伤害原意。

例如："境内西湖如明镜，千峰凝翠，洞壑幽深，风光迤逦。"译文："Hangzhou's West Lake is like a mirror, embellished all around with green hills and deep caves of enchanting beauty."原文用了"千峰凝翠""洞壑幽深""风光迤逦"等成语，翻译时切忌死译，应根据英语习惯，译出其意义。

景点介绍的英译应考虑外国客人的特点和中外文化差异，在达意的基础上，务求语言的华丽，唤起外国读者的兴趣，并使他们了解基本的中国文化。

三、历史典故的翻译

历史典故折射着民族的发展历史，凝结着民族的聪明智慧。无论是英文典故，还是汉语典故，多源于生动形象的寓言故事，其中寓意发人深省。通过译者的翻译，一个民族的文化瑰宝在另一个民族文化中能否依旧焕发异彩，这是翻译需要解决的问题。

(一)英汉历史典故对比

中国历史久远，汉语言文化更是源远流长，博大精深，而英语在近800年才得到较快的发展。从古代英语发展到近代英语，英语大量吸收借用其他语言，词汇量得到了极大丰富。英语中，较古老的典故多源于希腊、罗马神话或《圣经》，而正统的典故多成典较晚。莎士比亚时代相当于我国明末，而蒲柏与狄更斯时代相当于我国晚清。因此，英语典故带有时代特征。

英语典故在喻体选取比较方面多有相似之处。英汉典故中皆有以人设喻,如英语中的Shylock 和汉语中的"姜太公钓鱼";以事物设喻,如英语中的"kick the bucket"和汉语中的"三顾茅庐";以地名设喻,如英语中的"carry coals to Newcastle"和汉语中的"东山再起"。有些英汉典故不仅喻体形式相同,喻体形象相同,其寓意也完全一样。例如"walls have ears"与"隔墙有耳"。但这类形义相同的英汉典故在翻译中为数不多。

由于历史环境、地理风俗的不同,大多数英汉典故只是部分对应或者根本不对应。例如,英语的"meet one's water-loo"与汉语的"败走麦城",两者虽然寓意相同,但在喻体选取、设喻形式和使用上均存在差异。

英汉语言文化带有独具风格的民族色彩,这在英汉成语以及习语上表现尤为明显。如英语中的"paint the lily"与汉语中的"画蛇添足"。从《圣经》的天使报喜图中可以看出,西方人心目中百合花本来是"清白"与"贞洁"的象征,洁净素雅,高贵美丽。为百合花饰粉抹彩,破坏原有的雅致,自然是多此一举,徒劳无功。而汉文化中的蛇本来没有脚,画蛇添足反而使蛇不能称之为蛇。两个典故虽然渊源各异,但在表达"多此一举"的意义上却有异曲同工之妙,但同时各具民族特色。

(二) 英汉历史典故的翻译策略

历史典故的翻译虽然没有一成不变的固定模式,但也应遵循一定的原则。

(1) 直译或直译加解释

有些汉语典故涉及的概念英语本来就有,直译后不仅使原意顺利传达而且原文喻体形象也得到保留。而有些喻体形象在英语里原本没有,也可采取直译。这样保留了原文的意义和形象,同时,大量的外来词汇融入汉语,丰富了汉语文化,促进了两种文化的交融和共同进步。

例如:"冷战""cold war";"武装到牙齿""armed to the teeth";"鳄鱼的眼泪""crocodile tears"直译不仅可以被读者接受,而且能更好地再现原文。

一些典故如果采取直译,读者不能完全理解,如果采取意译,又丧失了原有的风格和形象。这时可以采取直译加解释的办法,这样能够保持原有的意义、形象和语言风格,使读者容易理解其潜在含义。例如:"有乐必有苦"可以翻译为"There is no rose without a thorn."

(2) 意译或意译加改造

不同民族的语言在形象和意义的结合方式上往往存在差异。一些典故中的形象在英语中虽然可以复制,但这种形象复制之后却丧失了原有的意义。这时,形象只能让位或牺牲,意译就变得理所当然。例如:"生于富贵之家""born with a silver spoon in one's mouth"。

如果英汉典故大致相等,差别仅在于形象或风格,翻译时,只需略加改造即可,同时又接近原文典故的结构和习惯,这就是意译加改造的方法。例如:"一花不是春"或"独木不成林",英语虽然找不到与此完全对应的谚语,但"one swallow does not make a summer""一燕不成夏"却和原文基本相同。又如:"无风不起浪",译为"no smoke without fire"也能为读者所接受。

(3) 等值典故互相借用

有些英汉典故在对方语言中可以找到与之对等的典故或俗语、成语,两者在意义、想象或风格上均有相似或相近之处，翻译时就可以采取等值互相借用法。例如"隔墙有耳"译为"Walls have ears."没有走意，形象和风格也得以保留。有很多成语典故可以用这种方法套用。

例如："山中无老虎，猴子称霸王。"等同于"Among the blind the one-eyed man is king.""英雄所见略同"等同于"Great minds think alike.""有志者事竟成"等同于"Where there is will, there is a way."

典故的互相借用是有条件的，不能在任何情况下都使用。一组对应的汉语和英语即使意思相近或形式相似，二者的确切含义和感情色彩也多有细微甚至很大的差别，所以不能随便借用，要结合具体的语言环境和意义综合考虑。

(三)对译者提出的要求

由于典故翻译的特殊困难，翻译时应根据具体情况及上下文的不同含义作具体处理。对典故的翻译一定要灵活处理，不能机械地生搬硬套，望文生义，要全面充分考虑到背后的民族文化。

语言是民族文化的载体，习语又称语言的精华。从对英汉典故的对比和翻译中可以看出，习语是民族文化的镜子。因此，要准确生动地互译英汉典故，翻译者要明确辨认英汉典故的相似性和差异性，不断提高自身语言能力和文化鉴赏能力，掌握从整体上、深层次上理解驾驭英汉语言的能力，进而达到跨语言跨文化交际的目的。

四、译文欣赏

颐和园，荟萃了中国古代园林，位于北京西郊。作为临时皇宫，颐和园建于1153年，并于1888年重建。颐和园内有万寿山和昆明湖。园内长廊上绘有精美的画作，为世界上最长的走廊，1992年被列入《吉尼斯世界纪录大全》。这条走廊连接慈禧太后处理国家事务的居住区和游览区。

[译文]

The Summer Palace, featuring the best of China's ancient gardens, is located in the western suburb of Beijing. The palace was built in 1153 as a temporary imperial palace. It was rebuilt in 1888. The Summer Palace consists of the Longevity Hill and the Kunming Lake. The Long Corridor, painted with exquisite paintings, was included in the Guinness Book of World Records in 1992 as the longest corridor in the world. The corridor links the area where Empress Dowager Cixi handled state affairs with the residential and sightseeing areas.

丽江古城位于云南省丽江市，是一座以纳西族为主的古镇，始建于1127年。古城的道路以丽江产的彩色鹅卵石铺就，城内有许多明清时代建造的石桥及牌坊。大部分住宅均由泥土、木头建造而成。古城内描绘宗教题材的宫廷壁画始于明代。丽江一直保持着纳西族的东巴文化传统。

[译文]

Lijiang ancient city, located in Lijiang, Yunnan Province, is an ancient town inhabited mainly by the Naxi minority people. The town was founded in 1127. The roads in the town are paved with colored pebbles produced in Lijiang, and there are many stone bridges and memorial archways built during the Ming and Qing Dynasties. Most of the residences are made of earth and wood. Palace murals depicting religious themes were painted during the Ming Dynasty. The traditional Dongba Culture of the Naxi ethnic group has been preserved in Lijiang.

秦始皇帝陵位于陕西省省会西安市以东35公里的临潼区。陵墓的建造,历时38年,涉及70多万名工人。多年来,共出土了5万余件重要文物。1980年两辆青铜马车出土,是迄今为止发现的最大最完整的铜车马。1974年,当地农民在秦始皇陵东约1.5公里处打井时发现秦始皇的地下兵马俑坑。三个墓穴中最大的有6 000个真人大小的兵马俑。秦俑被誉为"世界第八大奇迹"。

[译文]

Qinshihuang's Mausoleum is located in Lintong District, 35 kilometers east of Xi'an, capital of Shaanxi Province. Construction of the mausoleum lasted 38 years and involved over 700 000 workers. Over the years, a total of 50 000 important cultural relics have been unearthed. In 1980, two bronze painted horse-drawn chariots were unearthed. They are the largest and most complete bronze chariots and horses discovered so far. In 1974, farmers who were digging a well about 1.5 kilometers east of Qinshihuang's Mausoleum discovered three vaults containing Qinshihuang's Buried Legion. The largest of the three vaults contains 6 000 life-size terra-cotta warriors and horses. The collection of warriors is often dubbed the "eighth wonder of the world".

五、实践练习

翻译下列短文。

(1)峨眉山是中国四大佛教名山之一,位于四川省峨眉山市西南7公里处。山上有150座寺庙。山上有3 000多种植物和2 000种动物。乐山大佛位于四川省乐山市闽江河东岸。佛是雕刻出来的悬崖,高70.7米,是中国最大的坐尊如来佛祖。佛像的雕刻始于713年,于803年完成。佛陀的身体有排水系统,防止水土流失。

(2)承德避暑胜地,被称为"避暑山庄",位于河北省北部承德市,是清代皇帝夏天避暑和处理政务的场所。该避暑胜地的建设时间是从1703年到1792年,是规模最大、保存最完整的皇家离宫。周围的许多风景区都是华南著名的园林,外八庙的建筑以蒙古族、藏族和维吾尔族等少数民族的建筑风格为特色。

第九章 科技文本的翻译

一、论文摘要的翻译

摘要又称概要、文摘或内容提要,是科技论文中十分重要的组成部分。它通常放在题目和作者之后,文章正文之前,是以提供文献内容梗概为目的,不加评论和补充解释,简明、确切地记述文献重要内容的短文。摘要是科技论文的浓缩,可以使读者在尽可能短的时间内了解文章的研究内容,并决定是否有必要进一步阅读全文。国家标准 GB7713—87 中规定:"报告、论文一般均应有摘要,为了国际交流,还应有外文(英文)摘要"。可见,科技论文英文摘要直接关系到科研成果在世界范围传播和交流;同时国际上一些重要检索机构,如美国工程索引(EI)对非英文论文通过阅读英文摘要来判定是否收录。因此,高质量的摘要英译对于增加中文科技期刊和论文的被检索和摘引率、吸引读者和扩大学术影响意义重大。

一般而言,摘要的基本构成要素包括研究目的、方法、结果和结论。从语言运用看,摘要慎用长句,句型力求简单;无空泛、笼统、含混之词;不主张用"本文""作者"等主观性表述,代之以较为客观的第三人称。此外,摘要字数也有限制。学界有关科技论文摘要的翻译原则趋于一致。如魏羽、高宝萍提出了摘要翻译的四大要求:(1)结构严谨,表达明确,语义确切;(2)用第三人称;(3)要使用规范化的名词术语;(4)缩略语、略称、代号在首次出现时必须加以说明。例如:

摘要:二语习得有其自身的规律,对二语习得过程的充分了解有助于外语教学。将二语习得理论运用到英语口语课堂教学中,能更好地发展学生的语言交际能力,有助于培养出新时代所需的英语人才。

[译文] As second language acquisition has its own principles, foreign language teaching can benefit from a sound understanding of its processes. When SLA research is applied to spoken English teaching, students will develop better communicative competence to meet the needs of the new age.

——摘自《外语与外语教学》,2006 年 06 期

摘要:向心结构和离心结构是结构主义的重要概念,在中国语言学界的影响极为深远。但是,这一组概念在句法上并不形成真正的对立,用来解释汉语"的"字结构及相关现象也不成功,所以不值得保留,可以用较为简单的短语结构式来代替。

[译文]Endocentric construction and exocentric construction are two fundamental concepts of structuralism and have been influential among Chinese linguists. However, these two constructions do not contrast with each other in syntax. They are not very useful in explaining syntactic phenomena like the Chinese DE construction. They could be subsumed under a unified structural representation.

——摘自《外语教学与研究(外国语文双月刊)》,2007年04期

以上两则摘要均采用了直译的翻译方法,译文流畅易懂。翻译时,其英文摘要均从内容、信息呈现的先后顺序等各个方面照应汉语摘要。一般而言,学术论文的英语摘要大都采取直译法。然而,直译并不是机械地一句对一句、一词对一词的完全死译。例如:

摘要:(1)大数据成就了互联网,互联网促使了学习方式的变化和发展。(2)因此,面对信息化学习方式的变革,外语教学范式必须得到重新构建,而范式的重构必须考虑教学对象、教学环境以及教学的生态平衡等因素,以促进学生智慧学习和深度学习能力的发展。

[译文](1)Big Data technology facilitates the birth of Internet, which triggers the growth of IT-based learning modes. (2)In face of the changes of leaning modes, we need to reconstruct the norms of foreign language teaching. (3)To do it, we should take these factors such as students' identity, teaching environments and the balance of teaching ecology into consideration, thus promoting students' ability of smart learning and deep learning.

——摘自《外语电化教学》,2017年04期

原汉语摘要有两个句子,而英语摘要却有三个句子,似乎不太对应。但稍加分析便可发现,该英文摘要的第2、3句实际上与原汉语句子中第2句完全对等,只是英语版本为了行文方便,将其分为两句表述。

除此以外,还可采取意译。即翻译时,无须完全照搬汉语摘要,可只将其大意表达出来,进行适当改动。例如:

摘要:(1)近年来,读后续写引起了外语教学领域的关注,但探讨主要集中在理论层面,对于其促学效果的实证考察还相对匮乏。(2)因此本研究通过一项实验,全面呈现了读后续写对中国学生英语写作语言准确性、复杂性和流利性发展的影响。(3)实验结果显示,读后续写可以有效提升学习者的语言产出表现,特别是在准确性和复杂性方面,效果尤为明显。(4)研究指出,读后续写是内容创造与语言模仿的有机融合,即可凸显语言输入、激发学习者注意形式,又能优化语言输出、加快新知识的吸收,是提高外语教学效率的可靠途径。

[译文](1)Recent years has seen much interest amongst foreign language teaching researchers in the role played by the continuation task in foreign language learning. (2)In spite of the theoretical importance of this learning task, however, empirical evidence remains sparse. (3)This study examined the effect of the continuation task on second language learners' written accuracy, complexity, and fluency by comparing the performance of two groups of second language learners: one group wrote following text reading in six continuation tasks, and the other group wrote on six given topics without text reading. (4)The comparison revealed that the continuation task generated more gains on accuracy and complexity than the topic writing task. (5)However, there was no significant difference between the two groups on the development of fluency. (6)The implications of these findings from the perspective of cognitive psychology are discussed.

——摘自《现代外语(双月刊)》,2015年03期

该中文摘要共有四句,然而英文摘要却有6句。仔细对比后会发现,此英文摘要并没有严格按照中文摘要的内容进行翻译,而是进行了适当的增译和删减。例如,中文摘要中第二

句提到"本研究通过一项实验",而英文摘要第三句却对其具体内容进行了补充"by comparing the performance of two groups of second language learners: one group wrote following text reading in six continuation tasks, and the other group wrote on six given topics without text reading"。中文摘要第三句仅仅提到"实验结果显示,读后续写可以有效提升学习者的语言产出表现,特别是在准确性和复杂性方面,效果尤为明显。"英文摘要第四句"the comparison revealed that the continuation task generated more gains on accuracy and complexity than the topic writing task."对其进行了对应翻译,还补充了第五句"However, there was no significant difference between the two groups on the development of fluency",对研究结果进行了更加详细的补充。然而,原中文摘要第四句的内容却在英文摘要中进行了删减翻译。

一般来说,论文摘要的翻译可以分为三步走:首先,通过上下文的关系,弄清原文的词汇含义、语法及逻辑关系,正确理解论文摘要的内容;其次,通过筛选词汇和合理排列,组织句子各部分,恰当表达论文摘要原文的意思;最后,通过与原文对照检查,仔细校核,推敲译文语言并润色文字。除了遵循以上要点之外,还需注意和掌握一些细节问题及技巧。

1. 多用被动语态。被动语态能较好地表现客观性,主语部分可集中较多的信息,起到信息前置、鲜明突出的作用。因此,在介绍研究对象、研究所用的设备、手段时都常常使用被动语态。例如,"本文介绍了一种新的……方法"译为"In this paper, a new method is described for…";"本文对……进行了分析"译为"In this paper, an analysis of…was carried out…"。主动语态可以较好地突出作者的努力,所以在介绍目的和结论时多用主动语态。例如,"研究得出结论……"译为"It concludes that…";"研究结果表明……"译为"The result shows that…";"研究发现……"译为"It finds that…"等。

2. 正确选用时态。一般而言,论文的英文摘要经常使用的时态有三种:一般过去时,一般现在时和现在完成时。其中,一般现在时使用最为广泛,常常用来介绍研究目的、内容、结果、结论等客观事实。例如:"本文旨在/试图……"译为"This paper aims at/attempts to…";"本论文提出/探讨……"译为"This paper presents/discusses…";"本文表明……"译为"This paper demonstrates/shows/indicates…"等。现在完成时一般用来说明论题的发展背景,通常表示已取得的成果,已完成的工作。一般过去时常常用来介绍已进行的研究、实验、调查等,用于说明某一具体项目的发展情况。例如:

摘要:本文采用定量的研究方法对近10年(2006—2016)中国学术期刊刊载的有关基于网络学习英语听力的研究进行分析与评述,旨在揭示现有基于网络学习听力研究的总体情况,发现:(1)近10年来国内基于网络学习听力研究大致可以分为两个阶段;(2)国内针对基于网络学习英语听力研究主要焦点聚集于教学模式与方法改革、学生听力能力培养、听力策略培训等方面;(3)实证性研究比重呈逐年增长态势。

[译文]Aiming to reveal the existing literature on web-based L2 listening, this paper presents a quantitative analysis of relevant articles that have been published in CNKI from 2006 to 2016. The outcomes show that: (1) two stages of the development concerning the number of web-based English listening research articles can be identified; (2) in terms of research content, more attention has been paid to the teaching of listening, cultivation of self-learning capacity and strategies training; (3) the number of empirical studies has increased steadily.

——摘自《外国语文(双月刊)》,2017年05期

二、科技报告的翻译

科技报告是关于科研项目或科研活动的正式报告或情况记录,是研究、设计单位或个人以书面形式向提供经费和资助的部门或组织汇报其研究设计或项目进展情况的报告。它是以积累、传播和交流为目的,由科技人员按照有关规定和格式撰写,真实而完整地反映科研人员所从事科技活动的内容和经验的特种文献。与图书和期刊文献相比较,它的篇幅可长可短,但其内容新颖广泛、专业性强、技术数据具体,因而是科研人员、工程技术人员的优先参考资料,它对于交流各种科研思路、推动发明创造、评估技术差距、改进技术方案、增加决策依据、避免科研工作中的重复与浪费,促进科研成果转化为生产力起到了积极的作用。广义上讲,我国目前正式公开发行的科技报告有国研报告、商业报告、中国国防科技报告。一般而言,报告的专业性较强,包含大量专业术语,此外,报告形式多样,结构复杂。因此,翻译科技报告时,要把握好报告的结构特点,理清长句逻辑,掌握专业术语含义,对报告进行准确翻译。例如:

本年度主要在格密码数学问题研究、格密码体制安全性分析和对称密码算法分析模型建立方面进行研究。

[译文] We focus on the mathematics problems of lattice cryptography, cryptanalysis of lattice cryptosystems, and the cryptanalysis of symmetric ciphers according to the project proposal.

本年度投入了大量的人力和物力开展文献资料总结和野外调查工作,初步将西部山区大型滑坡地质结构类型划分为"弱面"控制型,"关键块体"型,"软弱基座"型和"采空区"控制型4大类。

[译文] Large amount of man power and resources were used to carry out literature review and site investigation, this year. The characteristics of large scale landslides in west China were preliminarily divided to four groups, which are weak interface controlled, key block controlled, weak foundation controlled and goaf controlled landslides, respectively.

痴呆与轻度认知障碍是我国卫生领域重大疾病,给社会和家庭带来了沉重负担。本项目在国家和省部级40余项基金资助下,对痴呆与轻度认知障碍的流行病学、发病机制和临床诊治进行了系统的研究,取得了显著成果,具体如下。

[译文] Dementia and mild cognitive impairment are the most common neurodegenerative disease and the leading cause of dementia in the elderly. Sponsored by over 40 national and provincial funds, our project aims to study systematically the epidemiology, pathogenesis, diagnosis and treatment of dementia and mild cognitive impairment. We've got tremendous achievements through all these years' hard work, which were listed as follows.

从以上三则科技报告示例可以发现,不同的学科领域,均有自己的一套专业术语。可谓是"行话"琳琅,"术语"满目。因此,在翻译过程中,为了使读者更好地了解报告内容,译者应该注意涉猎多领域的专业词汇,尽量保持文本与专业术语翻译的一致性。此外,还要注意调整句式,使得译文更符合译入语的语言特点。例如:

概念是人类意识、思维、语言、智慧等其他高级认知过程的基础,是认知系统的核心成分。我们旨在基于多年对语言概念的研究经验,结合概念认知研究的前沿理念和现代脑网络特性的最新分析方法,系统建构人类概念认知的脑网络系统,拟解决以下三个关键问题。

[译文] Concepts are the basic elements of human thought, subserving a wide range of cognitive functions, such as language, object recognition and use, and is at the heart of cognitive neuroscience research. On the basis of past experience with language, concepts, and brain network analyses, we aimed at constructing the brain network basis of human conceptual system, specifically targetting three issues.

本研究旨在梳理古今文献中脾脏象理论,阐明"脾主运化、统血"等脾脏象理论的基本概念、基本原理、基本规律,为整个研究提供理论支撑。按照任务书的计划,2013年度完成了规定任务,包括古代医籍的收集整理,近10年现代脾脏象理论相关文献的收录整理,初步研究脾脏象理论的内涵及框架结构,研究脾脏象理论数据库的结构,研究项目的信息管理平台的结构等任务。

[译文] The research is to study the visceral theory of spleen in ancient and modern literature, to expound the basic concepts, basic principles and basic rules of the visceral theory of spleen in transformation and transportation and controlling blood, so as to provide theoretical support for the entire research work. The work on the visceral theory of spleen in the research specification for the year of 2013 has been completed, including the collection of ancient medical books and the related modem literatures for the late 10 years, preliminary study on the connotation and frame structure, and the studies on the structure of the database and the structure of the information management platform for the entire research works, etc.

在课题实施过程中,培育水产新品种10个,其中已通过国家水产原种和良种审定委员会审定的5个,待审定的5个;培育新品系9个。建立了39个试验基地。申请专利40项,其中已获授权16项(其中国家发明专利12项),申请24项(其中国家发明专利22项);制定技术标准23项,其中已颁布15项(行业以上标准9项),申请8项(行业以上标准6项);获国家级奖励2项,省部级奖励6项;出版专著8部,合计300余万字,发表研究性论文172篇,其中SCI、EI收录39篇;培养博士研究生19人,硕士研究生68人。课题组圆满完成项目计划任务,并荣获科技部"十一五"国家科技计划执行优秀团队奖。

[译文] During the implementation of this project, ten new varieties of aquaculture species were obtained, five of which have been authorized by The National Approval Committee for Aquatic Species and Varieties. Nine new strains were obtained. 39 experiment bases were established. 40 patent applications were made, among which 16 were authorized, including 12 national invention patents. 23 industrial standards were drawn up, 15 of which were issued. The project partners have been awarded two national level and six provincial level scientific prizes, published eight books and 172 research papers, including 39 published in peer-reviewed SCI or EI journals. The project team also includes 19 Ph. D students and 68 master's degree students. The task group has fulfilled all scheduled tasks, and received the Excellence Team Award for Implementation of "The Eleventh Five Year Plan" National Science and Technology Programme, from the Ministry of Science and Technology.

三、专利说明书的翻译

专利文献是一种依法公布新技术的出版物，是以比较统一而固定的格式和书写方法，记载各国新的发明创造的技术成果说明书。专利说明书(patent specification)是专利文献的核心内容，它是用以说明发明的内容和取得的权利要求范围的文件。专利通常包括发明专利(Invention or Creation)、实用新型(Utility Model)及外观设计(Design or Mask)三种类型。一般而言，科技专利说明书是技术发明者向消费者全面、明确地介绍产品名称、用途、性质、性能、原理、构造、规格、使用方法、保养维护和注意事项等内容而写的准确、简明的文字材料。因此，它是非常重要的技术信息源，尤其对产业界来说，专利文献具有较高的使用价值和参考价值。由于专利文献是一种承载技术信息、法律信息的特殊文献，专利翻译比普通文本的翻译更为严谨。翻译人员不但要有功底深厚的英文水平，还需有相关领域的背景知识。例如：

本发明的实施例涉及照明装置技术领域。

[译文] Embodiments of the present invention relate to the technology field of a lighting device.

"实施例"是指对发明或者实用新型的优选的具体实施方式的举例说明，即将本发明付诸实现的最佳实例。通常，此词会被译为"embodiment"。这对于初次接触专利翻译的人员来说是比较有挑战的。然而，专利的术语常常具备程式化特点。所谓程式化是指同类语篇大致相同的体例与表达方式，对于这类程式化专利术语的翻译，"套译"这种翻译方法不失为一种很好的选择。所谓套译，是指完全照搬、套用相关英文的翻译。这种翻译策略适用于一切程式化文体的翻译，尤其适用于高度程式化的专利说明书部分内容的翻译。例如：

发明内容。

[译文] Summary of the Invention.

相关申请的交叉引用。

[译文] Cross Reference to Related Application.

类似的表达还有：Field of the Invention(技术领域), Background of the Invention(技术背景), Brief Description of the Drawings(附图说明), Detailed Description of the Invention(具体实施方式)等。这几大标题都是英文专利说明书中的惯用词组，通常有其固定译法。除此以外，还可套译一些常用的固定句型。

本发明的一个主要目的/另一个目的/再一个目的是……

[译文] A(n) main/another/further object of the present invention is to (do)…OR It is a (n) main/another/further object of the present invention is to (do)…

本发明提供了一种(装置/方法/工艺名称)，由……构成/包括……，其中……

[译文]The present invention provides a (name of a/an apparatus/method/process), consisting of/comprising…/including…,wherein…

结合附图和对本发明的多种实施例及以下对附图的详细说明,可更全面地理解本发明。

[译文]The disclosure may be more completely understood in consideration of the following detailed description of various embodiments of the disclosure in connection with the accompanying drawings.

本专利申请要求于××××年××月××日提交的美国临时专利申请号×××××××和于××××年××月××日提交的美国临时专利申请号×××××××的优先权,以上两个临时专利申请的公开内容以引用方式全文并入于此。

[译文]This application claims the benefit of U. S. Provisional Patent Application Nos. ××××××× , filed ×× ××, 20××, and ××××××× , filed ×× ××, 20××, the disclosures of which are incorporated by reference herein in their entirety.

此外,由于专利文献是技术文件和法律文件的结合物,需按专利法的有关规定撰写,因此会出现一些固体词以体现专利文体特有的严谨风格。

凡政府机构或为政府机构效力而使用本发明的,均可以授予专利特许证,免交专利使用费。

[译文]The invention described <u>herein</u> may be manufactured, used and licensed by or for the Government for government purpose without the payment to us of any royalty <u>thereon</u>.

此句中的 herein 指 in that place, in that(在那里),thereon 即 then, as the result of that(于是,因此)。这些单词也常常出现在国际商务合同中。因此,对于这类单词的翻译,可考虑采取参译法。

四、译文欣赏

摘要:(1)本研究通过对我国一所重点外语院校8位老教师的深度访谈,探究外语教育传统(1949—1978)中的写作教学实践,剖析写作教学实践的基本要素和特征,总结写作教学实践的核心理念。(2)研究结果表明,外语教育传统中的写作教学立足于教学和育人的完整性和统一性,追求写作的真实性和思想性,重视实践的互动性和主体性,强调教和学的过程性和形成性。(3)研究最后针对我国当下的外语写作教学提供了启示。

——摘自《外语界》,2017 年 05 期

[译文]
(1) Through in-depth interviews with 8 senior teachers at a key foreign language university in China, this study makes an investigation into the writing instruction practice in China's tradition of foreign language education (1949 – 1978). (2) It analyzes the fundamental elements and features of their writing instruction, and reexamines the core concepts of foreign language writing and writing instruction. (3) The study results show that the traditional writing instruction, oriented towards the whole-person teaching and education, pursues authenticity and thoughts, emphasizes learner agency and interactions between readers and writers, and goes through formative teaching and learning processes. (4) The study finally provides some implications for

foreign language writing instruction in China.

研究主要目标为通过双方合作研究尝试构建起中国危险化学品安全评估框架及相应技术体系,在此框架下合作开展部分新型污染物的环境行为研究、风险评价研究,提升双方研究水准,推动学科发展;通过项目建立中美化学品环境行为及风险评价研究中心,搭建平台推动双方在危险化学品安全评估领域的长期深入的合作研究与广泛交流,建立起双方全面、互信、长期的合作关系;通过研究促进人才培养和队伍建设工作。

[译文]

The main objective of the project through the cooperation is trying to build up China Dangerous Chemicals assessment framework and the corresponding technical system. Under the framework of cooperation, we are supposed to study the environmental behavior and risk assessment of new pollutants to enhance mutual research standards, and promote academic development. Through the project, we hope to establish Sino-US research center of environmental behavior and risk assessment of chemicals, and build a platform to conduct in-depth study and extensive exchanges and cooperation in the field of chemical safety assessment. We hope this project can help us to establish a comprehensive, mutual trust, long-term relationship to promote personnel training and team building.

本发明的实施例可以在不脱离本发明的精神和范围的情况下进行多种修改和更改。因此,应当理解,本发明的实施例不应限于以下所述的示例性实施例,但应受权利要求书及其任何等同形式中阐述的限制的控制。

[译文]

Embodiments of the present disclosure may take on various modifications and alterations without departing from the spirit and scope of the disclosure. Accordingly, it is to be understood that the embodiments of the present disclosure are not to be limited to the following described exemplary embodiments, but is to be controlled by the limitations set forth in the claims and any equivalents thereof.

五、实践练习

翻译下列短文。

(1)摘要:翻译能力是译者在翻译工作中所需的潜在知识体系、技能体系及相关职业素养。本文将西方翻译能力模式分为以语言能力为中心的模式、多元要素翻译能力模式、专业领域(法律)翻译能力模式和最简翻译能力模式。文章分析指出西方翻译能力模式具有重视双语语言能力、翻译技术能力和翻译服务能力,关注专业领域翻译能力,注重实证和实际应用等特点,并从教学目标、课程体系、教学方法等方面讨论了西方翻译能力模式研究对我国 MTI 翻译能力培养的启示意义。

(2)湖泊在国家经济社会发展、生态文明建设中发挥着十分重要的作用。湖泊综合治理与保护极具挑战性,底泥是湖泊生态系统的重要组成部分,它与湖泊富营养化和水质安全直接相关。湖泊底泥污染控制理论技术一直是湖泊综合治理和环境保护工程建设的关键科技难题。针对我国湖泊污染的严峻形势及污染控制的突出问题,项目涉及我国20多个主要湖泊,以底泥污染过程认知——底泥原位治理/环保疏浚——基底重建——生态修复——水质改善为主线,围绕底泥污染控制重大理论技术创新和工程应用,开展了长期、系统和综合对比研究,取得了如下重要成果。

第十章　商务文本的翻译

一、商标、品牌的翻译

商标(Trademark)指商品生产者或经营者为使自己的商品在市场上同其他商品生产者或经营者的商品相区别,而使用于商品或其包装上,由文字、图案或文字和图案的组合所构成的一种标记。商标是一个法定概念,而品牌(Brand)是一个市场概念。品牌通常具有丰厚的内涵,它不仅仅是一个标志和名称,更蕴含着生动的精神文化,体现着企业的价值观,抒发着人的情怀。如"可口可乐"的品牌内涵远不止"cocacola"几个字所构成的标志和名称,它体现了美国几代人乐观向上的人文文化和精神。商标是企业品牌宣传和产品推销的利器。因此,在对其进行翻译时应在遵循"以产品为中心、以目标受众为导向"、考虑商标词汇形态以及文化因素的影响基础上,根据不同情形,采取灵活多变的翻译策略。

一般而言,商标、品牌词通常包括普通词汇,如"Apple"(苹果)、"吉利"(Geely)等;专有名词,如"Disney"(迪士尼)、"McDonald's"(麦当劳)、"Chanel"(香奈儿)、"Longines"(浪琴)、"AVON"(雅芳)等;及臆造词汇,如"Volvo"(沃尔沃)、"Media"(美的)、"Lenovo"(联想)等。

商标、品牌翻译方法一般有音译法、意译法以及音意结合法。所谓音译,是指根据原文发音和译文发音的相似性,运用谐音字词对商标进行翻译。例如:

娃哈哈。

［译文］Wahaha.

"娃哈哈",一个巨大的饮料王国,其产品深受中国消费者的喜爱,在中国销售相当成功。据说之所以叫"娃哈哈",原因有三:一是好读好记,小孩子容易接受;二是它能形象地表现小孩子得到娃哈哈后的开心喜悦之情,很乐观积极;三是有一首广为流传儿歌叫《娃哈哈》,方便品牌传播。在国外市场,"娃哈哈"这一商标的译名采用了直接音译"Wahaha"。"haha"这一拟声词发音简单响亮,读起来朗朗上口,不仅可以给消费者留下深刻印象,也能带给人们愉悦。然而,值得注意的是,一般的汉语拼音对西方人而言只是一个音符。因此,虽有少数成功案例,但完全单纯地采用拼音翻译商标仍然比较冒险。如果拼音翻译不能使目标客户产生美好联想,也无法传达其源语言所蕴含的丰富内涵时,则可考虑谐音译法。

雅戈尔。

［译文］Youngor.

"雅戈尔"品牌是国家第一批"中国驰名商标",也是国家第一批"重点支持和发展的名牌出口商品"品牌。其商标采用谐音音译,译为"Youngor",与英文单词"young"的比较级"younger"相似,从而表明该品牌服装可以给人带来更多活力,巧妙地迎合了成功男士的消费心理。

海信。

[译文] Hisense.

"海信"是中国电器的知名商标,其英文商标采用谐音音译为"Hisense",来源于"High Sense",意指"高灵敏度、性能卓越",从而突出了该品牌产品的特点。除此以外,像"康佳"(Konka)、"立白"(Liby)、"达芙妮"(Daphne)等也都采用了相同的翻译方法。

直译是指在译语中选取与原语商标名称语义对应、文化意义相符的词汇进行翻译。例如:

永久牌(自行车)。

[译文] Forever.

"永久牌"自行车是上海永久股份有限公司生产的自行车品牌,在首届"中国驰名商标"消费者评选获"中国驰名商标"称号。其英文商标被直译为"Forever",巧妙地突出了该品牌自行车"经久耐用,直到永远"的优良品质,迎合了消费者的期待。

公牛。

[译文] Bull.

"公牛"品牌于1995年在宁波慈溪创立,主要生产国内领先的高档开关插座、转换器等。"牛"在中西方文化中都是强壮、有活力及生命力旺盛的代表。因此,将"公牛"直译为"Bull"可以巧妙地表明该品牌对自己的定位:"成为消费者心中的插座第一品牌""插座专家与领导""插座 = 公牛"。

小天鹅。

[译文] Little Swan.

1997年,"小天鹅"商标被认定为中国洗衣机行业第一枚驰名商标,现如今已赢得全球3 000多万消费者的喜爱,成功地实现了由国内家电制造商向国际家电制造商的转变,全力打造国际名牌。其英文译名"Little Swan"巧妙地让人联想到天鹅的洁白无瑕与美丽,同时也会给消费者该品牌洗衣机也能洗出像白天鹅般洁净衣物的积极暗示。

新东方。

[译文] New Oriental.

"新东方"作为中国教育培训领域的领头羊,在基础教育、职业教育、教育研发、出国咨询、文化产业等方面均取得了骄人业绩。其英文译名"New Oriental"也巧妙地表达出其想要成为"New"——中国优秀的、令人尊敬的、有文化价值的教学机构的美好愿景。

音意结合法是基于原商标的发音和意义进行翻译的方法,此方法可以充分发挥译语的优势,可谓音意兼备。例如:

格力。

[译文] Gree.

中国空调驰名商标"格力"采用音意结合的译法,将其英文商标译为"Gree",该英文单词不仅发音与原中文商标相似,还具有"优越""杰出"之意。此译法音义俱佳,巧妙地表明了该品牌产品质量卓越,性能杰出的特点。

乐凯。

[译文] Lucky.

"乐凯"是中国的一种胶卷老品牌,是胶卷行业的唯一可以与世界品牌柯达和富士并存,并且一直在中国胶卷市场上鏖战了多年的"三国演义"。其英文商标译为"Lucky",在英语中意味着幸福和好运,巧妙地迎合了人们的需求。因此,也深受外国人的欢迎。

除了上述方法以外,商标翻译有时还需跳出原文的局限,结合目标语语言习惯,把握产品要素,创造性地译出产品的卖点。例如:

狗不理。

[译文] Go Believe.

"狗不理"是天津的百年金牌老字号,是中华饮食文化的典范之作。其英文商标"Go Believe"采用了谐音音译与创译法相结合的方式,巧妙地表达了"狗不理"包子质优物美,值得人们信赖的特点。

二、商务广告的翻译

商务广告是指商家为了推销产品或提供服务,通过报纸、广播、电视等媒体进行宣传,从而激发消费者兴趣和购买动机的信息传播活动。广告文体是一种具有很高商业价值的实用文体,通常具有语言简明扼要、新奇独特、生动有趣、能在瞬间引起读者(观众)注意并刺激其产生强烈的购买欲望的特点。一则商业广告,通常会包括商标和广告语两个部分。翻译时,应遵循忠实、统一的原则,尽可能地体现原文的文体特点。此外,译文应充分体现广告的信息功能和劝说功能,要有美感,还应考虑文化差异,注意不同顾客群体的文化价值观,遵循社会文化习惯,进行恰当的文化转化。

想要皮肤好,早晚用大宝。

[译文] Applying "Dabao" morning and night makes your skin a real delight.

此则广告采用直译,"delight"一词巧妙地迎合了消费者的心理,并说明了定期使用该产品能够延缓皮肤衰老、深入滋润等特点。例如:

汰渍到,污渍逃。

[译文] Tide's In, Dirt's Out.

汰渍洗衣粉的这则广告富有对称性,其语言简洁明了,形象生动,巧妙地迎合了顾客的消费心理。翻译时,应尽量与原文结构保持一致。例如:

滴滴香浓,意犹未尽。

[译文] Good to the last drop.

这则是麦斯威尔咖啡的广告,译文采用意译,通过"连最后一滴也不放过"的意象来反衬咖啡的美味。例如:

简约而不简单。

[译文] Simple Yet Sophisticated.

这则利郎男装的广告语,简单明了。译文采用意译,巧妙地运用语言的形式美,押头韵,不仅突出了该品牌服饰时尚简约、古典俊雅、不求外显而求内涵的特点,还巧妙地强调了该品牌男装是时尚与传统的完美结合。

百闻不如一印。

[译文] Copying makes you believing.

这则是佳能复印机的广告,套用了中国谚语"百闻不如一见"。英译时,仿拟英文中的"Seeing is believing",文本读起来朗朗上口,使人印象深刻。

不到三亚,枉来海南。

[译文] A visit to Hainan would not be completed without visiting Sanya.

此句广告语在翻译时巧妙地运用了双重否定,不仅能够引起旅行者的注意,而且极具诱惑。

本品可即购即食,食用方便。

[译文] (Always) Ready to serve.

该广告词是一则食品广告的节选,若直译为:"Opening and eating immediately."易使人产生"不吃掉,食品马上会坏掉"的消极联想。因此,在进行广告翻译时,可适当进行意译。要注意,广告翻译不是表象文字的简单吻合,而应是信息和语言内涵上的紧密契合。

有备无患,随身携带,有惊无险。

[译文] A friend in need is a friend indeed!

这是一则治疗心脏病的名为"速效救心丸"的药物广告。此广告语运用反复和排比的修辞手法,巧妙地表明了该药品的优越品质及卓越功效。翻译此广告语时,译者直接引用了英文谚语:"A friend in need is a friend indeed!",虽与原文结构完全不同,但却非常巧妙地将药品比作"朋友",增加产品人情味与可信度的同时也表明了其功效。

原来生活可以更美的。

[译文] Media: It's your idea.

"美的"是我国著名的家电品牌,其汉语的广告词不仅融入了"美的"商标,还巧妙地迎合了人们追求美好生活的心理,暗示出该品牌产品可以美化生活。英译时,将其英文商标名称"Media"分解为"My idea",巧妙地抓住了西方文化中崇尚个人主义、尊重个人观点的特征,从而表明了该品牌的宗旨就是把顾客的"idea"变为现实,反映出顾客至上的经营理念。

衣食住行,有龙则灵。

参考译文:Your everyday life is very busy; our Long Card can make it easy.

这则是中国建设银行的广告语,译文中的"Long Card"指"龙卡"。翻译时应特别注意"龙"在中西文化中的差异。"龙"是中国人心目中喜气吉祥的代表,但在西方眼中却是邪恶凶残的代名词。因此,译文中"Dragon"被转译为汉语拼音"Long"。除此以外,在进行汉英翻译时,还应该注意 phoenix(凤凰),magpie(喜鹊),butterfly(蝴蝶),white elephant(白象),cock(鸡)等词的文化内涵。

三、商务合同的翻译

商务合同是指有关各方在进行某种商务合作时,为了确定各自的权利和义务而正式依法订立的、并且经过公证的、必须共同遵守的协议条文。按贸易方式的性质和内容,可将合同分为销售或购货合同(sales or purchase contract)、技术转让合同(contract for technology transfer)、合资或合营合同(contract for joint venture or joint production)、补偿贸易合同(contract for compensation trade)、国际工程承包合同(contract for international engineering projects)、涉外信贷合同(contract for credits and loans)等。一般来说,商务合同主要由名称(title)、前言(preamble)、正文(main body)和结尾(final clauses)四个主要部分组成。

商务合同是一种实用文体,兼有商务和法律语篇特有的特征,但同时又有其独有的特色。商务合同整体上语言精练、逻辑清晰,表达上力求严谨、准确,具有权威性和威慑力。因此,译文的语言必须符合文本的类型特征和实际意义。在我国的商务贸易业务中,合同一般都采用中英两种语言文字写成,且两种文本有相同的法律效力。一般而言,商务合同的翻译需要注意以下几点:忠实原文;符合国际惯例;尽量使用规范的法律用语。其翻译准则主要是:用词准确严谨(Accuracy and Faithfulness)、译文规范完整(Standardization and Completeness)、译文通顺(Expressiveness)。例如:

第一次董事会会议应在公司营业执照签发后一个月内召开。

[译文] The first board meeting shall be convened within one month after the issuance of the company's business license.

商务合同具有法律效力,因此,翻译时宜选用正式的书面语,且尽量避免词义弹性大的日常用语。此参考译文中的"convene"属于书面词语,语义比较明确,指"召集、召开",没有其他联想意义,而单词"call"为多义词,还可表示"打电话、拜访等",比较容易引起歧义。

例如:货到目的港后即行付清余款。

[译文] The balance shall be settled upon the arrival of the goods at the port of destination.

此译文没有使用"after",是因为"after"对时间的限定比较模糊,到货后的很多天依然可以理解为"after",因此,选择词语"upon"与原文的语意更加吻合,翻译更为准确。

例如:卖方在此保证:货物符合质量标准,无一瑕疵。

[译文] The seller hereby warrants that the goods meet the quality standard and are free from all defects.

商务合同中经常使用一些古体词来体现合同文本严密、庄重的文体特征,常见的有:"hereby, hereof, hereinafter, therefore, whereof"分别表示"兹、特此""本、此""在下文、以下""因此""关于那事(物)"。通常这类词是由here,there,和where与in,on,after,by,with,under,of等构成。一般来讲,here指"本合同(the contract)",there指"上文刚刚提到的名词或事件",where指what或which。此译文中的"hereby"表示"by means of or by reason of this""特此,由此,兹"的意思。

例如:本合约由甲方和乙方签订。

[译文] This contract is made and entered into by and between Party A and Party B.

"签订合约"可译为"make a contract"或"enter into a contract",将两者并列使用,取其共义,完全避免了语言疏漏可能引起的误解。同义词"by"和"between"的连用,不仅体现了合同的缔约人,而且反映了当事人之间的合同缔约人关系,更贴切地表达了原文意旨。翻译合同时,可适当多用成双成对的同义词和并列词语来限定或确定或强调其意义。

例如:双方可在必要时通过协商修改本合同。

[译文] The parties may, through consultation, make amendments to and revisions of this Contract as and when the need arises.

例如:本协议双方应履行协议规定的义务。

[译文] Each party to this Agreement shall fulfill or perform any of the obligations under this Agreement.

fulfill 的法律含义是"to do everything which is promised in a contract",强调的是合同的一方履行合同与所规定的该方的那部分具体义务,而 perform 的法律含义是"to do what one party is obliged to do by a contract",它泛指双方在合同中的各项责任和义务都应得到履行。

例如:本合同的修改只有在双方签字并在原审批主管机关批准后才能生效。

[译文] The amendments to or alterations of this Contract become effect only after they are signed by both parties and approved by the original approving authorities.

此外,合同语言中有一些约定俗成具有稳定性和规范性特点的套语,熟悉和正确使用这些套语,可以在翻译中起到事半功倍的作用。

例如:兹特立约为据,并由订约双方协议如下:……

[译文] NOWTHESE PRESENTS WITNESS that it is hereby agreed between the parties hereto as follows:…

例如:我方于_____年____月____日签署本文件,并于_____年____月____日接受该文件,特此为证。

[译文] IN TESTIMONY WHEREOF we have hereto signed this document on _____ (date) accepted on _____ (date).

例如:本合同由双方代表签字后生效,一式两份,双方各执一份,特此立据。

[译文] IN WITNESS/TESTIMONY WHEREOF, this contract shall come into effect after the contract in question is made and signed by the parties hereto in duplication, and either party will hold one copy.

例如:本合同用中英文两种文字写成,两种文字具有同等效力。本合同共_____份,自双方代表签字之日生效。

买方代表(签字):_____
卖方代表(签字):_____

[译文] This contract is executed in two counterparts each in Chinese and English, each of which shall deem equally authentic. This contract is in _____ copies, effective since being signed by both parties.

Representative of the buyer (authorized signature):_____
Representative of the seller (authorized signature):_____

四、商品说明书的翻译

商品说明书,也可称为产品说明书、产品描述、操作指南、用户手册或说明书,英文又称"instruction""book of instruction""operating instruction""operating manual""user's manual""direction""description"等,是提供商品所有重要信息和如何使用商品的说明性文件,是商品不可缺少的附带品之一。商品说明书一般具有宣传产品,指导消费(advertising products, guiding consumption);传播消息,促进消费(expanding news,stimulating consumption)及传播知识,创造品牌(spreading knowledge,creating the brand)的作用。因此,在国际贸易中,商品说明书的翻译质量十分重要。

商品说明书按其形式可分为手册式说明书、插页式说明书、标签式说明书及印在包装上的说明书。其形式虽有不同,但均是说明文文体。说明文的风格可概括为 PEA(plain 语言直白,efficient 信息充分,accurate 表达确切)。因此,翻译商品说明书时,应注重知识性和科学性,翻译的目标是为了让目的消费者准确、详细地了解产品,译者应尽量以客观、准确的语言描述介绍商品的特征、功效及主要事项等内容,语言要通俗易懂,行文通畅,符合逻辑。

例如:保存于常温干燥处。

[译文] Store dry and at room temperature.

例如:不使用相机时,请取出电池。

[译文] When not using the camera, remove the battery.

例如:红灯亮时即可切断电源。

[译文] When the red indicator is on, the switch can be turned off.

例如:如有不适及过敏症状,请立即停止使用。

[译文] Please stop using it in case of discomfort or sensitive symptom.

例如:如果包装已打开或有损坏迹象,请勿购买。

[译文] Do not purchase if box has been opened or shows signs of tampering.

例如:开瓶前充分摇匀,开启后三日内饮完。

[译文] Give the bottle a good shake before opening and drink up within three days.

例如:本产品系纯天然蜂蜜。可调入温开水饮用,亦可调入牛奶咖啡中饮用,还可抹于面包食用。

[译文] This refined honey is free from any additives and it can be used as sugar or jam.(注:中文商品说明书多使用主动语态来描述商品特征和使用方法,在译为英文时,可以作为被动语态译出。)

翻译时,译者需对原文理解透彻、入理,而不仅仅满足于对表层信息的转述。

例如:绿源苔干有治疗心脏病、神经官能症、消化不良、贫血诸功效。

[译文] Lvyuan Taigan can be served as a medical diet for those who are suffering from heart failure, neurosis, indigestion and anemia.

说到"治疗",我们一般会想到"cure"。但是通过理解商品说明书的上下文,我们可以发现"绿源苔干"是一种绿色健康食品,不是药品,并不能真正治疗疾病,所以译文中没有使用"cure",而是译为"be served as a medical diet for those who are suffering from",通过此种译法,可以较为准确地把绿源苔干的"食疗"功效翻译出来。

此外,由于文化的不同,语言的差异以及不同民族对同一事物所产生的不同心理感受,一种语言中的特殊概念在另一种语言中常常会出现语义上的空缺及理解上的背向。因此,为了提高译文的可读性,有时需要对不完全适合用译入语表达的原文和对不符合读者欣赏习惯的描写进行必要的删节和改写。

例如:它保持了酱香浓郁、典雅细致、协调丰满、回味悠长等特点。

［译文］It possesses the unique style and flavor and is an extensively enjoyable drink.

原文中的"酱香浓郁、典雅细致、协调丰满、回味悠长"一般是中文形容白酒口感好的常用说法,然而在西方,人们很少喝白酒,更不会有这样特殊复杂的形容白酒口感的说法。因此,直译的翻译方法在此处是行不通的,我们可将其译为"is an extensively enjoyable drink",帮助西方读者更好地理解,同时,也使得译文十分简洁贴切。

例如:本产品是根据中医理论"腰为肾之府""肾为先天之本""脾为后天之本"及"内病外治"的医理,采用高科技方法研制的保健药品。

［译文］This product is a new kind of healthcare medicine developed on the basis of TCM theory about kidney with the latest high technology.

原文中"腰为肾之府""肾为先天之本""脾为后天之本"及"内病外治"这些中医理论,一般消费者并不是十分了解。况且对于外国读者而言,这样的表述更是艰深难懂。因此,译文中将此部分全部删除,译为简洁的"TCM theory about kidney"这一通俗的缩略术语,更加有助于读者们的理解。

五、译文赏析

(1)玉兰油晚霜广告词(节选)

玉兰油晚霜是一种夜晚使用的特别护肤霜,能充分发挥夜晚的魔力。无油脂,轻柔,舒适,让皮肤一面自然呼吸,一面吸收玉兰油晚霜的特殊营养。

一夜之中,每时每刻,玉兰油晚霜使您的皮肤始终保持湿润,增强皮肤的自然再生能力,舒展细微皱纹,让您的皮肤显得更轻柔更年轻。

Night of Olay is special night care cream, created to make the most of the magic of the night. It is greaseless and remarkably light to touch, a sheer pleasure on your skin, allowing it to breathe naturally while it absorbs this special nighttime nourishment.

Hour after quiet hour all through the night, Night of Olay enhances your skin's own natural renewal by bathing it in continuous moisture, easing tiny dry wrinkle lines and encouraging the regeneration of softer younger looking skin.

此部分内容为玉兰油晚霜广告语的核心部分,翻译时应注意英汉语言的特点,如汉语是意合型语言,讲究形散而神不散,所以零句(没有主谓的句子)较多。此外,句中的动词没有形态变化。因此,汉译英时,要注意妥善处理零句,根据英语行文习惯及上下文语境,将某些散句组合成长句或者复合句(如:将"无油脂,轻柔,舒适,让皮肤一面自然呼吸,一面吸收玉兰油晚霜的特殊营养。"译为"It is greaseless and remarkably light to touch, a sheer pleasure on your skin, allowing it to breathe naturally while it absorbs this special nighttime nourishment.")另外,当多个动词出现在一个句子中时,也要注意理清它们之间的关系。(如:将"玉兰油晚霜是一种夜晚使用的特别护肤霜,能充分发挥夜晚的魔力。"译为"Night of Olay is special night care cream, created to make the most of the magic of the night.")

(2)在合作期间,由于地震、台风、水灾、火灾、战争或其他无法预见并且对其发生和后果不能防止和避免的不可抗力事故,致使直接影响合同的履行或者不能按约定的条件履行时,遇有上述不可抗力事故的一方,应立即将事故情况通知对方,并应在15天内提供事故的详细情况及合同不能履行,或者部分不能履行,或者需要延期履行的理由的有效证明文件。此项证明文件应由事故发生地区的公证机构出具。按照事故对履行合同影响的程度,由双方协商决定是否解除合同,或者部分免除履行合同的责任,或者延期履行合同。

Should either of the parties to the contract be prevented from executing the contract by force majeure, such as earthquake, typhoon, flood, fire, war or other unforeseen events, and their occurrence and consequences are unpreventable and unavoidable, the prevented party shall notify the other party without any delay, and within 15 days thereafter provide detailed information of the events and a valid document for evidence issued by the relevant public notary organization explaining the reason of its inability to execute or delay the execution of all or part of the contract. Both parties shall, through consultation, decide whether to terminate the contract or to exempt part of the contract according to the effects of the events on the performance of the contract.

此部分内容为合同中通用条款的不可抗力(force majeure)条款示例。需注意的是:Should 一般用于条件句,商务合同中多使用"Should + S + V"结构,使用这种条件句时,发生条件句中所描述情况的可能性较小。如果该条件句所描述的情况发生了,那么主句所描述的事宜必须完成。

(3)KC-14、KC-16 型窗式房间空气调节器,具有20世纪80年代先进水平。它采用了先进的滚动转子式全封闭制冷压缩机和高效率的涤翅式散热片。具有体积小、重量轻、噪声低、耗能少、使用安全、性能可靠、外形美观等特点。它能自动调节室内温度,并有一定的除湿能力,使用于宾馆、医院及家庭等要求舒适环境的房间。本空气调节器享有盛誉,深受国内外用户信赖。

With the advanced level of the 1980s, it adopts the modern Rotary Hermetic Compressor and the unique cross fin coil type with high efficiency super slit fins. Characterized by compact, light weight, low noise, less energy consumption, excellent function and an elegant shape, it is safe for use and automatic in adjusting the room temperature as well as in dehumidifying. It is suitable for the rooms of hotels, hospitals and homes where comfortable environment is needed. It wins a high reputation and is widely trusted at home and abroad.

此部分内容为窗式房间空气调节器的推销说明书。一般而言,在产品说明书中,会经常提及产品所采用的技术,经常运用英文表达"It adopts…"。此外,介绍产品"具有……特点或特征"时,会经常运用英文表达"Characterized by…"。

六、实践练习

翻译下列短文。

(1)四季岛旅游宣传广告语(节选)

金色的沙滩,诱人的海鲜,四季岛是男女老幼向往的海滨胜地!

碧海蓝天,风光绮丽,四季岛拥有您所期望的休闲逸趣。在这,您可以进行无数种水上运动,也可以休闲地躺在沙滩上,尽情享受阳光的沐浴。

这儿还有美味佳肴!我们的厨师为您准备了丰盛可口的美食,从广东名菜到华北小吃,应有尽有!

（2）基于本协议授予的独家代理权，甲方不得直接或间接地通过乙方以外的渠道向新加坡顾客销售或出口第三条所列商品，乙方不得在新加坡经销、分销或促销与上述商品相竞争或类似的产品，也不得招揽或接受以到新加坡以外地区销售为目的的订单，在本协议有效期内，甲方应将其收到的来自新加坡其他商家的有关代理产品的询价或订单转交给乙方。

（3）江苏家具系选用优质木料制作。做工精湛，拆装便利，造型美观大方，结构坚固耐用，辅以雕刻、镶嵌等工艺，具有传统的民族风格。近年来又吸取现代家具的特点，适合多种居住条件，经济实惠，更受广大消费者的欢迎。

主要产品有：卧房套装家具、餐厅家具、各类书架，品种繁多，欢迎各地客商选购，也承接来料订货。

第十一章 法律文本的翻译

一、协议条约的翻译

社会集团或个人处理各种社会关系、事务时常用到"契约"类文书,包括合同、议定书、条约、公约、联合宣言、联合声明、条据等。协作的双方或数方,为保障各自的合法权益,经双方或数方共同协商达成一致意见后,签订书面材料。鉴于现在对外交流事例逐渐增多,跨文化、语言的协约条款中汉译英的翻译愈显重要,最常见的是公司之间的合同翻译。Contracts are agreements between equal natural persons, legal persons and other organizations for the purpose of establishing, altering and terminating mutual civil rights and obligations. (Contract Law of People's Republic of China)合同是平等主体的自然人、法人、其他组织之间设立、变更、终止民事权利义务关系的协议。

协议条约若译文不准确或不严谨,势必会引起不必要的政治、经济纠纷。翻译失真则是法律翻译的大患,比如有的译者在涉外销售合同的翻译中把"earnest money",即具有担保性质的"定金"译成"订金",以致在外商违约时,"订金"被解释为预付款,致使外商逃脱了双倍返还定金的责任。其语言保持程式化、准确性、严谨性、一致性、庄重性、简明化等特点。

法律上合同、协议书等正式文件的开头语常出现"特此",因此,"兹"在英文中意思相当于 by means of, by reason of this, 书面的表达方法是 hereby。在条款中需要强调时也可用。它的位置一般置于主语后,紧邻主语。如我们谨达成如下本协议,we hereby reaches this agreement。通过对以上事实的说明,我们提出如下建议……With all that stated, we hereby advise as follows...例如:

特此证明,据我们所知,上述声明内容真实,正确无误,并提供了全部现有的资料和数据,我们同意,应贵方要求出具证明文件。

[译文] We hereby certify to the best of our knowledge that the foregoing statement is true and correct and all available information and data have been supplied here; thus, we agree to provide documentary proof upon your request.

业主特此立约保证在合同规定的期限内,按合同规定的方式向承包人支付合同价,或合同规定的其他应支付的款项,以作为本工程施工、竣工及修补工程中缺陷的报酬。

[译文] The Employer hereby covenants to pay the Contractor in consideration of the execution and completion of the Works and the remedying of defects therein the Contract Price or such other sum as may become payable under the provisions of the Contract at the time and in the manner prescribed by the Contract.

在表示上文已提及的"在本合同中、本文件中……"时,英文与之相对的是 hereof,表示"of this…",我们便可把该 hereof 视为"of this Companies Act"理解。一般置于要修饰的名词的后面,与之紧邻。

任何一方都可以根据本终止条款通知另一方终止本协议。

[译文] Either party may terminate this Agreement by giving notice to the other party in accordance with Termination Clause hereof.

当某一条款中需要作进一步规定或在作规定时语气上表示转折,在中译英时,应加上"provided that"。有时从中文上看,尽管没有"但规定""进一步规定"的词语,但英文写作时,应加上该词组。其用法与 if 或 but 非常类似,汉语中的意思相当于"倘若/如果"或"但"。

不论港口习惯是否与本款规定相反,货方都应昼夜地,包括星期日与假日(如承运人需要),无间断地提供与提取货物。货方对违反本款规定所引起的所有损失或损坏,包括滞期应负担赔偿责任。

[译文] Whether the custom of the Port is contrary to this Clause or not, the owner of the goods shall, without interruption, by day and night, including Sundays and holidays (if required by the carrier), supply and take delivery of the goods. <u>Provided</u> that the owner of the goods shall be liable for all losses or damages including demurrage incurred in default on the provisions hereof.

该短语放在句首,引导出的是法律英语中的一个条件分句,与 if,when 或 where 引导的条件句没有本质上的差异。

如果在本合同约定的租期届满后,业主接受租金或中间收益,不应视为业主放弃了合同的任何条款或违反了任何条款,也不应该视为以延期或其他方式重新租赁。

[译文] <u>Provided that</u> the acceptance of rent or mesne profits(中间收益) by the Landlord after the expiration of the term of the tenancy hereby created shall not be deemed to operate as a waiver or breach of any of the terms hereof nor as a new periodic tenancy by way of holding over or otherwise.

但如果该短语之前存在一个主句,则它表示的是一个与之前的陈述相反的"例外"。相当于 with the exception of…翻译成"但"。法律界通常称呼这类句子为"但书"(proviso)。

租赁期间届满,当事人可以续订租赁合同,但约定的租赁期限自续订之日起不得超过二十年。(合同法)

[译文] At the end of the lease term, the parties may renew the lease, provided that the renewed term may not exceed twenty years commencing on the date of renewal.

不少从事法律文书写作的人喜欢在"但是"后面大做文章:写完一个条件后,往往觉得意犹未尽或者需要再补充一点什么,所以最佳的做法是来一段"但书",看起来有点晦涩难懂,但那恰恰表明法律英语的书面性强、较为严谨,有时也是应为对历史案例的参照和沿袭而表达受限。"但书"内也可再加上一些花色,如将该词大写,或再增添一个 always 之类的强调词,PROVIDED ALWAYS HOWEVER that…

在法律文件中表示"订立本协议"可用以下 4 个动词:sign(make,conclude or enter into)

this agreement,按照同义词连用的写作特点,可用上述 4 个动词中的两个来表示)。例如:

本合同双方,××××公司(以下称甲方)与××××公司(以下称乙方),在平等互利基础上,通过友好协商,于××××年××月××日在中国××(地点),特签订本合同。

[译文] This Contract is hereby made and concluded by and between ×××× Co. (hereinafter referred to as Party A) and ×××× Co. (hereinafter referred to as Party B) on ××× (Date), in xx (Place), China, on the principle of equality and mutual benefit and through amicable consultation.

如果甲方向乙方提供含有专项培训费的专业技术培训,甲方可以补充订立培训协议作为本合同的附件,约定服务期和违约金。

[译文] If Party A provides professional and technical training to Party B with special-item training expense, Party A can make the training contract to stipulate service term and liquidated damages as an attachment to this contract.

汉英翻译协议条约时,还要注意"应该""必须"等的措辞,了解 may、shall、should、will、may not、shall not 等词语的法律内涵尤其必要。例如:

双方首先应通过友好协商,解决因合同而发生的或与合同有关的争议。

[译文] The parties hereto shall, first of all, settle any dispute arising from or in connection with the contract by friendly negotiations.

第一条 甲方应尽快在本协议生效后,且最迟在本协议生效后六十天内,有关特许产品的全部技术与销售信息递送到乙方地址。

[译文] Article 1 Party A shall deliver to Party B as soon as possible after this Agreement becomes effective, but in any event within 60 days thereafter, at Party B's address set forth above, all the Technical and Sales Information, relating to Licensed Products.

协议条约较为严谨,也比较强调客观因素,忌加入情感因素,一般都会运用"必须"或"应该"等措辞,表示法律上可以强制执行的义务(Obligation),如未履行,即视为违约,并构成某种赔偿责任。按照常理,"必须"或"应该"与英文的 should,have to 等同,例如有译者把"合营企业所需的机器设备……在同等条件下,应尽量在中国购买"译成"…a joint venture should give first priority to Chinese sources"。译文中以"should"来译"应当",非常不妥。一是因为"应"在法律条文中就是"must""have to"即汉语"必须"之意。而"should"在此方面的意味不及"must"和"have to"强,甚至尚不及"ought to"强。二是因为"should"表示法律义务,只表示一般义务或道义上的义务。例如:

在受益人向发出修改通知的银行表示接受修改内容之前,原信用证的条款和条件对受益人仍然有效。受益人应当发出接受或拒绝受该修改的通知。

[译文] Before the beneficiary said to accept the amendment from the bank that advised such amendment, the terms and conditions of the original credit is still valid for the beneficiary. So the beneficiary should give the notification of acceptance or rejection of the amendment.

但此处显然不是,因此存在误译的情况。"shall"在法律文件中有其特殊的含义,并不是单纯的将来时,而是表示强制性承担法律或合同所规定的义务,带有指令性和强制性,是一种法律义务,是使用频率最高的词之一。在合同中在表达"应该"或"必须"做某事时,应用"shall"而不能用"must"或"should",但有时可用"will",力度比 shall 弱。

董事会会议应由董事长召集、主持;若董事长缺席,原则上应由副董事长召集、主持。

[译文]The board meeting shall be convened and presided over by the Chairman. Should the chairman be absent, the vice-Chairman shall, in principle, convene and preside over the board meeting.

在合同中表示语气较弱的假设,表示"万一"或"如果"等时,多翻译成"should"。例如:

双方必须严格遵守合同规定,如单方违约,任何一方有权终止合同。

[译文]Both parties shall strictly comply with the contract provision. Should one party break the contract, the other party is entitled to cancel it.

二、立法文本的翻译

戴维麦林克夫的经典研究《法律的语言》(1963)的开篇之句:"法律是一项措词的职业"表明了法律语言的使用者对语言表达中细微之处的重视程度是任何别的领域的语言使用者所无法比拟的。立法的语言要求严格,同样立法文本的翻译要求准确性及精确性(Accuracy and Precision),一致性及同一性(Consistency and Identity),清晰及简练(Clarity and Concision),专业化(Professionalism),语言规范化(Standardized Language)。

所谓语言规范化主要是指在法律翻译中使用官方认可的规范化语言或书面语,以及避免使用方言和俚语。虽然在法律文书的起草和翻译中有许许多多的清规戒律(如慎用被动语态、外来词、缩略词等),但有一点必须强调,那就是必须采用官方用语(词),尤其是现行法律中已有界定的词语。法律用语是每个国家正式程度最高的语言,是其所管辖下的所有地区中通用的语言。例如,英国的法律概念不但在英国本土通行,在往日的属地即所有英联邦国家和地区内也一概通行。正因为如此,一名原先在澳大利亚执业的大律师可被加拿大政府聘为法官而无须再去接受专业训练。如果在受同一个法律体系管辖的地区内,法律用词、用语上各行其是,那么法律在实施的过程中势必乱套。

在进行法律文书汉译英翻译过程中,有时会碰到不少汉语意义相同的词,但这些词在不同的搭配中和特定的上下文中,是有明显区别的,译者一定要注意语言的逻辑性,勤查专业工具书。例句:"正式协议"和"正式声明"这两条术语中的"正式"就不能盲目地套用,必须弄清它们之间的不同含义。第一个"正式"是指"符合规定的";第二个"正式"是表示"官方权威性的"。"正式协议"译成"formal agreement","正式声明"译成"official statement"。

《中华人民共和国宪法》是中华人民共和国的根本大法,规定拥有最高法律效力,翻译这样的文本没有多少发挥的余地,主要是直译,但切忌翻译腔。汉英翻译不同于英汉翻译的是理解汉语,表达英语,这难免要受汉语习惯的影响,在选词、造句中总会有点"汉式英文"的味道。这仿佛是汉译英过程中的通病,但我们在汉英翻译中应尽量避免受汉语思维习惯的影响,要多注意两种语言的差异,使译文准确、流畅,一气呵成。例如:

中华人民共和国是工人阶级领导的、以工农联盟为基础的人民民主专政的社会主义国家。

[译文]The People's Republic of China is a socialist state under the people's democratic dictatorship led by the working class and based on the alliance of workers and peasants.

国营经济是社会主义全民所有制经济,是国民经济中的主导力量。国家保障国营经济的巩固和发展。

[译文]The state economy is the sector of socialist economy under ownership by the whole people; it is the leading force in the national economy. The state ensures the consolidation and growth of the state economy.

我国著名资产阶级启蒙思想家,翻译界的老前辈严复根据自己的翻译实践,曾提出过"信、达、雅"翻译标准。"信"即译文要忠实于原作内容,对于法律文本,特别是立法文本更是如此。立法语言所表述的内容是全体公民的行为规范,是人们的行为准则,同时也是司法人员的执法依据。因此,立法者要通过语言文字的准确运用来表述国家的立法思想和具体的法律内容,以便司法人员和全体公民能清楚地了解作为一个国家的公民,他们拥有哪些权利,承担哪些义务,从而明白哪些行为是被允许的,哪些行为是被禁止的,哪些行为是要受到鼓励或制裁的,以及一旦出现违法行为会产生什么样的后果及其应负什么样的法律责任。真正使人们准确理解法律内容,严格依法办事,做到有法必依、执法必严、违法必究,那么在"立法"这个环节上,就必须使法律条文的表述做到明确无误。语言必须准确、确凿、严密,这是法律的社会职能决定的。

本细则的解释权,属于中华人民共和国财政部。

[译文]The right of interpreting the Detailed Rules and Regulations belongs to the Ministry of Finance of the People's Republic of China.

"解释"在汉英词典上可译成:"construe""explanation""exposition""interpretation",但这个句子的"解释"是指对法律条文的正式解释,选择"interpretation",较为恰当。句中谓语动词"belong to"用得欠妥,"belong to"的含义是"属于……的财产",这里的"属于"是指"权利、权力等为……所有",故应选用"reside in"更为合适。整个句子为 The right of interpreting the Detailed Rules and Regulations resides in the Ministry of Finance of the People's Republic of China.

虽然立法文本中较为严谨,但也不是一点发挥的余地也没有,可以根据上下文,做一些减法,避免按部就班,却较为冗长。如"本法所称……,是指……",一般译成"This term…as mentioned in this Law refers to…"或者"This term…as referred to in this Law means",这两种译法都较为正式,但过于直译,如果译成"…in this Law means"或者"…herein means"则更为简洁。事实上,单就"本法"的翻译也是五花八门,其主要原因就在于"法"的译法不一。按照《现代汉语词典》第296页上的解释,法"包括法律、法令、条例、命令、决定等",因此,"法"的译法就有"law(法律)""act(法令,决议)""enact(法令,法规,条例)""regulation(s)(条例)""rule(s)(法则,细则)""statute(法令,法规,成文法)""code(法典)""moastlre(s)(措施,办法)""decree(政令,命令)""resolution(决议,决定)"等。由此可见,在翻译"本法"的"法"时一定要谨慎。

刑法中经常使用"不得"等字句表达禁止性规范,庄重严肃,简洁明快。"不得"一般译作 shall not,然而"不能"常译为 may not,这和英文中一些否定表达方法对应一致,故不再重复。

没收财产是没收犯罪分子个人所有财产的一部分或者全部。在判处没收财产的时候,不得没收属于犯罪分子家属所有或者应有的财产。(《刑法》第五十九条)

[译文] Confiscation of property refers to the confiscation of part of all of the property personally owned by a criminal. When a sentence of confiscation of property is imposed, property that the criminal's family member owns or should own shall not be subject to confiscation.

典型法律禁令字句在汉译英的过程中通常译为 be prohibited 句式。

禁止证券交易内幕信息的知情人和非法获取内幕信息的人利用内幕信息从事证券交易活动。

[译文] Persons possessing inside information relating to securities trading and persons obtaining such information unlawfully are prohibited from making use of such inside information in securities trading activities.

禁止任何人利用任何手段扰乱社会秩序。扰乱社会秩序情节严重,致使工作、生产、营业和教学、科研无法进行,国家和社会遭受严重损失的,对首要分子处五年以下有期徒刑、拘役、管制或者剥夺政治权利。

在立法文本中有禁止,自然也有必须要遵守的法律规定。在该领域的翻译专家的实践中,尤其是在具权威性法律文献的翻译实践中,以 must 对应"必须"的惯例似乎早已确立。

中华人民共和国公民必须遵守宪法和法律,保守国家机密,爱护公共财产,遵守劳动纪律,遵守公共秩序,尊重社会公德。

[译文] Citizens of the People's Republic of China must abide by the Constitution and the Law, keep state secrets, protect public property and observe labor discipline and public order and respect social ethics.

三、讼诉文书的翻译

法律文本需要强调用词的专有性,即必须掌握一定的法律术语。诉讼文本是应用于法庭的文本,最具有法律语言的特征。案情陈述书 statement of case,辩护律师 defense attorney,当事人 party,被告 defendant,侵权行为 tort,委托辩护 entrusted defense,未成年人法庭 juvenile court,无罪判决 acquittal,先予执行申请书 application for advanced execution,裁定 order,驳回上诉 withdraw appeal。

虽然一般意义上,诉讼文本中的词或词组能在汉英字典中找到相应的单词,但也要按照具体的情境进行分析。例如:陪审团宣告被告谋杀罪不成立。译文:The jury acquitted the respondent of the charge of murder. 分析:该句中的"被告"一词应用"the accused",而不能用"respondent",因为"respondent"指的是民事案件的答辩人即被告,尤指离婚案的被告(defendant in a civil case, especially, in a divorce one),而"the accused"则是刑事案件的被告(the person charged in a criminal case),从这方面看来,虽然都是"被告",但此"被告"非彼"被告"也。民事案件的"原告"和"被告"分别为"plaintiff"和"defendant";离婚案件的"原告"和"被告"分别为"petitioner"和"respondent";海事案件的"原告"和"被告"分别为"libellant"和"libellee";刑事案件的"自诉人/公诉人"和"被告人"则分别为"private prosecutor/public prosecutor"和"the accused"。

李明在中国居住期间没有受过刑罚的记载。

[译文]Li Ming has not been punished according to the criminal law during his living in China.

分析：此句中的"not to be punished"与表示一段时间的 during 短语连用不恰当,况且,此句证明的是"没有受过刑罚的记载",而"触犯刑律"也应译成"commit an offence against the criminal law"。另外,"居住"这个词选用"residence"而不用"living",更强调一个住所的永久性和合法性。

改译成：Li Ming has no record of committing offences against the criminal law during his residence in China.

不难看出,如果译者不熟悉这些词语,就很难准确反映当事人在诉讼中的地位,也就会造成误解,让法律条文丧失其精确性(preciseness)。

另外在法律文本中,需要注意的是同一性原则,Henry Weihofen 在其所著《法律文体》一书中告诫译者 Don't be Afraid to Repeat the Right Word! 因此在汉译英过程中,为了维护同一概念、内涵或事物在法律上始终同一,避免引起歧义,词语一经选定后就必须前后统一,旨在保证法律文字的准确。"未成年人"在英文中可翻译成"infant",和"minor"两个词。当我们在翻译同一材料时,如果选定"infant",下文就不能用"minor",这样就会造成歧义,缺乏一致性。

被告(宝洁公司)从未以任何方式向原告(雇员)施加精神压力。被告可以拿走原告的文档和他使用的电脑,这是公司的规章制度所规定的,其目的是防止公司的商业秘密被泄露。

[译文]The defendant (P&G) never exerted any spiritual pressure in any form on the claimant, the defendant was free to take away all the plaintiff's files and the computer he had been using, strictly in accordance with the company's stipulations, and that such actions were aimed at preventing the company's trade secrets from being disclosed.

译文中对原文中的"原告"用了两个不同的词,即"claimant"(索赔者,从严格的法律意义上讲,它是指仲裁案件中的"申诉人")和"plaintiff"(原告),这在翻译法律文件时是不允许的。否则,读者会以为是两个不同的主体。

文学性语言要求生动,有鲜明的语言特色,在翻译文学作品中要尽量保持原汁原味,即使是下层人物的污秽语言,例如地方方言或俚语也要照搬,才能达到"神似""化境"等境界。法律语言需要遵循严肃性和纯洁性等原则,事实上,在法律文件的供词中会涉及犯罪分子的方言,帮派的黑话和行话,有时龌龊得不堪入耳,如某些地方把嫖妓说成"拍婆子",在翻译过程中不需要用 shag,bonk 等来传神,这种地方色彩的俚语用大众能够明白的,即全国通用的书面语言表达是最合理、切实可行的办法,没有必要绘声绘色地描述。

四、译文欣赏

社会主义的建设事业必须依靠工人、农民和知识分子,团结一切可以团结的力量。在长期的革命和建设过程中,已经结成由中国共产党领导的,有各民主党派和各人民团体参加的,包括全体社会主义劳动者、拥护社会主义的爱国者和拥护祖国统一的爱国者的广泛的爱国统一战线,这个统一战线将继续巩固和发展。中国人民政治协商会议是有广泛代表性的统一战线组织,过去发挥了重要的历史作用,今后在国家政治生活、社会生活和对外友好活动中,在进行社会主义现代化建设、维护国家的统一和团结的斗争中,将进一步发挥它的重要作用。

[译文]In building socialism it is essential to rely on workers, peasants and intellectuals and to unite all forces that can be united. In the long years of revolution and construction, there has been formed under the leadership of the Communist Party of China a broad patriotic united front which is composed of the democratic parties and people's organizations and which embraces all socialist working people, all patriots who support socialism and all patriots who stand for the reunification of the motherland. This united front will continue to be consolidated and developed. The Chinese People's Political Consultative Conference, a broadly based representative organization of the united front which has played a significant historical role, will play a still more important role in the country's political and social life, in promoting friendship with other countries and in the struggle for socialist modernization and for the reunification and unity of the country.

中华人民共和国各民族一律平等。国家保障各少数民族的合法的权利和利益,维护和发展各民族的平等、团结、互助关系。禁止对任何民族的歧视和压迫,禁止破坏民族团结和制造民族分裂的行为。国家根据各少数民族的特点和需要,帮助各少数民族地区加速经济和文化的发展。各少数民族聚居的地方实行区域自治,设立自治机关,行使自治权。各民族自治地方都是中华人民共和国不可分离的部分。各民族都有使用和发展自己的语言文字的自由,都有保持或者改革自己的风俗习惯的自由。

[译文]All nationalities in the People's Republic of China are equal. The state protects the lawful rights and interests of the minority nationalities and upholds and develops a relationship of equality, unity and mutual assistance among all of China's nationalities. Discrimination against and oppression of any nationality are prohibited; any act which undermines the unity of the nationalities or instigates division is prohibited. The state assists areas inhabited by minority nationalities in accelerating their economic and cultural development according to the characteristics and needs of the various minority nationalities. Regional autonomy is practiced in areas where people of minority nationalities live in concentrated communities; in these areas organs of self-government are established to exercise the power of autonomy. All national autonomous areas are integral parts of the People's Republic of China. All nationalities have the freedom to use and develop their own spoken and written languages and to preserve or reform their own folkways and customs.

任何一次解雇,如果是基于相关法律,或辞职信是在决定期限内,于合同到期前递交的,将能让当事人强制执行以下行为:主动终止支付与工资数额相等的赔款,并在合同的剩余期限内,不损害其他可能的赔偿。

然而,对于一个有确定期限的劳动合同,或一份已被明确定义的工作,在固定任期内发生重大渎职事,或当事人之间已达成协议,合同可以提前终止。因重大过失而终止的有确定期限的合同,首先终止合同的一方应当在48小时内将此事告知另一方。

[译文]Any dismissal which is not done basing on the reasons provided for the law or resignation made before the expiry of a contract for a determined period compels the party that takes initiative of termination to pay an indemnity equivalent to the remuneration for the remaining contract period without prejudice to other compensation which may be paid.

However, the contract of employment for a determined period or for a well defined work can be terminated before the fixed term in case of gross negligence or agreement between the parties. Where the contract for a determined period is terminated due to gross negligence, the party causing the contract to be terminated shall notify the same to the other party within forty eight (48) hours.

五、实践练习

翻译下列短文。

(1) 合营企业设董事会,其人数组成由合营各方协商,在合同、章程中确定,并由合营各方委派和撤换。董事长和副董事长由合营各方协商确定或由董事会选举产生。中外合营者的一方担任董事长的,由他方担任副董事长。董事会根据平等互利的原则,决定合营企业的重大问题。

董事会的职权是按合营企业章程规定,讨论决定合营企业的一切重大问题:企业发展规划、生产经营活动方案、收支预算、利润分配、劳动工资计划、停业,以及总经理、副总经理、总工程师、总会计师、审计师的任命或聘请及其职权和待遇等。

董事会是合营企业的最高权力机构,决定合营企业的一切重大问题。董事会成员不得少于3人。董事名额的分配由合营各方参照出资比例协商确定。董事的任期为4年,经合营各方继续委派可以连任。

董事会会议每年至少召开一次,由董事长负责召集并主持。董事长不能召集会议时,由董事长委托副董事长或其他董事负责召集并主持董事会会议。经1/3以上董事提议,可以由董事长召开董事会临时会议。董事会会议应当由2/3以上董事出席方能举行。董事不能出席的,可以出具委托书委托他人代表其出席和表决。董事会会议一般应当在合营企业法定地址所在地举行。

(2) 普通法发源于约12世纪的英格兰,那时一套传统法律第一次被整合在一起。普通法的名称是基于这样一个事实,即是一套对于整个英国都很普通的法律,而不是用于不同社区或部落的不同的法律。

普通法的显著特征之一是其发展是基于使用而不是像民法典体系那样被编纂而成的条例要求强制施行。(立法是指由一个像议会这样的代表机构制定法律或法规。法律编纂是指把一些本质类似的法律汇总到一部新的、包含面更广的法律中。)

普通法的发展基于诸多法庭判例的结果。每一个法庭判例都为下一次类似案件的审理提供了依据。经过几个世纪以及数千的法庭判例,这一过程形成了一套包含社会方方面面、基于社会总体共享的原则的法律。

有几个核心的原则指导着普通法,虽然这些原则并不是普通法所独有的。这些原则包括:

(1) 个人权利与国家权力同在;

(2) 对抗性;

(3) 无罪推定;

(4) 判例法来自审判和先例;

(5) 判例法与成文法同在,大多数情况下,与宪法同在。

第十二章　文学文本的翻译

一、诗词的翻译

诗是一种最古老的文学形式,它是伴随着音乐舞蹈产生的,而人们常常吟唱诗,诗又称为诗歌。一直以来对于诗歌的翻译就争论不休,分为两大阵营即诗之不可译(Untranslatability)与诗之可译(translatability)。Robert L Frost 认为诗就是在翻译中失去的那种东西。在巴西诗人和翻译家奥古斯都·德·坎波斯看来,诗歌不应只属于一个国度而应该属于更广阔的国度,译者有权帮助诗歌跨越语言的障碍,以实现全人类共同欣赏之目的。郭沫若提出的"以诗译诗"及闻一多所说的以"诗笔"译诗也是诗歌翻译的一种准则。

翻译诗歌的难点在于意境、诗歌的形式和文化因素三点,其一,意境本身是一种抽象的艺术形态,但这种抽象的形态,却能够表达出诗歌的本质甚至灵魂;其二,诗的形式包括其内部的韵律以及外部的形式,韵律就像是诗歌的声音,是诗歌的音乐特征,而外部形式就像是诗歌的外衣,是诗歌区别于其他文学作品的一个重要特点;其三,无论诗歌还是诗歌翻译都与其所处的文化背景密切相关,诗歌的文化因素决定了诗歌翻译不仅是一种跨语言,也是一种跨文化的行为。诗人和诗歌在不同时代和不同文化中往往扮演不同的角色,也正是文化背景的差异增加了诗歌翻译的难度,诗歌译者和诗人从不同的文化背景出发对诗歌翻译也进行过迥异的阐释。据此看来,译者既要承认和正视诗歌翻译中存在的难度。

但是也不可否认诗歌的可译性。佳译是在反复不断的译诗实践中产生的,译者需要在具体的翻译过程中,积极调动思维和自身的知识储备,努力再现原诗本身在音、形、意三方面的美感,传达原诗的"意美""音美"和"形美"。意美指的是语言的深层结构,即"语言背后的语言""言外之意""弦外之音"传达出诗的意境美。意境本身是一种抽象的艺术形态,但这种抽象的形态,却能够表达出诗歌的本质甚至灵魂。

天净沙·秋思 Autumn Thinking-to the tune of Sky Scours Sand
马致远 by Ma Zhiyuan(赵甄陶译)
枯藤老树昏鸦,Withered vines, olden trees, evening crows;
小桥流水人家,Tiny bridge, flowing brook, hamlet homes;
古道西风瘦马,Ancient road, wind from west, bony horse;
夕阳西下,The sun is setting,
断肠人在天涯。Broken man, far from home, roams and roams.

译文首先以一系列的意象进行直译,枯藤、老树、黄昏时的乌鸦传神地表达出诗歌时间、地点的大语境,第二句以小桥、流水、人家传达出诗人对温馨家庭的渴望,转而在第三句以瘦马在西风中飘零传达出第三幅图片孤独、漂泊的旅人形象。对此诗的翻译不下十种,其中以该例译文诗句最短,又较好地传达了原作的节奏感和押韵美。更为重要的是,它很好地传递了原词中的意境美,译文用几乎与原词等同的字数,以意象的叠加堆砌重新构建了一个郁郁不得志的游子独自漂泊的形象。

汉语的音美和英语的音美有所不同,汉语是声调语言(tone language),汉语的四声构成了发音的抑扬顿挫,产生了一种音乐的特征。同时,汉语基本上是单音节而英语是重音语言(intonation language),英语单词多是多音节,英语中约有1200个音节,有重音,但没有四声。由于语音的特性,汉语诗歌的格律为"平仄律",英语诗歌的格律为"轻重律"。因此,利用发音的特点形成的语言游戏很难英汉互译。例如,汉语诗歌的叠字较多,在声韵上形成一种气势,激发荡气回肠的情感,而英语很少用叠词来表达思想的徘徊。所以就要用别的方法传达出汉语的音韵之美。

译者可采用语义对等翻译来传达音之美。翻译中的语义对等是翻译理论中的一个新模式。奈达坚信不同语言具有同等的表达力,"一种语言所能表达的,必然能用另一种语言表达出来,除非形式是所表达意义的一个基本组成部分……翻译,就是在目的语中以最自然的对等语再现源语的信息,首先是意义,其次是文体。"(Nida and Taber, 1969)

奈达的"动态对等"翻译基本思想可以概括为以下三句话翻译是交际活动、翻译主要是译意、为了译意,必须改变语言的表达形式。具体地说,就是在词汇、语法、语义等语言学的不同层次上,不拘泥于原文的形式,只求保存原作的内容,用译文中最切近而又最自然的对等语将这个内容表达出来,他从读者反应出发,认为理想的译文应该使译文接受者阅读译文时的反应与源语文本读者阅读源语文本时的反应相同。因此,在翻译中要想实现语义等值,译者必须在特定的语境中,仔细分析原文的语义。例如:

夜夜相思更汤残。(韦庄《洗溪沙》)

[译文]Each night I long for you till the water clock the fades. (许渊冲译)

夜夜所表达的意思同"每"相近,英语可译成 each, every 等词,若不强调"每一个",可用复数形式来译。

吴山点点愁(白居易《长相思》)

[译文]The southern hills reflect my woe. (许渊冲译)

译文用"hill"来形容远山很小、很多。

音美指的是节奏和韵律,人们总是将诗与歌联系起来,认为诗歌是"带有音乐性的思想";诗即是歌,歌既是诗。要保持诗歌的神韵,音、形皆美才能堪称诗歌翻译典范。如,欲去又依依(韦庄《女冠子》)you'd go away but stop to stay. (许渊冲译)"依依"在翻译时变成以 S 音押头韵,stop, stay 再现了双声叠韵,起到了加强节奏、渲染气氛的作用读者似乎可以感觉到诗中人物那种留恋徘徊、不忍分离的心理状态使整个句子读起来音韵十分优美,传达出依依不舍的情感。

再例如:李白的《早发白帝城》(Departure from the empire town at dawn)

早辞白帝彩云间,Bidding the town farewell when morning clouds hang low,

千里江陵一日还,A long trip through canyons I made in a mere day,

两岸猿声啼不住,Monkey cries were heard on either bank all through the day,

轻舟已过万重山。While the boat passed by mountains in a low.

一三句押韵，二四句押韵，在句式上朗朗上口，保持了古诗词的音韵和形似。

形美主要是指诗歌的体裁、用词、句子结构、表现手法以及比喻手段等方面与原文一致。外部形式就像是诗歌的外衣，是诗歌区别于其他文学作品的一个重要特点，拟声词和颜色词在翻译时运用得好也能促进在音和形上的一致。如：车辚辚，马萧萧。（杜甫《兵车行》）Chariots rumble, and hordes grumble.（许渊冲译）这里将汉语的拟声词译成英语拟声词，音、形达到了完美的统一。

关于音美和形美，我们再来欣赏许渊冲先生所译刘禹锡的《竹枝词》：

杨柳青青江水平，Between the willows green the river flows along,

闻郎江上唱歌声。My beloved in a boat is heard singing a song.

东边日出西边雨，The west is veiled in rain, the east basks in sunshine,

道是无晴还有晴。My beloved is as deep in love as the day is fine.

这例译文采用抑扬格六音步，形式工巧，又采用 aabb 韵式，较好地传达了原诗的形美和音美。

诗歌是一种结合了意境、外形与声音的完美的艺术整体，而每一首诗的内涵与外部形态都是独一无二的。因此，翻译诗歌绝不是一项简单的工作，是要尽可能多的再现原诗的艺术魅力。首先要求译者具有丰富的想象力诗歌翻译，尤其当翻译名作佳作之时，更需要译者丰富的想象力。因为愈是伟大的作品，其语言越精练含蓄，其内涵的延展性也越大。中国古典诗词向来讲究意境，一首诗中往往有着"溢出它自身"的东西。译者必须使用最准确的词语，向读者传递原诗最深远的意义和诗人最丰富的情感。在翻译的整个过程中，我们都应该尽自己最大的努力去寻找恰当并且生动的词语来翻译诗歌。在反映原诗内容的基础上，译者还应该提高对自身的要求，准确地再现原诗中的意境，以便在内涵、韵律、意境上都能与译文保持一致。

二、散文的翻译

散文是文学中常见的体裁，它选材广泛，结构灵活，表现手法多样，如叙事，抒情，议论等，主要特点是：体物写志，行散神聚，"形散"是指散文运笔如风，不拘形式，清淡自然；"神聚"指意旨明确，紧凑集中，既散得开，又收得拢。优美的散文艺术性在于新颖的构思、充沛的感情、丰富的想象、简洁精粹的语言和耐人寻味的意境，散文也常常被比作小而境界深邃的园林。散文同时也是美文，在阅读散文过程中，读者不自觉地享受着美的熏陶。

翻译散文时，译者在忠实原文内容、使译文表达自然流畅的基础上，还应注重把握原文的写作风格，再现原文的美学特征。俄国著名翻译家吉加切奇拉泽在《文艺翻译与文学交流》一书中谈到文艺翻译的总的指导原则时认为："理想的文艺翻译首先是在艺术上，而不是在语言上和原文一致。即使达不到这一目标，也应全力以求，离目标越近越好"。在加氏看来，作家的思想表现在文字形象以及一定的语调和节奏结构上，他认为文艺翻译的过程也应当根据上面的模式进行。不过译者不能机械地重复创作过程的所有阶段，译者应努力把通过文字形象表达的原作的思想用另一种语言再现出来，当然同时要有兼顾文学文本所特有的语调、节奏和句构特点，作为文学翻译形式之一的散文翻译，自然也要求译者在传译过程中，不仅要传达出原文的语流，节奏和句子结构等语义信息，更应着重传达原文的艺术神韵,以使目标读者在读译文时可以获得和原文读者读原文时同样的语义和美学的双重享受。

散文的形式美主要表现在原文的句式和使用的修辞手法上。许多作家都有自己独特的风格,风格就是作者表达意思时表现出来的个人特点,即所谓的"文如其人"。散文译文如果脱离了原文内容,无论其形式如何华丽,也毫无审美价值可言。朱自清的散文文字质朴,没有过多的修饰语,语言朴素、自然、平实,因此在翻译朱自清先生的作品时,译文也需要形、神兼备,才能体现原文的神采。例如:

燕子去了,有再来的时候;杨柳枯了,有再青的时候;桃花谢了,有再开的时候。(朱自清《匆匆》)

[译文]Swallows may have gone, but there is a time of return; willow trees may have died back, but there is a time of regreening; peach blossoms may have fallen, but they will bloom again. (朱纯深译)

去的尽管去了,来的尽管来着,去来的中间,又怎样地匆匆呢?(朱自清《匆匆》)

[译文]Those that have gone have gone for good, those to come keep coming; yet in between, how swift is the shift, in such a rush? (朱纯深译)

朱先生的散文内容美主要体现在工整对称的句式和各种修辞手法,或借景抒情,或借物言志。译者很好地传达了朱先生字里行间透露出的对时间的无奈,进而生发出珍惜时间、珍惜生命的感叹。

冰心"文笔细腻委婉,清新隽丽",语言质朴平实、深入浅出、简洁凝练。文章虽短,但含义隽永、寓意深刻、充满哲理,反映出作者深邃的智慧、敏锐的洞察力,以及对于生命内涵的感知。文学作品的艺术性越高,语言风格越独特,翻译起来就越困难。例如:

雨声渐渐的住了,窗帘后隐隐的透进清光来。推开窗户一看,呀!凉云散了,树叶上的残滴,映着月儿,好似萤光千点,闪闪烁烁的动着。(冰心《笑》)

[译文]As the rain gradually ceased to patter, a glimmer of light began to filter into the room through the window curtain. I opened the window and looked out. Ah, the rain clouds had vanished and the remaining raindrops on the tree leaves glistened tremulously under the moonlight like myriads of fireflies. (张培基译)

连夜雨雪,一点星光都看不见。(冰心《雨雪时候的星辰》)

[译文]It had been snowing all night, not a single star in sight. (张培基译)

冰心的文字简洁明快,翻译时再现作者的写作风格、原文的语言特色和文章的韵味并非易事,尤其是翻译散文、诗歌这类文体时,一定要挖掘出语言层面下的深层意蕴。

英语通常采用形合法连接,而汉语却用意合法连接。英语造句用各种"形式手段"来连接词、语、分句或从句,注重显性接应,表达语法意义和逻辑关系;而汉语通过词语或分句的"含义"表达语法意义和逻辑关系。汉译英至关重要的一步就是弄清汉语各句之间的逻辑关系。张培基先生在翻译散文时,使用适当的句型表现逻辑关系,译文通俗易懂。例如:

那年冬天,祖母死了,父亲的差使也交卸了,正是祸不单行的日子。——《背影》

[译文]Misfortunes never come singly. In the winter of more than two years ago, grandma died and father lost his job.

原文事实在前,结论在后;译文结论在前,事实在后。调整结论与事实的顺序,更符合西方人逻辑思维习惯。

世代为地主耕种,家境是贫穷的,和我们来往的朋友也都是老老实实的贫苦农民。——《母亲的回忆》

[译文]From generation to generation, they tilled land for landlords only to eke out a bare subsistence.

"only to"表明一种结果关系。

可是她的时间大半给家务和耕种占去了,没法照顾孩子,只好让孩子们在地里爬着。——《母亲的回忆》

[译文]But she was too busily occupied with household chores and farming to look after the kids so that they were left alone crawling about in the fields.

这句话中 too...to 表示一种逻辑上的因果关系,so that 表示结果。

从理论上说,英语语言与汉语语言相比,英语句子"常常是环扣相嵌,盘根错节,句中有句",是所谓的树式结构。而汉语以散句、松句、紧缩句、省略句、流水句等短句居多,是所谓的链式结构。可见,在汉英翻译中,使用英语长句是理所当然的,也是符合语言规律的。但翻译家往往也要视翻译的文本写作风格而定,张培基先生在充分把握英汉两种语言的异同的基础上,结合原文的风格,译文的英语短句屡见不鲜。

例如,在《差不多先生》(Mr. About-the-Same)一文中,有这么一段话:

差不多先生的相貌和你和我差不多。他有一双眼睛,但看的不很清楚;有两只耳朵,但听得不很分明;有鼻子和嘴,但他对于气味和口味都不很讲究。他的脑子也不小,但他的记性却不很精明,他的思想也不很细密。

[译文]Mr. Cha Buduo has the same physiognomy as you and I. He has a pair of eyes, but doesn't see clearly. He has a pair of ears, but doesn't hear well. He has a nose and a mouth, but lacks a keen sense of smell and taste. His brain is none too small, but he is weak in memory and sloppy in thinking.

译文句子多为简单句和并列句,主要使用普通的形容词、副词和动词等,以达到言简意赅。译文干净、利落,通俗易懂,给人一种清爽自然之美,而没有盘根错节之迷惑。与原文短小精悍的形式保持了一致,松散的句式也传递出原文差不多先生的神韵。

散文中也经常会用到一些修辞手法,暗喻较为常用,那么在翻译时需要如何去做才能传达出原文的神韵?例如,弓儿似的新月,挂在树梢。——《笑》(明喻) The crescent new moon looked as if hanging on the tips of the trees. 译文仍然用比喻的修辞手法翻译原文的比喻,但却转移了喻体,"弓儿似的"如果直译成 bow-like,看似形象,但不符合英语对新月的描述习惯,译文将比喻落在了动作上,形象地再现了"新月挂树梢"的样子。例如:什么有轮齿的锯子啦,有两个耳朵的刨子啦?——《木匠老陈》(暗喻) such as the saw with toothed blade, the plane with two ear-like handles. 因为文化原因,外国人可能对原文中的实物及暗喻不太清晰,所以需要用增词法进行进一步说明,并且也符合英语表达习惯。

明喻在散文中也经常出现。例如:像针尖上一滴水滴在大海里,我的日子滴在时间的流里,没有声音,也没有影子。(朱自清《匆匆》)

[译文]Like a drop of water from the point of a needle disappearing into the ocean, my days are dripping into the stream of time, soundless, traceless.

此译文把明喻把完全展现出来,形成强烈的对比,让读者明白比喻的贴切与微妙。

三、小说的翻译

  小说是作者对社会生活进行艺术概括,通过叙述人的语言来描绘生活事件,塑造人物形象,展开作品主题,表达作者思想感情,从而艺术地反映和表现社会生活的一种文学体裁。在文学翻译过程中,译者除接触语言外,也接触了语言背后的文化内涵。例如《水浒传》(*Outlaws of the Marsh*)的写作风格是以民间口语为基础的书面语,风格洗练、明快、富有表现力,人物语言的个性化也有很高的成就。

  王进分付道:"……你与我将这些银两去岳庙里和张牌买个三牲煮熟,在那里等候。我买些纸烛,随后便来。"

  [译文] Wang Jin said, "... You and Corporal Zhang buy and cook the three kinds of sacrificial meat, and wait for me. I'll join you just as soon as I've bought some sacrificial paper ingots and candles." (translated by Sidney Shapiro)

  对译者来说,一篇或一部译作的成功与否,很大程度上取决于译者能否有效地将源语文化移植到目标语文化之中。沙博理把张牌翻译成 Corporal Zhang,Corporal 在英文中的意思是下士,纸烛翻译成 paper ingots(纸元宝)and candles,他想方设法使译文能够被目的语读者接受。又如:

  已到了腊月廿九日了,各色齐备,两府中都换了门神,联对,挂牌,新油了桃符,焕然一新。(《红楼梦》第五十三回)

  [译文] In both mansions, new door-gods had been pasted up on all the doors, the inscribed boards at the sides and over the tops of gateways had been repainted, and fresh 'good luck' slips — auspicious couplets written in the best calligraphy on strips of scarlet paper — had been pasted up at the sides of all the entrance. (translated by David Hawkes)

  什么是门神,对联,桃符又是什么,估计外国人没有几个能答得上来,读起来只能一头雾水。语言是文化的载体,语言的文化内涵涉及一个民族的政治、经济、社会、历史、风俗、习惯等各方面,是一个民族知识、经验、信仰、价值、宗教、时空等观念的总和。而汉语和英语在文化内涵上的差异就十分显著。美籍意大利学者劳伦斯·韦努蒂(Lawrence Venuti)于1995年在他的名著《译者的隐身——部翻译史》(*The Translator's Invisibility: A History of Translation*)中提出了归化和异化的概念:异化以源语或者原文作者为归宿,归化以目的语或者译文读者为归宿。归化法的翻译方法(Domesticating method)将源语与目的语之间语言上和文化上的彼此差异降到最低,用目的语读者熟悉的语言和文化表达源语的语言和文化,使译文更透明、通顺、易懂,为两种语言更有效的交流扫除了语言和文化上的障碍。沙博理和霍克思显然在翻译中采取了归化的翻译方法,最大限度地以目的语读者为归宿,降低中英文化上的差异。

  但归化法也遭受不少非议,例如,雨后春笋的归化翻译就是 like mushrooms after rain,再翻译成中文就是如雨后蘑菇,虽然目的语的读者更明白了,却丢了中国原文化的喻意,有人建议还是译为 bamboo shoots after a spring rain 较好,采取的就是异化翻译。与归化翻译相对应的是异化翻译,美籍意大利学者劳伦斯·韦努蒂(Lawrence Venuti)是异化翻译的代表人物。他通过彻底研究考察西方翻译史,批评当代英美翻译流派中,以奈达为代表的通顺的归化翻译是将英语中透明话语的限制强加在每一种外国文化上,以强化英美文化的规范,对英美文化而言,这是一种殖民的表现。他反对归化翻译,主张用异化翻译表现外国文本在语言和文化上的差异,这样,译者就从原来支配他们写作的规范中解放出来,保持外国文本的独特性,不仅有效地传达了源语文本的意义,也忠实地再现了源语的语言特色和文化内涵。从文化交流的角度来看,异化的翻译有利于不同的民族之间加深对彼此的了解与认识,同时,异化的翻译通过彰显各民族在语言和文化上的独特性,试图消除不同语言在文化地位上的不平等,使翻译真正成为不同文化之间的对话与交流。例如,纸老虎 paper tiger,叩头 Kowtow,功夫 Kung Fu,炒面 chaw main。钱钟书的《围城》里有一句是这样的:"忠厚老实人的恶毒,像饭里的沙砾或者出骨鱼片里未净的刺,会给人一种不期待的伤痛。"英文版的《围城》(*Fortress Besieged*)是这样翻译的,"The viciousness of a kind, simple-hearted soul, like gritty sand in rice or splinters in a deboned fish, can give a person unexpected pain."译文尊重原文的文化差异。以下再举几个例子:

忠厚老实人的恶毒,像饭里的沙砾或者出骨鱼片里未净的刺,会给人一种不期待的伤痛。

[译文]The viciousness of a kind, simple-hearted soul, like gritty sand in rice or splinters in a deboned fish, can give a person unexpected pain.

李梅亭多喝了几杯酒,人全活过来,适才不过是立春时的爬虫,现在竟是端午左右的爬虫了。

[译文]After a few glasses of wine, Li Meiting had fully revived. Whereas before he had been an insect of early spring, now he was an insect of Dragon Boat Festival time.

李先生再有涵养工夫也忍不住了,冲出房道:"猪猡!你骂谁?"阿福道:"骂你这猪猡。"

[译文]Losing his patience, Li burst from his room, demanding, "You swine, whom are you cursing?" Ah Fu replied, "I'm cursing you, you swine."(translated by Jeanne Kelly & Nathan K)

无论是第一句话里的"像饭里的沙砾或者出骨鱼片里未净的刺"还是第二句你的"立春时的爬虫",抑或第三句中的"猪猡"都是带有浓郁的中国文化特色的比喻,但译者并没有回避,而是直译了。好处和坏处都显而易见。过度归化的翻译忽略语言之间的差异性,使译文失去其源语本身的特色,读起来像译者所写而非原作者所写的;而过度异化的翻译则使得译文晦涩难懂,同样不利于文化的传播与交流。

实际上,归化和异化能够达成相对的统一。例如:

屋里呢,他越来越觉得虎妞像个母老虎。小屋里是那么热,憋气,再添上那个老虎,他一进去就仿佛要出不来气来。(《骆驼祥子》)

[译文]At home, Tigress seemed more and more to live up to her name. The little room were hot and stifling, and with Tigress there he found them suffocating.

"越来越觉得虎妞像个母老虎"翻译成"live up to",作了一下转换也是恰到好处的。我们可以想见,归化的翻译,因为其通俗易懂、易于传播的优势,还将长期受到普通读者、批评家和出版商的欢迎;与此同时,在国际政治、经济、文化交流日益频繁的今天,随着各国人民受教育程度的普遍提高和互相之间了解认识的不断加深,异化的翻译不仅将被越来越多的读者所接受而且将在促进不同文化的交流与融合、保护世界文化多样性的方面,发挥更积极的作用。

四、译文欣赏

上邪！
我欲与君相知
长命无决衰
山无棱
江水为竭
冬雷震震
夏雨雪
天地合
乃敢与君绝

[译文]
Oh heaven high!
I will love him
Forever till I die.
Till mountains crumble,
Rivers run dry.
In winter thunder rumbles,
In summer snow fall far and high.
And the earth mingle with the skies,
Not till then will my love die.

　　我最大的爱好是沉思默想。我可以一个人长时间地独处而感到愉快。独享欢乐是一种愉快，独自忧伤也是一种愉快。孤独的时候，精神不会是一片纯粹的空白，它仍然是一个丰富多彩的世界。情绪上的大欢乐和大悲痛往往都是在孤独中产生的。孤独中，思维可以不依照逻辑进行。孤独更多地产生人生的诗情——激昂的和伤感的。孤独可以使人的思想向更遥远更深邃的地方伸展，也能使你对自己或环境作更透彻的认识和检讨。

　　[译文]My greatest avocation is musing. I can stay by myself for a long time without feeling disconsolate in the least. Happiness enjoyed alone is a pleasure, so is sorrow tasted privately. In solitude, the mind is not a complete blank; it remains a rich and colorful world. Solitude often induces ecstasy or anguish, and allows thinking to wander in a random way. She inspires the mood for poems, passionate or pathetic. She also enables people to think further and deeper and to have a more thorough understanding and examination of themselves and their environment.

　　可是我却哭了。哭那陌生的、但却疼爱我的卖灶糖(candy)的老汉。后来我常想，他为什么疼爱我呢？无非我是个贪吃的、因为丑陋而又少人疼爱的吧。等我长大以后，总感到除了母亲，再没有谁能够像他那样朴素地疼爱过我——没有任何希求，也没有任何企望的。我常常想念他，也常常想要找到我那个像猪肚子一样的烟荷包。可是，它早已不知被我丢到哪里去了。

[译文]But I cried for the strange old candy peddler who had been so fond of me. Later on, I wondered why. For no other reason than that I was a foolish little thing who loved candy, with few to love me because of my plain face. When I glow up, I could never forget that apart from my own mother, no one had loved me so fondly and so disinterestedly, with no expectations whatever. I often think of him now, and have tried to find that tobacco pouch that had looked like a piece of pork liver. But I don't know what became of it.

五、实践练习

翻译下列短文

(1) 丑石

我常常遗憾我家门前的那块丑石呢：它黑黝黝地卧在那里，牛似的模样；谁也不知道是什么时候留在这里的，谁也不去理会它。只是麦收时节，门前摊了麦子，奶奶总是要说：这块丑石，多碍地面哟，多时把它搬走吧。

于是，伯父家盖房，想以它垒山墙，但苦于它极不规则，没棱角儿，也没平面儿；用赘破开吧，又懒得花那么大气力，因为河滩并不甚远，随便去掬一块回来，哪一块也比它强。房盖起来，压铺台阶，伯父也没有看上它。有一年，来了一个石匠，为我家洗一台石磨，奶奶又说：用这块丑石吧，省得从远处搬动。石匠看了看，摇着头，嫌它石质太细，也不采用。

它不像汉白玉那样的细腻，可以凿下刻字雕花，也不像大青石那样的光滑，可以供来院纱捶布；它静静地卧在那里，院边的槐荫没有庇孤它，花儿也不再在它身边生长。

(2) 幸福

许多人认为当他们富有，取得成功时，幸福自然就会随之而来。我告诉你：事实并非如此。世界上有很多富人，但是他们却很痛苦，犹如生活在地狱中。

在我看来，如果你是通过运气或是不诚实的手段而获得钱财，你会知道那并不是辛苦挣来的钱；如果通过利用别人或是伤害别人而获得钱财，你不会因此高兴。你会认为自己是个卑鄙的人。长期的幸福是建立在诚实，有成果的工作，贡献和自尊的基石上的。

幸福并不是终点，而是种过程。那是一个持续地通过诚实，有成果的工作为他人奉献的过程，这样做也会让你感到自己是一个有用的且有价值的人。如果你等待某些事情的发生或依靠生活的外部环境来让你自己感到幸福，你总也不会感到满足，总会有些事与你失之交臂。

附录 1　实践练习参考译文

第一章　绪论

（一）翻译下列短语。

(1) acquire knowledge
(2) educational level
(3) quality-oriented education
(4) community work
(5) fundamental interest
(6) official statement
(7) single youth above the normal marriage age
(8) vicious circle
(9) job market
(10) International community

（二）翻译下列句子。

(1) You are on the waiting list.
(2) The book is available in the library.
(3) They should follow the teacher's advice.
(4) Who has never tasted bitter doesn't know what is sweet.
(5) What's unique for a nation is also precious for the world.
(6) Beijing first saw the beginning of the May 4th Movement.
(7) His parents were happy with his success in the national college entrance examination.
(8) If we are frequently exposed to English, we will master it naturally.
(9) Our cooperation is based on mutual respect and mutual trust.
(10) We are deeply impressed by the hospitality of your people.

第二章　汉英语言对比

翻译下列句子。

(1) My suggestion is that he should quit smoking at once.
(2) I am no drinker, nor smoker.
(3) This pupil is a good writer.
(4) He is both a bibliomaniac and a lover of calligraphy.
(5) These rustic lassies are good singers.
(6) The government called for the establishment of more technical schools.
(7) I am an amateur actor. He is a better player than I.
(8) Vietnamese War is a drain on American resources.
(9) Every morning she would go to the lake area for a walk.
(10) He objected that the plan is not practical.

第三章 汉语词汇的翻译

（一）翻译下列短语。
(1) get on the bus / train
(2) to go up (or to mount) a hill
(3) to go to work; to be on duty
(4) to be taken in
(5) to get angry, feel vexed / anxious
(6) to make progress
(7) to freeze
(8) to mount a horse
(9) to perform
(10) to take up an official post
(11) to attend class, go to class, give a lesson to
(12) to be addicted (to sth.)
(13) appeal to the higher authorities for help
(14) to visit, to drop in, come or go to see sb.
(15) to board a plane

（二）翻译下列句子。
(1) He was a man of few words, but of all smiles. His smile was natural and friendly.
(2) Overwhelmed with grief, Qu Yuan drowned himself in the Miluo River with a large stone in his arms.
(3) They shouldn't return evil for good.
(4) This is the beauty of being alone. For the moment, just let me indulge in this profusion of moonlight and lotus fragrance.
(5) One of the characteristics of Chinese language is the predominance of the verb.
(6) All peace loving people demand the prohibition of atomic weapons.
(7) The maiden voyage of the newly-built steamship was a success.
(8) Lin Zexu believed that a successful ban of the trade in opium should be preceded by a destruction of the drug itself.

（三）翻译下列句子。
(1) He is a man who hoes his own potatoes.
(2) You are really casting pearls before swine.
(3) What is learned in the cradle is carried to the grave.
(4) I don't want to hang on my parents sleeves.
(5) He knows he can depend on his family, rain or shine.

（四）翻译下列句子。
(1) That's a business of their own, why would you get involved in?
(2) You know all the bits and pieces of trifles of other families. You are really well informed.
(3) Braving the wind and dew, Wang Mian traveled day after day past large posting stations and small, till he came to the city of Jinan.
(4) The enemy troops threw the whole village into great disorder.
(5) If you are willing to marry me, you will enjoy the luxuries all your life.

第四章 汉语成语的翻译

(一) 用两种方法翻译下列成语。
(1) 直译：to lure the tiger out of the hills
    意译：to lure the enemy from his base
(2) 直译：be like a dog counting on its master's backing
    意译：be a bully under the protection of a powerful person

(3)直译:shout in the east and strike in the west

意译:look one way and row another / sell the dummy

(4)直译:be engraved in one's heart and bones

意译:remember to the end of one's life

(5)套译:to kill the goose that lays the golden eggs

直译:to drain the pond to catch all the fish

(6)套译:to help a lame dog over a stile

直译:send charcoal in snowy weather

(7)套译:as poor as Job

直译:have nothing but four bare walls in one's house

(8)套译:cast pearls before swine

直译:play the lute to a cow

(9)套译:paint the lily

直译:draw a snake and add feet to it

(10)直译:Blessings do not come in pairs and calamity never comes singly.

意译:Luck comes but once but trouble comes in droves.

(二)翻译下列句子。

(1)Looking around the empty room, she told herself with a wry smile, "nothing but four bare walls."

(2)He is utterly confused by this problem.

(3)This added fuel to the fire of the old lady's anger. "Who ordered coffins?" she screamed.

(4)If this was a time of triumph for the many, it was a painful period for the few.

(5)He sat there and watched them, so changelessly, so changing, so bright and dark, so grave and gay.

(6)He carelessly glanced through the note and got away.

(7)"Whoever they are, they are letting the wolf into the fold!"

(8)Don't say anything about it; we mustn't wake a sleeping dog, why not keep an eye on what they engage in?

(9)Wild flowers and old pines on the precipice, with birds singing in fragrance, form a beautiful scene full of life and vitality.

(10)He was smooth and agreeable.

第五章　汉语句子的翻译

翻译下列句子。

(1)Peking Opera is the most popular and influential opera in China.

(2)In the Sui and Tang Dynasties, the technology of block printing was invented, and therefore the spead of printing was increased.

(3)When Chou Enlai's door opened they saw a slender man of more than average height with gleaming eyes and a face so striking that it boarded on the beautiful.

(4)The violent tornado that struck in August last year has aroused great attention among scientists throughout world. Seven countries suffered a great loss from it.

(5)The best cook sometimes makes bad dishes.

(6)In the doorway lay at least a dozen of umbrellas of all sizes and colors.

(7)Sweet scents, such as the smell of roses or almonds, could help to relieve pain but the effect only seem to work in women.

(8) I know today many guests will extend their congratulations by delivering speeches, for which we are waiting.

(9) The indirect effects of tourism are even greater, accounting for an estimated US $184 billion of economic activity and contributing to some 54 million jobs.

(10) No matter what you are interested in, you may well find something in Beijing museums that fit your interests: museums about agriculture, architecture, nature, geology, outer space, etc., about almost everything.

第六章 汉语篇章的翻译

翻译下列短文。

(1) Yes-Man or No-Man, Determines the Fortune of a Nation

"Nuo" (meaning "yes") is the pet word of yes-men, who are obedient to every order and say "nuo, nuo" to everything. Such people bow and scrape to everybody obsequiously and agree to everything servilely, never care whether it is right or wrong.

"E, e" ("e" means "speak frankly") is used to describe no-men, the opposite of yes-men, who dare to speak up the truth and to argue when they don't see eye to eye with others.

A saying was popular and widespread in the pre-Qin days (that is before 221 B.C.) that "it is better if there is one no-man who dares to say 'no' than there are a thousand yes-men who always say 'yes'". This shows that straight forward argument was respected then, even there was only a single person fighting a lonely battle. However, as time went by, fewer and fewer people dared to speak up the truth, and finally such people reduced to become "rare species". Many people felt they didn't have enough time to curry favor, therefore, how could they have the mind or mood to speak up the truth? The Analects recorded Master Confucius' saying: "A true gentleman is calm and at ease, the small man is fretful and ill at ease." Some scholars didn't follow the master's sincere and earnest teaching and thus they failed to live up to be gentlemen. They were never calm or at ease, and as a result, fret seemed to follow them all the time like their own shadows.

For many years the annual sessions of the National People's Congress (NPC) and the Chinese People's Political Consultative Conference (CPPCC) have followed an established practice of "meetings of solidarity without the least dispute". In last few years, things have changed greatly as there have emerged arguments on some issues. Some representatives and committee members are very outspoken when discussing state affairs. A number of them even voiced different opinions concerning some "major policies" of certain governmental departments. There were debates among them while some of them even challenged certain ministries or commissions of the State Council. Each voiced his or her own opinion, putting forward various remarks and suggestions.

As a matter of fact, it is only fine to hear different opinions and suggestions. There is an essay which analyses the simplified Chinese character 会 (which means "meeting") in this way: Its upper part is the character 人 meaning "people", while its lower part is the character 云 meaning "speaking". Only in this way can we claim to enjoy a normal political life in a truly democratic atmosphere, and only in this way can we pool the wisdom of everyone and benefit our courses.

But the annual sessions of the NPC and CPPCC at some grass-root levels have become no more than routines, at which the representatives and committee members shake hands with each other when coming to the meeting, clap their hands when the meetings open, raise their hands to show their unanimous support when voting, and wave their hands to say good-bye to each other when the meetings come to an end. What good is there for such costly meetings?

A few leaders are still not used to hearing different opinions raised by those attending such sessions, especially when heated debates take place. They do not know that true democratic consultation means letting every one have their say, and that real wisdom requires one to listen to both sides. True gentlemen remain on good terms with each other despite their different opinions, and true harmonious common understanding should be reached through discussion over different opinions. It would only give people a false impression if there is not the least challenge or opposition in the whole nation concerning matters however important or complicated. People in ancient times laid much stress on having one no-man who dared to speak up the truth rather than having a thousand yes-men who agreed to everything. This showed their candidness and broad mind. It is far more significant and valuable when there is even one fearless no-man who is outspoken and voices his disagreement straight forwardly than there are a thousand slavishly obedient yes-men who did nothing but curry favor.

(2) One Third of Our Lifetime

What is the significance of life? Is there any gauge to measure it? It would be very difficult, of course, trying to advance an absolute standard. However, the significance of one's existence can more or less be rated by examining his attitude toward life and work.

Since ancient times all people of accomplishment are very serious about their lives. While they are alive, even if there is only one day left to live, they try to work as hard as they can and learn as much as possible, never letting a single day slip by without any gain. This is true of the working people as well as of the great statesmen and great thinkers in our history.

In the chapter "Foods and Goods" of The Chronicles of the Han Dynasty, the great historian Ban Gu states: "In winter people stay indoors. Women get together to spin hemp threads at night. They manage to work forty-five days in a month." It sounds strange. How come there are forty-five days in a month? Let us look at its annotations given by Yanshigu: "They gain half a day's time every night and, they have forty-five days in a month."

Now it's clear. Our ancestors had, earlier than the westerners, learned how to calculate workdays accurately and reasonably. They had also learned how calculate day shift and night shift as well.

It is common knowledge that there are only thirty days in a month. Counting the time of one night for half a day, our forefathers managed to expend the month by fifteen days. In this sense the night time gained amounts to one third of our lives, doesn't it?

This one third of life is not only treasured by the working people but also by the great statesmen in our history. In the chapter "Criminal Law" of The Chronicles of the Han Dynasty, Ban Gu also states: "The First Emperor of the Qin Dynasty set a good example in being industrious, disposing of lawsuits during the day and reading at night ," This is about how he tried to find time to read at night.

To some people the The First Emperor of the Qin isn't a pleasant name to recall but there is no denying that he was a great figure in the history of China. Even BanGu has an impartial opinion of him.

Liu Xiang, the great scholar of the Han Dynasty, cites in his historical Anecdotes many princes of the Spring and Autumn period and Warring States period who paid great attention to learning.

Why did the people in the set such great store by the night time? I think this is positive proof of their attitude toward the one third of their lives. This is exactly what we should learn from them.

第七章 新闻文本的英译

翻译下列短文。

(1) Increasingly popular bike-sharing services in China have helped ease traffic congestion in big cities, according to a recent report. The report, published by domestic map and navigation provider Amap, Chinese

Academy of Transportation Sciences and Tsinghua-Daimler Center for Sustainable Transportation, said nearly 80% of China's 100 biggest cities saw improved local traffic conditions in the second quarter of 2017. This is the first time the "congestion index" has shown signs of going down since Amap launched the index across the country in 2014. People's means of transportation changed a lot and traffic congestion eased as bike-sharing services quickly expanded in many cities, the report said. According to bike-sharing company ofo Inc, among the top 20 cities hosting most of ofo's bikes, 19 of them have seen improved traffic conditions. In Beijing, congestion in over half of the main metro stations during rush hour has decreased by 4.1% compared to last year, according to Amap.

(2) A new report on China's "left-behind children" said that nearly 30% of rural students were left behind by both of their parents. More than half of rural children left behind by both of their parents see their parents less than twice a year, according to *Chinese Left-behind Children's Psychological Conditions White Paper* released by "On the Road to School", an NGO that provides financial and psychological help to left-behind children. In a sampling of 14 868 people from 17 provincial-level regions in China, 58.1% of rural students are left behind in their hometowns, with 26.1% left by both of their parents, according to the report. The report estimated as many as 10 million rural students could have been left behind by both of their parents. According to an official of the Ministry of Civil Affairs, a special campaign is being carried out to keep all rural left-behind children under guardianship by the end of 2017, *Beijing News* reported. If the left-behind children are not under any guardianship and their migrant worker parents cannot be reached, the children would be sent to other relatives or foster institutes for temporary care, the ministry said.

第八章　旅游文本的英译

翻译下列短文。

(1) The Emei Mountain is one of China's four famous Buddhist Mountains. It is located 7 kilometers southwest of Emeishan City, Sichuan Province. There are 150 temples on the mountain. The mountain features more than 3 000 plant species and 2 000 varieties of animals. Leshan Giant Buddha is located on the east bank of the Minjiang River in Leshan city, Sichuan Province. The Buddha is carved out of a cliff and, being 70.7 meters tall, is the largest sitting Buddha in China. Carving of the Buddha started in 713 and was completed in 803. The body of Buddha has a water drainage system to prevent erosion.

(2) Chengde Summer Resort, known as "The Mountain Hamlet for Escaping the Heat", is located in northern Chengde, Hebei Province. Qing Emperors used to spend their summer days handling state affairs at the resort. Construction of the resort lasted from 1703 to 1792. It is the largest and best-preserved imperial palace outside the capital. Many of the scenic spots around the resort's lake area mimic famous landscaped gardens in southern China, and the buildings of the Outer Eight Temples feature architectural style of minority ethnic groups such as Mongolian, Tibetan and Uygur.

第九章　科技文本的英译

翻译下列短文。

(1) Abstract: Translation competence can be defined as the potential knowledge system, skill system and relevant professionalism required in translation work. This paper classifies the translation competence models in the West into four categories, namely the linguistic competence centered model, multicomponent model, professional (legal) translation competence model and minimalist model. It summarizes that the translation competence models in the West are characterized by emphasis on bilingual sub-competence, translation technology sub-competence and translation service provision sub-competence, interest in professional translation competence, and focus on

empirical studies and their application in translation programs. The paper further discusses the implications of the translation competence models in the West for China's MTI competence cultivation in terms of teaching objectives, curriculum design, teaching methodology and so on.

(2) Lakes play a very important role in the national economic and social development as well as ecological civilization construction. The theory and technology of lake sediment pollution control has been a key technological problem in the comprehensive management of lakes and the construction of environmental protection engineering. Aiming at the grim situation of lake pollution in China and the outstanding problem of pollution control, the project is related to more than 20 major lakes in China. By taking the cognition of sediment pollution process — sediment in-suit treatment / environmentally-friendly dredging — base reconstruction — ecological restoration — water quality improvement as the main line, a long-term, systematic and comprehensive comparative study has been carried out around the major theoretical and technological innovation and engineering applications of sediment pollution control. The following important results have been obtained.

第十章 商务文本的英译

翻译下列短文。

(1) A holiday resort for the tourists of all ages with splendid beaches and tasty seafood dishes!

Siji Island has everything conceived for relaxation. It has the most spectacular view with clear water and blue sky. Here you can practice numerous water-sports or just laze on the beaches, soaking up the sun.

What's more, our chefs will prepare food for you that is as varied as it is delicious; you will find it hard to choose from the range of Cantonese favorites to North China specialties.

(2) In consideration of the exclusive rights granted herein, Party A shall not, directly or indirectly, sell or export the commodity stipulated in Article 4 to customers in Singapore through channels other than Party B; Party B shall not sell, distribute or promote the sales of any products competitive with or similar to the above commodity in Singapore and shall not solicit or accept orders for the purpose of selling them outside Singapore. Party A shall refer to Party B any enquiries or orders for the commodity in question received by Party A for other firms in Singapore during the validity of this agreement.

(3) Jiangsu furniture is made of selected wood of superior quality, exquisite in workmanship, easy to fix and unfix, elegant and decent in patterns, tight in structure and durable in use. In addition to crafts as carving and inlaying on, thus successfully showing traditional native features, characteristics of modern fashion have been adopted in recent years, both economical and practical, so that it is suitable for various residences and, wins high popularity among consumers.

Here are our main products: bedroom suits, dining-room suits, bookshelves of various designs, etc. Buyers and businessmen from all parts of the world are welcome to make their choices and orders, and we also accept orders for processing supplied materials.

第十一章 法律文本的英译

翻译下列短文

(1) A joint venture shall set up a board of directors, the member and composition of which shall be specified in the contract and articles of association by the parties to the joint venture through consultation. The directors shall be appointed and replaced by the parties. Chairman or vice-chairman shall be determined by the parties to the joint venture through consultation or elected by the board of directors. Where the Chinese party or the foreign party assumes the office of chairman, the other party shall be the vice-chairman. The board of directors shall decide

important matters concerning the joint venture on the principles of equality and mutual benefit.

As its functions and powers, the board of directors shall, in accordance with the provisions of the articles of association of the joint venture, discuss and decide all important matters concerning the joint venture, namely, the enterprise expansion plan, plans for production and business activities, budget for revenues and expenditures, profit distribution, plans concerning labor and wages and winding up, as well as the appointment or engagement of the general manager, deputy general manager, chief engineer, chief accountant, and auditors and their functions and powers, and salaries and benefits.

The board of directors shall be the highest authority of a joint venture. It shall decide all major matters concerning the joint venture. The board of the directors shall consist of no less than three members. The number of directors to be appointed by each party shall be determined through consultation by the parties to the joint venture with reference to the proportion of their respective capital contribution.

The term of office for each director shall be four years. Such term shall be renewed when a director is re-appointed by the original appointing party to the joint venture. The board meeting shall be convened at least once a year, which shall be called and presided over by the chairman of the board. If the chairman is unable to call the meeting, he shall appoint the vice-chairman or another director the power to call and preside over the meeting. The chairman may convene an interim meeting upon a proposal made by more than one third of the total number of directors. The board meeting shall be held only when over two-third of the directors are present. If a director is unable to attend the meeting, he may issue a power of attorney to appoint a proxy to represent him and vote on his behalf. The board meeting shall generally be held at the location of the joint venture's legal address.

(2) This system developed from a set of traditional laws first brought together in England around the 12th Century. The name derives from the fact that it was one set of laws "common" to the whole kingdom, rather than different sets of laws used by individual communities or tribes.

One of the distinguishing features of common law is that it developed through usage rather than being imposed by codified legislation as with the civil code system. (Legislation means laws - sometimes also called statutes-that are made by a representative body such as a parliament. Codification is when individual laws of a similar nature are bundled together under one new, overarching law.)

Common law developed based on the outcomes of individual court cases. Each court case provided a basis for judging the next case of a similar nature. Over the centuries and many thousands of court cases, this process led to a body of laws covering most aspects of society and based on principles shared by the society in general.

There are several core principles which guide common law, though they are not necessarily unique to it. These include:

(1) The rights of the individual exist alongside those of the state;
(2) It is adversarial;
(3) It has a presumption of innocence;
(4) It develops case law through judgments and precedents;
(5) Case law co-exists with statute law and-in most cases-a constitution.

第十二章 文学文本的英译

翻译下列短文

(1) An Ugly Stone

I used to feel sorry for that ugly black piece of stone lying like an ox in front of our door; none knew when it was left there and none paid any attention to it, except at the time when wheat was harvested and my grandma, seeing the grains of wheat spread all over the ground in the front yard of the house, would grumble: "This ugly stone takes so much space. Move it away someday."

Thus my uncle had wanted to use it for the gable when he was building a house, but he was troubled to find it of very irregular shape, with no edges nor corners, nor a flat plane on it. And he wouldn't bother to break it in half with a chisel because the river bank was nearby, where he could have easily fetched a much better stone instead. Even when my uncle was busy with the flight of steps leading to the new house he didn't take a fancy to the ugly stone. One year when a mason came by, we asked him to snake us a stone mill with it. My grandma put, "Why net take this one, so you worst have to fetch one from afar." But the arson took a look and shook his head; he wouldn't take it for it was of too fine a quality.

It was neither like a fine piece of white marble on which words or flowers could be carved, nor like a smooth big bluish stone people used to wash their clothes on. The stone just lay there in silence, enjoying no shading front the pagoda trees by the yard, nor flowers growing around it.

(2) On Happiness

Many people think that when they become rich and successful, happiness will naturally follow. Let me tell you that nothing is further from the truth. The world is full of very rich people who are miserable as if they were living in hell.

To my mind, If you obtain wealth through luck or dishonest means, you will know that it is ill earned money. If you get your money by taking advantage of others or by hurting others, you will not be happy with it. You will think you are a base person. Long — term happiness is based on honesty, productive work, contribution, and self — esteem.

Happiness is not an end; it is a process. It is a continuous process of honest, productive work which makes a real contribution to others and makes you feel you are a useful, worthy person. If you wait for certain things to happen and depend on external circumstances of life to make you happy, you will always feel unfulfilled. There will always be something missing.

附录2 短文翻译练习

练习1

譬如那些苍黑的古柏,你忧郁的时候它们镇静地站在那儿,你欣喜的时候它们依然镇静地站在那儿,它们没日没夜地站在那儿,从你没有出生一直站到这个世界上又没了你的时候。

譬如暴雨骤临园中,激起一阵阵灼烈而清纯的草木和泥土的气味,让人想起无数个夏天的事件;譬如秋风忽至,再有一场早霜,落叶或飘摇歌舞或坦然安卧,满园中播散着熨帖而微苦的味道。

味道是最说不清楚的,味道不能写只能闻,要你身临其境去闻才能明了。味道甚至是难于记忆的,只有你又闻到它你才能记起它的全部情感和意蕴。所以我常常要到那园子里去。

练习2

但蚂蚁金服在美国的尝试还显示出,科技正大举破坏全球老牌巨头的统治地位,特别是在金融领域。尤其值得注意的是,在银行和其他传统公司受到的挑战中,越来越多新贵挑战者或是中国面孔,或背后有中国资本。这反过来又突显了一些中国企业已在全球一举成名。

一些分析师认为,阿里巴巴在全球电商领域的重要竞争对手——亚马逊(Amazon)推出类似支付宝的产品只是时间问题。他们还提到了印度,阿里巴巴在印度移动支付公司 Paytm 持有40%的股份,且对该公司的战略方向拥有否决权。

所有这些都是金融业大转型的一部分。我们正处于一个区块链技术有望给金融交易的清算和结算方式带来革命性变化的时代。如果成功,银行在金融体系的这些部分也将变得不那么重要,这将有利于新的精通数字技术的运营商。而这种转变在狗年只会加速。

练习3

来美国求学的中国学生与其他亚裔学生一样,大多非常刻苦勤奋,周末也往往会抽出一天甚至两天的时间去实验室加班,因而比起美国学生来,成果出得较多。我的导师是亚裔人,嗜烟好酒,脾气暴躁。但他十分欣赏亚裔学生勤奋与扎实的基础知识,也特别了解亚裔学生的心理。因此,在他实验室所招的学生中,除有一名来自德国外,其余5位均是亚裔学生。他干脆在实验室的门上贴一醒目标牌:"本室助研必须每周工作7天,早10时至晚12时,工作时间必须全力以赴。"这位导师的严格及苛刻是全校有名的,在我所待的3年半中,共有14位学生被招进他实验室,最后博士毕业的只剩5人。1990年夏天,我不顾别人劝阻,硬着头皮接受了导师的资助,从此开始了艰难的求学旅程。

练习4

科学就是探求真理。在探求真理的过程中,人们对客观规律的认识要经过艰苦曲折的过程。常常有这样的情形:由于研究的角度不同,掌握资料的差异,认识方法的不同,就会出现"横看成岭侧成峰,远近高低各不同"的情况,以至引起学术上的争论。因此,有作为的科学工作者都把反对的意见看作对自己的莫大的帮助,把对自己的批评当作最珍贵的友谊。正如歌德所说,"我们赞同的东西使我们处之泰然,我们反对的东西才使我们的思想获得丰产。"这都是因为,赞同的意见未必正确,反对的意见未必错误。退一步说,即使错误的反对意见,对自己的科学研究也是很有好处的。

练习 5

平日读报,看到一篇好的文章时,总有把它剪下来的欲望。然而有时拿起剪刀的时候,才发现背面的文章也很有意思,或者教你如何养生,或者关照你如何做人处世。只要你剪了正面的文章,这背面的文章就要受损,或者只剩下半块,或者缺了文章题目。常常因舍不得反而弄得无法再下剪子。反悔和遗憾是在所难免。其实生活就是这样,就像剪报纸一样,有时一件事的正反两面都是完美的,而我们又总是在关注一件事时才发现了另一件事。于是我们常常被绊住,闹得举棋不定。记得一位哲学家说过:"当一扇门关闭的时候,生活会为你开启另一扇门。"有时无意与被动的选择并不一定就是太坏的。人生在世,无论做什么,无论生活的涛浪把我们抛向何方,其实都有我们的风景与可为之处。别忘了,上苍随时都在为我们准备着另一扇门。当你的大门紧闭时,另一扇大门就一定会为你敞开。

练习 6

如果你觉得心有余力不足,觉得缺乏前进的动力,有时候你只需要改变思维的角度。试着训练自己的思想朝好的一面看,这样你就会汲取实现目标的动力,而不会因为消极沉沦停滞不前。一旦变换看问题的角度,你的生活会豁然开朗,幸福快乐会接踵而来。别交出掌握命运的主动权,也别指望局面会不可思议的好转。你必须与内心希望与热情步调一致。建立自信,敢于与困难短兵相接,而非绕道而行。记住,力量不是驾驭局势的法宝,无坚不摧的能力才是最重要的。请坚信,美好的降临并非不可能,失误也许是成功的前奏。将惶恐化作信任,学会超越担忧和疑虑。让"诚惶诚恐"的时光变得"富有成效"。不要挥霍浪费精力,将它投到有意义的事情中去。当你下意识品尝生命的欢愉时,美好就会出现。当你积极地看待生活,并以此作为你的日常准则时,你就会找到快乐的真谛。

练习 7

生活之乐趣来源于良好的情绪,信赖这些情绪,并任由它们如同鸟儿高翔于天空般地自由自在。生活的乐趣是无法靠姿态摆出来的,也无法用戴上一张面具来伪装。拥有这种乐趣的人们无须挂在嘴边,他们自然会焕发出快乐的气息。他们自己生活在快乐当中,也将这样的快乐自然而然地感染着他人,犹如是鸟儿就必将歌唱。直接追求生活的乐趣却只会使乐趣远离我们,它与幸福一样青睐胸有大志的人们。生活过得高雅、简单便会产生出乐趣。它是我们对生活的投入,而非所求。

练习 8

中国科技馆的诞生来之不易。与国际著名科技馆和其他博物馆相比,它先天有些不足,后天也常缺乏营养,但是它成长的步伐却是坚实而有力的。它在国际上已被公认为后起之秀。

世界上第一代博物馆属于自然博物馆,它是通过化石、标本等向人们介绍地球和各种生物的演化历史。第二代属于工业技术博物馆,它所展示的是工业文明带来的各种阶段性结果。这两代博物馆虽然起到了传播科学知识的作用,但是,它们把参观者当成了被动的旁观者。

世界上第三代博物馆是充满全新理念的博物馆。在这里,观众可以自己去动手操作,自己细心体察。这样,他们可以更贴近先进的科学技术,去探索科学技术的奥秘。中国科技馆正是这样的博物馆!它汲取了国际上一些著名博物馆的长处,设计制作了力学、光学、电学、热学、声学、生物学等展品,展示了科学的原理和先进的科技成果。

练习 9

中国保险监管机构出面提醒大家不要购买网络销售的"恋爱险"产品,称其为"虚假的"保险产品。中国大陆许多奇葩保险产品的销售方并没有获得销售此类产品的授权。如果能成功预测出一对恋人的恋情能维持多久,购买这种保险产品的客户就能赚上一笔,一般能达到付款的数倍。中国保监会周一在其网站上发布了风险提示,其中提到了"鹿晗恋爱险"。鹿晗是中国青少年的人气偶像,他公布恋情后,导致新浪微博宕机。数万名伤心的粉丝纷纷留言,表达对于他不再单身的失望之情。去年鹿晗在新浪微博公布恋情时,一些淘宝商家就推出了"鹿晗恋爱险",每份 11.11 元。如果这段恋情持续超过 1 年,商家将会双倍赔付。《人民日报》上月发表评论说,"恋爱险"及类似产品并非保险产品,更像是在赌博。中国保监会称:"公众人物'恋爱险'并非保险产品,不符合《保险法》规定"。

练习 10

著名爱尔兰诗人奥斯卡·王尔德(1854—1900)曾写道:"啊!趁你还拥有青春的时候好好享用吧。"他指出了一个重要的真理:人生旅途中青春是无价之宝。然而,近来的网络热词"佛系"却质疑了上述说法,它鼓励年轻人心态平和,尽量避免冲突 —— 换句话说,就是像佛陀一样生活。如今,中国网友还创造了一系列"佛系"衍生词来形容这一相似的心态。例如,"佛系学生"指的是适度学习的学生 —— 他们不会逃课,但也不会熬夜。还有"佛系父母",他们不会过多干涉孩子的生活,让他们自由发展。但不论如何,有一件事"佛系青年"应当铭记在心:面对失败要保持冷静,但同时也应该对课业、工作与生活充满热情,积极面对。

练习 11

日前,苹果公司两次为一名颜姓中国女子新买的 iPhone X 手机退款,因为它的人工智能面部识别技术无法区分她和她的一名中国同事。这位来自南京的颜女士向当地媒体透露,虽然自己亲手激活并设置了面部识别软件,但她的一名女同事却每次都能解锁她的 iPhone X 手机。后来她和同事一起去了最近的苹果店,店员认为是摄像头有问题,颜女士用退款又买了一部 iPhone X 手机。但是这部新手机还是出现了相同的问题,于是店员再次为她办理了退货并对颜女士表示,这应该不是摄像头的问题,而是软件本身的问题。《新闻周刊》联系苹果公司要求置评,但目前尚未收到回复。一名推特用户对此发表评论,批评"面容ID"功能的设计者"大概只在白人身上进行了充分测试"。

练习 12

长白山位于吉林省东南部,是中国的自然保护区之一,覆盖面积超过 20 万公顷,南北绵延 78.5 千米,西向东 53.3 千米。长白山具备健康的自然环境和生态系统,生存着世界著名的珍稀动物如东北虎、梅花鹿、紫貂等。

火山湖:它坐落在白头山,长白山的主峰,也是中国和朝鲜之间的一个边境湖。这个湖被 16 个奇异的山峰环绕着,是火山口,充满蓝色的水,被称为"天池"。该盆地湖海拔 2155 米,最大水深 313 米,面积 9.2 平方千米,是典型的高山湖泊。湖水不断流出,不会引起水位的明显变化。湖心岛表面光滑如镜,在许多奇异的形状上反射着奇形怪状的悬崖。

练习 13

这几天心里颇不宁静。今晚在院子里坐着乘凉,忽然想起日日走过的荷塘,在这满月的光里,总该另有一番样子吧。月亮渐渐地升高了,墙外马路上孩子们的欢笑,已经听不见了;妻在屋里拍着闰儿,迷迷糊糊地哼着眠歌。我悄悄地披了大衫,带上门出去。沿着荷塘是一条曲折的小煤屑路。这是一条幽僻的路;

白天也少人走,夜晚更加寂寞。荷塘四面,长着许多树,蓊蓊郁郁的。路的一旁,是些杨柳,和一些不知道名字的树。没有月光的晚上,这路上阴森森的,有些怕人。今晚却很好,虽然月光也还是淡淡的。路上只我一个人,背着手踱着。这一片天地好像是我的;我也像超出了平常的自己,到了另一世界里。我爱热闹,也爱冷静;爱群居,也爱独处。

练习 14

"1932 年 1 月 2 日上午 8 点,在芝加哥大学的课堂中,我得到了第二次生命——作为经济学家重生了。"本月早些时候出版的保罗·萨缪尔森回忆录中,他如是写道。他成为 20 世纪下半叶或许最具影响的经济学家。沉闷如经济学,他在该领域数分支都有著作于世,并因此成为第一位荣膺诺贝尔奖的美国经济学家。通过自己的畅销教材,他将数以百万计的人们引入了经济学领域。直至垂暮之年,萨缪尔森仍在谆谆教诲着经济领域中最闪亮的学者。其实,萨缪尔森在此 17 年前生于印第安纳州"钢都"加里市的一个波兰移民家庭中,当时正值家族兴旺。他儿时经历 1919—1921 年间经济衰退和墨西哥民工客串罢工,以及随后的繁荣萧条更迭,而这些早期的记忆对他的宏观经济理论产生了毕生影响。

练习 15

货物抵达目的地后 90 天内,如果质量、技术规格或数量发现与合同的规定不符(除过保险公司和运输公司的责任所负),买方应该依据中华人民共和国出入境检验检疫局的检验报告或者是卖方的调试人员在安装调试时出具的报告,有权要求替换或补偿,所有的费用(包括商检费、替补件来回运费、保险费、仓储费、货物装货卸货费等)均由卖方承担。卖方的质量保证为签订关于此批货物的验收报告后 12 个月内;由于货物内在的质量、差的做工、选材不当而造成操作中的货物损坏,买方应立即书面通知卖方,并同时随附中国商检局出具的检验报告作为索赔依据。

练习 16

阳光唇膏

阳光唇膏有各种色泽,可根据不同年龄、肤色、口型、时间、场合选用。年轻的姑娘用色彩鲜丽显得活泼,中年人用色调较暗的橙红显得庄重,唇小可将唇线适当扩大,光线明亮宜用淡色,背景较暗宜用深色,该唇膏可使唇部获得健康美丽的光彩。

练习 17

iPad 系苹果公司于 2010 年发布的一款平板电脑,该产品定位介于苹果的智能手机 iPhone 和笔记本电脑产品之间,它只有四个按键,与 iPhone 的布局一样。iPad 的功能很强大,是集影音娱乐办公于一体的平板电脑,可以收发邮件,浏览网页,听音乐,看高清视频,聊天,玩 3D 游戏,阅读电子书、报纸和电子杂志。你可以导航,还可以在 App Store 里下载各种各样的软件。iPad 的设计时尚,更加人性化,它轻小简约,操作简单,分辨率高,屏幕显示效果非常出色,用料更加环保,电池电量大,可以用很长的时间。iPad 配有自己的 CPU 和操作系统,以及核心技术。

练习 18

摘要:本研究旨在调查外籍专家、留学生和中国大学生对中国英文报刊中本土化英语的可理解度。研究方法采用文本分析、问卷调查和访谈,共收集 139 位受试的数据,留学生被分为英语水平高、中、低三组。结果表明:第一,外籍教师认为中国英文报刊中影响理解的表达主要是不常见的搭配或句式、中国特色术语及外宣语等。第二,中国大学生和留学生高水平组对本土化英语的理解难度不大,中水平组的理解难度略有增加,低水平组的难度最大。第三,中国大学生和留学生高水平组受试能够较准确地解释本土化英语,中水平组受试和低水平组受试大多数存在解释困难。

练习 19

本项目属于交通运输科学技术领域。我国道路基础设施建设和交通运输发展迅速。道路交通在给人们出行带来方便的同时,所产生的与节能环保相悖的问题日益突出。例如:交通噪声危害普遍;城市地下水补充不足和地表洪水泛滥;城市热岛效应加剧;冬季路面结冰行车滑移和撒盐除雪破坏环境;城市汽车尾气污染严重。传统的道路路面无法解决甚至会加剧上述问题。为此,长安大学自20世纪末起开展环保型路面技术攻关,主持了包括"十一五"国家科技支撑计划在内的课题研究,主要内容包含透水路面,低噪声路面,低吸热路面,融冰雪路面,分解尾气路面等环保型路面技术。在理论分析、材料开发、结构设计、施工技术等方面取得如下创新性成果。

练习 20

在人际关系问题上我们不要太浪漫主义。人是很有趣的,往往在接触一个人时首先看到的都是他或她的优点。这一点颇像是在餐馆里用餐的经验。开始吃头盘或冷碟的时候,印象很好。吃头两个主菜时,也是赞不绝口。愈吃愈趋于冷静,吃完了这顿宴席,缺点就都找出来了。于是转喜为怒,转赞美为责备挑剔,转首肯为摇头。这是因为,第一,开始吃的时候你正处于饥饿状态,而饿的吃糠甜加密,饱了吃蜜也不甜。第二,你初到一个餐馆,开始举筷时有新鲜感,新盖的茅房三天香,这也是以叫作"陌生化效应"吧。

参考译文

练习 1

For example, the dark old cypresses: when you're feeling melancholy, they are standing there sedately, and when you're feeling happy, they are still standing there sedately — they've stood there since before you were born and will go on standing there until you are no longer in this world.

Or a sudden rainstorm in the park touches off a pure green and muddy earth scent giving rise to memories of countless summer occurrences; or the autumn wind suddenly arrives, and there is an early frost, and falling leaves or tottering singing and dancing or calm and quiet sleep: the park is pervaded with an atmosphere of tranquility and a little bitterness.

Atmosphere is the most difficult thing to explain. My words can't convey this atmosphere; you have to be there and smell it for yourself. It's hard to remember, too: only when you smell it again will it bring back all the feelings connected with it. And so I must often go back to this park.

练习 2

But Ant Financial's attempted US play also shows how much technology is undermining the dominance of traditional global titans, especially in the financial sphere. It is especially noteworthy that many of the upstart challengers to banks and other legacy companies increasingly either have a Chinese face or Chinese capital behind them. That, in turn, underscores how some Chinese players have leapfrogged into prominence across the world.

Some analysts believe it is only a matter of time before Amazon, Alibaba's big competitor in global ecommerce, comes up with something comparable to Alipay. They also point to India, where Alibaba has a 40 percent stake in the mobile wallet company Paytm, and veto power over its strategic direction.

All this is part of a larger transformation in finance. We are in a time when blockchain technology holds out the potential for revolutionizing the way financial trades are cleared and settled. If it succeeds, banks will also become less relevant in those parts of the financial system, to the advantage of the new digitally savvy operators. And change is only likely to accelerate in the year of the dog.

练习 3

Like students from other Asian countries and regions, most Chinese students who come to pursue further education in the United States work on their studies most diligently and assiduously. Even on weekends, they would frequently spend one day, or even two days, to work overtime in their laboratories. Therefore, compared with their American counterparts, they are more academically fruitful.

My supervisor (advisor / tutor) is of Asian origin who is addicted to alcohols and cigarettes, with a sharp (an irritable) temper. Nevertheless, he highly appreciates the industry and the solid foundation knowledge of Asian students and has a particularly keen insight into the psychology of Asian students. Hence, of all the students recruited by his laboratory, except for one German, the rest five were all from Asia. He even put a striking notice on the door of his lab, which read, "All the research assistants of this laboratory are required to work 7 days a week, from 10 a.m. to 12 p.m.. Nothing but work during the working hours." This supervisor is reputed on the entire campus for his severity and harshness. In the course of the 3 and half years that I stayed there, a total of 14 students were recruited into his laboratory and only 5 of them stayed on until they graduated with their Ph D. degrees.

In the summer of 1990, ignoring the remonstrations (admonishments / dissuasions) from others, I accepted my supervisor's sponsorship and embarked on the difficult journey of academic pursuit (undertaking further studies in the United States).

练习 4

Science means the exploration of truth. In the process of exploring truth, people will have to experience tremendous hardships and difficulties before they can come to understand the objective laws. It is often the case that the differences in the research perspectives, the materials mastered, and the ways of understanding would lead to totally different results — as we might say, "a mountain becomes a hill when viewed horizontally and a ridge when viewed vertically, and it assumes totally different shapes when viewed from a short or a long distance, or from a high or a low position." — and even lead to academic disputes. Therefore, an accomplished scientist would regard opposing arguments as his most tremendous benefit and take others' criticism of him as the most precious friendship that he can ever obtain. In Gothe's words, "We take for granted what we are in favor of. However, only what we are opposed to can enrich our thoughts." This is all because the approving opinions are not necessarily justified while the opposing arguments are not necessarily unfounded. To put it in the least way, even the opposing arguments that are mistaken will be immensely beneficial to one's own scientific research.

练习 5

When I come across a good essay in reading newspapers, I am often inclined to cut and keep it. But just as I am about to do so I find the article on the opposite side is as much interesting. It may be a discussion of the way to keep in good health, or advice about how to behave and conduct oneself in society. If I cut the front essay, the opposite one is bound to suffer damage, leaving out half of it or keeping the text without the subject. As a result, the scissors would stay before they start, or halfway done when I find out the regretful consequence that inevitably causes my repentance. In fact that is what life is like: we are often faced with the two opposite aspects of a thing which are both desirable like newspaper cutting. It often occurs that our attention is drawn to one thing only after we are engaged in another. The former may be more important than the latter and give rise to a divided mind. I still remember a philosopher's remarks: "When one door shuts, another opens in life." So a casual or passive choice may not be a bad one. Whatever we do in our lifetime, wherever life's storm tosses us, there must be something we can achieve, some shore we can land, that opens up new vistas to us. Don't forget God always keeps an alternative door open for everyone. While the front door is closed, there must be another open for you.

练习 6

If your life feels like it is lacking the power that you want and the motivation that you need, sometimes all you have to do is shift your point of view. By training your thoughts to concentrate on the bright side of things, you are more likely to have the incentive to follow through on your goals. You are less likely to be held back by negative ideas that might limit your performance. Your life can be enhanced, and your happiness enriched, when you choose to change your perspective. Don't leave your future to chance, or wait for things to get better mysteriously on their own. You must go in the direction of your hopes and aspirations. Begin to build your confidence, and work through problems rather than avoid them. Remember that power is not necessarily control over situations, but the ability to deal with whatever comes your way. Always believe that good things are possible, and remember that mistakes can be lessons that lead to discoveries. Take your fear and transform it into trust; learn to rise above anxiety and doubt. Turn your "worry hours" into "productive hours". Take the energy that you have wasted and direct it toward every worthwhile effort that you can be involved in. You will see beautiful things happen when you allow yourself to experience the joys of life. You will find happiness when you adopt positive thinking into your daily routine and make it an important part of your world.

练习 7

Joy in living comes from having fine emotions, trusting them, giving them the freedom of a bird in the open. Joy in living can never be assumed as a pose, or put on from the outside as a mask. People who have this joy don not need to talk about it; they radiate it. They just live out their joy and let it splash its sunlight and glow into other lives as naturally as bird sings. We can never get it by working for it directly. It comes, like happiness, to those who are aiming at something higher. It is a byproduct of great, simple living. The joy of living comes from what we put into living, not from what we seek to get from it.

练习 8

The first generation of museumsis what might be called natural museums which, by means of fossils, specimens and other objects, introduced to people the evolutionary history of the Earth and various kinds of organisms. The second generation is those of industrial technologies which presented the fruits achieved by industrial civilization at different stages of industrialization. Despite the fact that those two generations of museums helped to disseminate / propagate / spread scientific knowledge, they nevertheless treated visitors merely as passive viewers.

The third generation of museums is those replete with / full of wholly novel concepts / notions / ideas. In those museums, visitors are allowed to operate the exhibits with their own hands, to observe and to experience carefully. By getting closer to the advanced science and technologies in this way, people can probe into their secret mysteries.

The China Museum of Science and Technology is precisely one of such museums. It has incorporated some of the most fascinating features of those museums with international reputation. Having designed and created exhibits in mechanics, optics, electrical science, theology, acoustics, and biology. Those exhibits demonstrate scientific principles and present the most advanced scientific and technological achievements.

练习 9

China's insurance watchdog has come out against the "love insurance" products sold online in the country, labelling them as "fake" policies. Chinese mainland's many such quirky online insurance policy peddlers do not have the authorisation to sell these products. Customers who buy such policies might make a certain amount, usually several times their initial payment, if they successfully predict how long a couple will date. In a post on its website on Monday, the China Insurance Regulatory Commission named one such policy concerning popular Chinese teen idol Lu Han, whose announcement about a relationship led to a rare breakdown of the servers at social media platform Weibo. Tens of thousands of his heartbroken fans left messages expressing their disappointment over him not being available any more. When Lu Han announced his relationship in a Weibo post last year, some Taobao shops rolled out a "Lu Han love insurance" priced at 11.11 yuan per policy. Purchasers could get double their money if he was still dating his girlfriend a year later. *People's Daily* said in a commentary last month that "love insurance" and similar products were something akin to gambling, rather than insurance policies. "These 'love insurances' involving celebrities are not insurance products as they do not meet the requirements listed in China's Insurance Law," said the commission.

练习 10

Famous Irish poet Oscar Wilde (1854—1900) once wrote: "Ah! Realize your youth while you have it." He pointed out the important truth about how precious youth is in one's journey through life. However, the popular internet slang word "Buddhist" is challenging this norm by encouraging young people to remain calm and peaceful and avoid conflict as much as possible — in other words, to live like a Buddha. Now, Chinese internet users are pairing the phrase with other words to describe a similar mindset. For example, "Buddhist students" are those who study just the right amount — they don't cut class, but they don't burn the midnight oil, either. There are also "Buddhist parents", who interfere little with their children's lives and let them develop however they like. But no matter what, there is one thing that "Buddhist youngsters" should keep in mind: You may want to keep a calm mindset regarding failure, but you should also be passionate and positive about school, work and life.

练习 11

A Chinese woman, identified only by her surname Yan, was offered two refunds from Apple for her new iPhone X, as the AI-powered facial recognition technology was unable to tell her and her other Chinese colleague apart. Yan from Nanjing in East China, told local news that despite personally activating and configuring the facial recognition software, her female work colleague was able to get into both devices on every single attempt. Yan then went with her colleague to the nearest Apple store. Thinking that a faulty camera was to blame, the store operator gave Yan a refund, which she used to purchase another iPhone X. But the new phone turned out to have the same problem, prompting the store worker to offer her another refund and suggesting to Yan that it was probably not an issue with the camera but with the software itself. Newsweek has reached out to Apple for comment. A response has not yet been received. One Twitter user has reacted by accusing the creators of Face ID to have only "properly tested on white people".

练习 12

Located in Southeastern Jilin Province, Changbaishan is one of China's nature preservation zones, covering an area of over 200 000 hectares, extending 78.5 kilometers north to south, and 53.3 kilometers west to east. It has a wholesome natural environment and ecosystem with world famous precious animals like Northeast Tigers, sikas, sables, etc.

The Crater Lake: It nestles on Baitoushan (The White-Head Mountain), the main peak of the Changbaishan and is also a border lake between China and Korea. Surrounded by 16 exotic peaks, the lake is the crater of a volcano, filled with blue waters, known as "The Heavenly Lake". The basin-shaped lake, 2 155 meters above sea level, and 313 meters deep at maximum, encompasses an area of 9.2 square kilometers. It's a typical high mountain lake. The lake waters keep flowing out, without causing apparent change in its water level. The surface of the Lake is smooth as a mirror, with the reflections of cliffs upon it in numerous exotic shapes.

练习 13

It has been rather disquieting these days. Tonight, when I was sitting in the yard enjoying the cool, it occurred to me that the Lotus Pond, which I pass by every day, must assume quite a different look in such moonlit night. A full moon was rising high in the sky; the laughter of children playing outside had died away; in the morn, my wife was patting the son, Run-er, sleepily humming a cradle song. Shrugging on an overcoat, quietly, I made my way out, closing the door behind me. Alongside the Lotus Pond runs a small cinder footpath. It is peaceful and secluded here, a place not frequented by pedestrians even in the daytime; now at night, it looks mare solitary, in a lush, shady ambience of trees all around the pond. On the side where the path is, there are willows, interlaced with some others whose names I do not know. The foliage, which, in a moonless night, would loom somewhat frighteningly dark, looks very nice tonight, although the moonlight is not more than a thin, grayish veil. I am on my own, strolling, hands behind my back. This bit of the universe seems in my possession now; and I myself seem to have been uplifted from my ordinary self into another world. I like a serene and peaceful life, as much as a busy and active one; I like being in solitude, as much as in company.

练习 14

"I was reborn, born as an economist, at 8.00 a.m. on January 2nd 1932, in the University of Chicago classroom," wrote Paul Samuelson in a memoir published earlier this month. He became probably the most influential economist of the second half of the 20th century. For his work in several branches of the dismal science he became the first American economics Nobel laureate. Through his bestselling textbook, he introduced millions of people to the subject. And right to the end he kept on mentoring the profession's brightest stars. His actual birth took place almost 17 years earlier in the steel town of Gary, Indiana, to a family of upwardly mobile Polish immigrants. His earliest memories — of the recession of 1919—1921 and strikebreaking immigrant workers from Mexico, and of the boom and bust that followed — shaped Mr Samuelson's macroeconomic views throughout his life.

练习 15

Within 90 days after the arrival of the goods at destination, should the quality, specification, or quantity be found in unconformity with the stipulations of the Contract except those claims for which the insurance company or not the owners of the vessel are liable, the Buyers shall, on the strength of the Inspection Certificate issued by the

State Administration for Entry-Exit Inspection and Quarantine of P. R. C. or the site inspection report issued by the seller's engineer, have the right to claim for replacement with new goods, or for compensation, and all expenses (such as inspection charges, freight for returning the goods and for sending the replacement, insurance premium, storage and loading and unloading charges etc.) shall be borne by the Sellers. As regards quality, the Sellers shall guarantee that if within 12 months from the date of signing the acceptance report of this machine, damages occur in the course of operation by reason of inferior quality, bad workmanship or the use of inferior materials, the Buyers shall immediately notify the Sellers in writing and put forward a claim supported by Inspection Certificate issued by the State Administration for Entry-Exit Inspection and Quarantine of P. R. C.

练习 16

Sun Shine Lipstick

There are many colors for choice according to the age, skin's color, mouth's pattern, time and occasion. Young girls use gay color which appears lively. Middle-aged ladies use somewhat dull orange red which appears solemn. Small lips may enlarge the contour of the lips by it. You may use light colors in bright condition and with deep colors under dark occasion. The lipstick makes the lips with healthy and beautiful gloss.

Sunshine Lipsticks

Sunshine Lipsticks. Various colors available. For different ages, complexions, lip-shapes, time and occasion. Bright colors make you a cute baby. Deep colors make you a dignified lady. If you have small lips, you can enlarge the lipline accordingly. In well-lit place, light colors are suitable. With gloomy background, deep colors are desirable. Sunshine Lipsticks make your face look vital with dazzling charm.

练习 17

iPad was issued by Apple Company in 2010, positioned between Apple's iPhone and laptop computers. It has only four buttons, with the same layout of iPhone. The function of iPad is very powerful, including video, entertainment and office — all in one of the Tablet PC. It can send and receive mail, browse the web, listen to music, watch HD videos, chat, play 3D games, read e-books, read newspapers and e-magazines. You can navigate and download all kinds of software in the App Store. iPad design is very stylish, more humane, light and small as well as simple. The operation is also very simple. With a high resolution, the screen display is quite good. The material of iPad is more environment-friendly. Its battery power provides longer support. You can use it for a long time. iPad has its own CPU, operating system and core technology.

练习 18

Abstract: The study aims to explore the intelligibility of English expressions with native features from English journals in China. 139 participants including experts from English-speaking countries, Chinese university students and international students took part in the study. Text analysis, questionnaires and interviews are adopted. International students are divided into 3 groups in terms of their English levels. The results are revealed as follows: first, according to experts from English-speaking countries, what affects intelligibility is unusual collocations, terms with Chinese characteristics and publicized expressions. Second, Chinese university students and higher achievers of international students could understand 10 sentences; intermediate achievers have some difficulty comprehending the expressions; lower achievers feel most difficult. Finally, Chinese university students and higher achievers could interpret the 10 sentences well, while most intermediate and lower achievers could not give the correct interpretations of the expressions.

练习 19

This project belongs to the field of transportation technology. Road infrastructure construction has developed quickly in China. While these roads provide a lot of convenience to travelers, the rapid pace of development has greatly increased the energy usage of our transportation network and increased the adverse environmental impacts caused by roadways. For example, the harm of traffic noise to people's health is widespread, urban groundwater recharge is insufficient and causing more surface flooding, urban heat island effects are expanding, salt-based deicing during the winter destroys the environment around our roads. In order to address these problems, new techniques and materials for building our roads must be found. Therefore, Chang'an University has been conducting research on the environmental impacts of pavement since the end of 20th century; taking charge on research including the "11th Five-Year" National Science and Technology Support Program, the main contents of which include environmentally beneficial technologies such as permeable pavement, low-noise pavement, lower heat-absorbing pavement, ice and snow-thawing pavement, and exhaust-decomposing pavement.

练习 20

We should not be so romantic on the interpersonal relationship. Human beings are interesting. They tend to see his or her advantages when contacting a person for the first time. This is just like the experience that we have a meal in a restaurant. When we begin to eat the first dish or the appetizer, the impression is good. And when eating the first two main courses, we also praise them greatly. As we continue to eat, we become calmer. Then after finishing the banquet, all the disadvantages are exposed. Therefore, we divert from happiness to rage, from praise to blame and fastidiousness, from acceptance to rejection. This is because, first, when you begin to eat, you are in a hungry state. Everything is delicious when you are hungry. Everything is tasteless when you are full. Second, as you come to a restaurant, you have a fresh feeling at the moment of raising your chopsticks. The newly built toilet is also fragrant in the first three days. This is the so-called "unfamiliar effect".

附录3 大学英语四级翻译历年真题及参考译文

真题1

华山位于华阴市,距西安120千米。华山是秦岭的一部分,秦岭不仅分隔陕南与陕北,也分隔华南与华北。与从前人们常去朝拜的泰山不同,华山过去很少有人光临,因为上山的道路极其危险。然而,希望长寿的人却经常上山,因为山上生长着许多药草,特别是一些稀有的药草。自20世纪90年代安装缆车以来,参观人数大大增加。

真题2

黄山位于安徽省南部。它风景独特,尤以其日出和云海著称。要欣赏大山的宏伟壮丽,通常得向上看。但要欣赏黄山美景,就得向下看。黄山的湿润气候有利于茶树生长,是中国主要产茶地之一。这里还有许多温泉,其泉水有助于防治皮肤病。黄山是中国主要旅游目的地之一,也是摄影和传统国画最受欢迎的主题。

真题3

泰山(Mount Tai)位于山东省中部。它是中国黄河流域古代文化的发祥地之一,被誉为"五岳"之首。因其山峰险峻,景色壮丽而闻名于世。中国历代帝王都把泰山当作天的象征,纷纷到此封禅(offer sacrifices to)、祭告天地。历史上的中国文化名人都曾登临泰山,留下诗文、墨宝。泰山风景区内,现有古建筑群22处,古遗址97处,历代石碑(stele)819块,历代刻石1800处,为研究中国古代历史、书法等提供了重要而丰富的实物资料。泰山不只是一座风景山,更是一座文化山。

真题4

珠江是华南一大河系,流经广州市,是中国第三长的河流,仅次于长江和黄河。珠江三角洲是中国最发达的地区之一,面积约11 000平方千米。它在面积和人口方面也是世界上最大的城市聚集区。珠江三角洲九个最大城市共有5 700多万人口。20世纪70年代末中国改革开放以来,珠江三角洲已成为中国和世界主要经济区域和制造中心之一。

真题5

长江是亚洲最长、世界上第三长的河流。长江流经多种不同的生态系统,是诸多濒危物种的栖息地,灌溉了中国五分之一的土地。长江流域(river basin)居住着中国三分之一的人口。长江在中国历史、文化和经济上起着很大的作用。长江三角洲(delta)产出多达20%的中国国民生产总值。几千年来,长江一直被用于供水、运输和工业生产。长江上还坐落着世界最大的水电站。

真题 6

黄河是亚洲第三、世界第六长的河流。"黄"这个字描述的是其河水浑浊的颜色。黄河发源于青海,流经九个省份,最后注入渤海。黄河是中国赖以生存的几条河流之一。黄河流域(river basin)是中国古代文明的诞生地,也是中国早期历史上最繁荣的地区。然而,由于极具破坏力的洪水频发,黄河曾造成多次灾害。在过去几十年里,政府采取了各种措施防止灾害发生。

真题 7

在中国文化中,红色通常象征着好运、长寿和幸福,在春节和其他喜庆场合,红色到处可见。人们把现金作为礼物送给家人或亲密朋友时,通常放在红信封里。红色在中国流行的另一个原因是人们把它与中国革命和共产党相联系。然而,红色并不总是代表好运与快乐。因为从前死者的名字常用红色书写,用红墨水写中国人名被看成是一种冒犯行为。

真题 8

随着中国的改革开放,如今很多年轻人都喜欢举行西式婚礼。新娘在婚礼上穿着白色婚纱,因为白色被认为是纯洁的象征。然而,在中国传统文化中,白色经常是葬礼上使用的颜色。因此务必记住,白花一定不要用作祝人康复的礼物,尤其不要送给老年人或危重病人。同样,礼金也不能装在白色信封里,而要装在红色信封里。

真题 9

在中国文化中,黄颜色是一种很重要的颜色,因为它具有独特的象征意义。在封建(feudal)社会中,它象征统治者的权力和权威。那时,黄色是专为皇帝使用的颜色,皇家宫殿全都漆成黄色,皇袍总是黄色的,而普通老百姓是禁止穿黄色衣服的。在中国,黄色也是收获的象征。秋天庄稼成熟时,田野变得一片金黄。人们兴高采烈,庆祝丰收。

真题 10

乌镇是浙江的一坐古老水镇,坐落在京杭大运河畔。这是一处迷人的地方,有许多古桥、中式旅馆和餐馆。在过去一千年里,乌镇的水系和生活方式并未经历多少变化,是一座展现古文明的博物馆。乌镇所有房屋都用石木建造。数百年来,当地人沿着河边建立起了住宅和集市。无数宽敞美丽的庭院藏身于屋舍之间,游客们每到一处都会有惊喜的发现。

真题 11

功夫(Kung Fu)是中国武术(material arts)的俗称。中国武术的起源可以追溯到自卫的需要、狩猎活动以及古代中国的军事训练。它是中国传统体育运动的一种,年轻人和老年人都练。它已逐渐演变成了中国文化的独特元素。作为中国的国宝,功夫有上百种不同的风格,是世界上练得最多的武术形式。有些风格模仿了动物的动作,还有一些则受到了中国哲学思想、神话和传说的启发。

真题 12

在山东潍坊市,风筝不仅是玩具,而且还是这座城市文化的标志。潍坊以"风筝之都"而闻名,已有将近 2400 年放飞风筝的历史。传说中国古代哲学家墨子用了三年时间在潍坊制作了世界上首个风筝,但放飞的第一天风筝就坠落并摔坏了。也有人相信风筝是中国古代木匠鲁班发明的。据说他的风筝用木头和竹子制作，飞了三天后才落地。

真题 13

云南省的丽江古镇是著名的旅游目的地之一。那里的生活节奏比大多数中国城市都要缓慢。丽江到处都是美丽的自然风光，众多的少数民族同胞提供了各式各样、丰富多彩的文化让游客体验。历史上，丽江还以"爱之城"而闻名。当地人中流传着许多关于因爱而生，为爱而死的故事。如今，在中外游客眼中，这个古镇被视为爱情和浪漫的天堂。

真题 14

今年在长沙举行了一年一度的外国人汉语演讲比赛。这项比赛证明是促进中国世界其他地区文化交流的好方法。它为世界各地的年轻人提供了更好地了解中国的机会。来自87个国家共计126位选手聚集在湖南省省会参加了从7月6日到8月5日进行的半决赛和决赛。比赛并不是唯一的活动，选手们还有机会参观了中国其他地区的著名景点和历史名胜。

真题 15

中国父母往往过于关注孩子的学习，以至于不要他们帮忙做家务。他们对孩子的唯一要求就是努力学习，考得好，能上名牌大学。他们相信这是为孩子好，因为在中国这样竞争激烈的社会里，只有成绩好才能保证前途光明。中国父母还认为，如果孩子能在社会上取得大的成就，父母就会受到尊敬。因此，他们愿意牺牲自己的时间、爱好和兴趣，为孩子创造更好的条件。

真题 16

在西方人心目中，和中国联系最为密切的基本食物是大米。长期以来，大米在中国人的饮食中占据很重要的地位，以至于有谚语说"巧妇难为无米之炊"。中国南方大多数种植水稻，人们通常以大米为食；而华北大部分地区因为过于寒冷或过于干燥，无法种植水稻，那里的主要作物是小麦。在中国，有些人用面粉做面包，但大多数人用面粉做馒头和面条。

真题 17

中国是世界上最古老的文明之一。构成现在世界基础的许多元素都起源于中国。中国现在拥有世界上发展最快的经济，并经历着一次新的工业革命。中国还启动了雄心勃勃的太空探索计划，其实包括到2020年建成一个太空站。目前，中国是世界上最大的出口国之一，并正在吸引大量外国投资。同时，它也在海外投资数十亿美元。2011年，中国超越日本成为第二大经济体。

真题 18

据报道，今年中国快递服务（courier service）将递送大约120亿件包裹。这将使中国有可能赶超美国成为世界上最大的快递市场。大多数包裹里装着网上订购的物品。中国约有百万在线零售商以及其竞争力的价格销售商品的机会，仅在11月11日，中国消费者就在国内最大的购物平台买了价值90亿美元的商品。中国有不少这样的特殊购物日，因此，快递能在中国扩展就不足为奇了。

真题 19

越来越多的中国年轻人正对旅游产生兴趣，这是近年来的新趋势。年轻游客数量和不断增加，可以归于他们迅速提高的收入和探索外部世界的好奇心。随着旅行多了，年轻人在大城市和著名景点花的时间少了,他们反而更为偏远的地方所吸引,有些人甚至选择长途背包旅行。最近调查显示,很多年轻人想要通过旅行体验不同的文化,丰富知识,拓宽视野。

真题 20

中国的互联网社区是全世界发展最快的。2010 年,中国约有 4.2 亿网民(netizen),且人数还在迅速增长。互联网的日渐流行带来了重大的社会变化。中国网民往往不同于美国网民。美国网民更多的是受实际需要的驱使,用互联网为工具发电子邮件、买卖商品、规划旅程或付款。中国网民更多是出于社交原因使用互联网,因而更广泛地使用 QQ、聊天室等。

真题 21

大熊猫是一种温顺的动物,长着独特的黑白皮毛。因其数量极少,大熊猫已被列为濒危物种。大熊猫对于世界自然基金会有着特殊意义。自 1961 年该基金会成立以来,大熊猫就一直是它的徽标。大熊猫是熊科中最稀有的成员,主要生活在中国西南部的森林里。目前,世界上大约有 1 000 只大熊猫。这些以竹为食的动物正面临许多威胁。因此,确保大熊猫的生存比以往更重要。

真题 22

为了促进教育公平,中国投入 360 亿元,用于改善农村地区教育设施和加强中西部农村义务教育(compulsory education)。这些基金用于改善教学设施,购买书籍,使 116 万多所中小学受益。资金还用于购置音乐和绘画器材,现在农村和山区的儿童可以与沿海城市的儿童一样上音乐和绘画课。一些为接受更好教育而转往城市上学的学生如今又回到本地农村学校就读。

真题 23

中国进一步发展核能,因为核电目前只占其总发电量的 2%。该比例在所有核国家中居第 30 位,几乎是最低的。2011 年 3 月日本核电站事故后,中国的核能开发停了下来,中止审批新的核电站,并开展全国性的核安全检查。到 2012 年 10 月,审批才又谨慎地恢复。随着技术和安全措施的改进,发生事故的可能性完全可以降低到最低程度。换句话说,核能是可以安全开发和利用的。

真题 24

中国的教育工作者早就认识到读书对于国家的意义。有些教育工作者 2003 年就建议设立全民读书日。他们强调,人们应当读好书,尤其是经典著作。通过阅读,人们能更好地学会感恩、有责任心和与人合作,而教育的目的正是要培养这些基本素质。阅读对于中小学生尤为重要,假如他们没有在这个关键时期培养阅读的兴趣,以后要养成阅读的习惯就更难了。

真题 25

中国结最初是由手工艺人发明的,经过数百年不断的改进,已经成为一种优雅多彩的艺术和工艺。在古代,人们用它来记录事件,但现在主要是用于装饰的目的。"结"在中文里意味着爱情、婚姻和团聚,中国结常常作为礼物交换或作用饰品祈求好运和辟邪。这种形式的手工艺代代相传,现在已经在中国和世界各地越来越受欢迎。

真题 26

"你要茶还是咖啡?"是用餐人常被问到的问题,许多西方人会选咖啡,而中国人则会选茶,相传,中国的一位帝王于五千年前发现了茶,并用来治病,在明清(the qing dynasties)期间,茶馆遍布全国,饮茶在六世纪传到日本,但直到18世纪才传到欧美,如今,茶是世界上最流行的饮料(beverage)之一,茶是中国的瑰宝。也是中国传统和文化的重要组成部分。

真题 27

很多人喜欢中餐,在中国,烹饪不仅被视为一种技能,而且也被视为一种艺术。精心准备的中餐既可口又好看。烹饪技术和配料在中国各地差别很大。但好的烹饪都有一个共同点,总是要考虑到颜色、味道、口感和营养(nutrition)。由于食物对健康至关重要,好的厨师总是努力在谷物、肉类和蔬菜之间取得平衡。所以中餐美味又健康。

参考译文

真题 1

Huashan (Mount Hua) is situated in Huayin City, 120 kilometers away from Xi'an. It is part of the Qinling Mountains, which divides not only Southern and Northern Shaanxi, but also South and North China. Unlike Taishan, which became a popular place of pilgrimage, Huashan was not well visited in the past because it is dangerous for the climbers to reach its summit. Huashan was also an important place frequented by immortality seekers, as many herbs grow there especially some rare ones. Since the installation of the cable cars in the 1990s, the number of visitors has increased significantly.

真题 2

Huangshan (Yellow Mountain) is located in southern Anhui Province. The area is well known for its unique scenery, especially sunrise and sea of clouds. To enjoy the magnificence of a mountain, you have to look upwards in most cases. To enjoy Huangshan, however, you've got to look downward. Furthermore, Huangshan's moist climate facilitates the growing of teatrees; therefore the mountain is one of China's premier tea-growing areas. In addition, Huangshan has multiple hot springs which help prevent and cure skin illness. Huangshan is one of China's major tourist destinations and the most frequent subject of photography and traditional Chinese painting.

真题 3

Mount Tai locates in the middle of Shandong Province. It is one of the birthplaces of the ancient culture along the Yellow River basin, and is regarded as the head of the Five Great Mountains. Mount Tai is celebrated for its precipitous peaks and magnificent sceneries. In Chinese history, emperors of all dynasties would take a journey to Mount Tai, which was considered as the symbol of heaven, to worship and offer sacrifices to the heaven and earth. The cultural celebrities in ancient China composed numerous pieces of poems and calligraphy works after they had toured Mount Tai. Currently, there are 22 ancient architecture complexes, 97 historic sites, 819 pieces of stele, 1 800 pieces of carved stones, which provide plenty of important material evidences to make researches on Chinese ancient history and calligraphy. Mount Tai is not only a mountain of scenery, but also a mountain of culture.

真题 4

The Pearl River, China's third longest river is a major river system in Southern China and flows through the city of Guangzhou second only to the Yangtze River and the Yellow River. As the densest region of cities and population in world and one of China's most developed areas, the Pearl River delta covers an extent of about 11 000 square kilometers and resides more than 57 million people in top 9 largest cities in this area. Since China's reform and opening in the late 1970s, Pearl River delta has become one of the major economic areas and manufacturing centers of China and the world.

真题 5

The Yangtze River is the longest river in Asia, and ranks third in the world. It flows through a variety of ecosystems and becomes a habit for many endangered species. Moreover, Yangtze River also irrigates one fifth of China's farmland, and the Yangtze River basin resides one third of China's population and plays an essential role in China's history, culture and economy. The Yangtze River delta accounts for as much as 20% of China's GNP. For thousands of years, the Yangtze River has always been used for water supply, transportation and industrial production. It also settles the world's largest hydro-power station.

真题 6

The Yellow River is the third longest river in Asia and sixth-longest river in the world, the word "Yellow" in its name was derived from the color of the muddy water. Originating in Qinghai province, the Yellow River flows through nine provinces, and it empties into the Bohai Sea. The Yellow River basin was the birthplace of ancient Chinese civilization and it was the most prosperous region in early Chinese history. However, the Yellow River also caused several sever damages because of frequent devastating floods. During the past decades, the government has taken a variety of measures to prevent it.

真题 7

In Chinese culture, red symbolizes good luck, longevity and happiness. Therefore, red can be seen everywhere on the Spring Festival and other happy occasions. Cash is often enclosed in a red envelope when given as a gift to family members and close friends. Another reason why red is popular in China is that people connect it with China's revolution and the Communist Party. However, red does not always mean good luck and happiness because in the old days, names of the dead were written in red, and thus writing Chinese names in red is considered an offensive act.

真题 8

With the Reform and Opening-up of China, many young people nowadays like to hold western wedding ceremonies. The bride wears white wedding gown because white is considered to symbolize purity. However, in tradition Chinese culture, white is the color for funerals. So, do bear in mind, white flowers should not be used as a gift to celebrate someone's recovery, especially not for the aged or those who are seriously ill. Similarly, cash, as a gift, should be enclosed in red envelopes rather than white ones.

真题 9

In Chinese culture, yellow is a very important color because of its unique symbolic meaning. In feudal society, it symbolizes the rulers' power and authority. At that time, yellow was the color for the emperor. The royal palace was entirely painted yellow and the imperial robe was always yellow too, but common people were forbidden to wear yellow clothes. In China, yellow also symbolizes harvest. When crops ripe in autumn, fields turn entirely golden, people celebrate the good harvest happily.

真题 10

Wuzhen is an ancient water town in Zhejiang province, which is located in the Grand Canal of Beijing and Hangzhou. This is a charming place, having many ancient bridges, Chinese style hotels and restaurants. Over the past one thousand years, the water system and lifestyle of Wuzhen has not experienced many changes, which is a museum showing ancient civilizations. All the houses in Wuzhen are built of stone and wood. For hundreds of years, the local people built homes and fairs along the river. Countless beautiful and spacious courtyards lie among the houses, thus the tourists would have a pleasant surprise when coming to here.

真题 11

Kung Fu is the common name of Chinese martial arts. The origin of Chinese Kung Fu can be traced back to the needs of self-defense, hunting and ancient Chinese military training. It is one of the traditional Chinese sports, which is practiced by both young and senior people. It has gradually become a unique element in Chinese culture. As a national treasure of China, Kung Fu has hundreds of styles, which is the most practiced martial arts form around the world. Some features imitate the animal actions and others are enlightened by Chinese philosophical thoughts, myths and legends.

真题 12

In Weifang City, Shandong Province, the kite is a cultural symbol of the city as well as a toy for children. Weifang is known as the City of the Kite because it has a long history of two thousand four hundred years in flying the kite. It is said by some people that Motse, one of the philosophers in ancient China spent three years in making the first kite in the world, and that the kite he made crashed the first day it flew in the sky. It is also believed by others that Luban, the greatest carpenter in ancient China invented the kite, and that his kite made of wood and bamboo flew for three days before it landed on the ground.

真题 13

Lijiang, an ancient town of Yunnan Province, is one of the most famous tourist destinations. Its pace of life is slower than that of most cities of China. There are many natural beauties everywhere in Lijiang and many ethnical minorities provide tourists with a great variety of cultural experience. Lijiang is also well-known as the "city of love" in history. Many stories about life and dying for love have spreaded widely among the locals. Nowadays, for tourists home and abroad, the ancient town is regarded as a paradise of love and romance.

真题 14

The Annual Chinese Speech Contest for Foreigners was held in Changsha this year. The contest was proved to be a good way to promote cultural exchanges between China and other regions all over the world. It provides an opportunity for young people around the world to understand China better. A total of 126 players from 87 countries gathered in the capital of Hunan province to participate in the semi-final and the final from July 6th to August 5th. Competition is not the only activity. Players also have a chance to visit famous and historical attractions in other parts of China.

真题 15

Chinese parents have frequently tended to pay too much attention to their children's study, so that children don't help them do the housework. Their only requirement for their children is to study hard, perform well in the exams, and go to a famous / prestigious university. They believe it is good for their children, because in such a highly competitive society, only good results could ensure a promising future. Chinese parents also believe that parents will be honored if their children can achieve great success in society. Therefore, they are willing to sacrifice their own time, hobbies and interests, to create much better conditions for children.

真题 16

In the eyes of the western, the basic food closest to China is rice. Rice has long occupied so significant a position in the diet of Chinese that there is a proverb "Even a clever housewife cannot cook a meal without rice". Rice is grown mostly in southern China where people usually take rice as their staple food, while it cannot be planted in northern China where the climate is either too cold or too dry for rice to grow. As a result, the main crop in the north is wheat. In China, flour is sometimes the main ingredient for bread but more often used to make buns and noodles.

真题 17

China is one of the oldest cultures in the world, from which much that constructs the foundation of the modern world is derived. China is witnessing the fastest development of its economy and experiencing a new industrial revolution. Also, China has started the ambitious program for exploring the outer space, including completing a space station by 2020. Currently, being one of the largest exporters in the world, China is attracting massive foreign investment. Simultaneously, it has invested billions of dollars overseas. In 2011, China surpassed Japan as the world's second-largest economy.

真题 18

It is reported that China's express courier service will deliver about 12 billion packages this year, which will make it possible for China to overtake the United States as the world's largest express market. Most packages are filled with items ordered online. China provides opportunities to millions of online retailers to sell goods at very competitive prices. Only on November 11th, Chinese consumers bought goods worthy of $9 billion from the nation's largest shopping platform. There are many such special shopping days in China. As a result, it is no surprise at all that the expansion of express can take place in China.

真题 19

Chinese young people in mounting numbers come to be interested in tourism, which is a new trend of this year. Rising number of young tourists, can be attributed to their rapidly increase income and the curiosity to explore the outside world. With the increase of traveling, the young spend less time in big cities and famous attractions; they are more attracted to remote locations. Some people even choose backpacking trip for long-distance. Recent survey indicates that many young people want to travel to experience different culture, enrich knowledge and broaden view.

真题 20

The Chinese Internet communities are developing at the highest speed in the world. There were about 420 million netizens in China in 2010 and this numbers keeps increasing rapidly. The growing popularity of the Internet brings about significant social changes. Chinese netizens are different from their American counterparts. The latter is more motivated by real needs. They use Internet as tools of sending emails, purchasing goods, doing research, planning tours or making payments. Chinese netizens use Internet for social reasons. Therefore, Internet forums, blogs and chat rooms are more widely used.

真题 21

Giant panda is a kind of tame animal with unique black and white fur. Because of the small numbers, panda is listed as endangered species. Panda has a special meaning toward the WWF. Since the founding of the fund in 1961, panda has been its symbol. Panda, which lives in the forest of the south-west of China, is the rarest in bear species. Nowadays, there are approximately 1 000 pandas in the world. These animals whose food is mainly bamboo are under serious threat. Thus, the survival of panda is much more important than ever before.

真题 22

In order to promote equality in education, China has invested 36 billion Yuan to improve educational facilities in rural areas and strengthen rural compulsory education in Midwest areas. These funds are used to improve teaching facilities, and purchase books, which benefit more than 160 000 primary and secondary schools. Funds are used to purchase musical instrument and painting tools as well. Now children in rural and mountainous areas can have music and painting lessons just like children from coastal cities. Some students who have transferred to city schools to receive a better education are now moving back to their local rural schools.

真题 23

China should further develop nuclear energy, because nuclear power currently accounts for only 2% of the total generating capacity. The proportion is in 30th among all nuclear-capable countries, which almost the lowest。 In March 2011, after the accident of Japanese nuclear power station, China stopped its nuclear energy development, with approvals for new nuclear power plants suspended, and national nuclear safety inspection carried out. Examine and Approval has been restored carefully since October, 2012. With the improvement of technology and safety measures, the possibility of nuclear accidents can be dropped to a minimum extent. In other words, the nuclear energy can be exploited and utilized safely.

真题 24

China's education workers have realized for a long time the importance of reading to the country. Some of them have suggested that a National Reading Day be set up since 2003. They stressed that people should read good books, especially the classic works. Through reading, people can better learn to be grateful, responsible and cooperate with others. However, the purpose of education is to cultivate these basic qualities. Reading is particularly important for primary and middle school students. If they don't develop the interest of reading during this crucial period, it is difficult to form the habit of reading later.

真题 25

The Chinese knot was originally invented by the craftsmen. After hundreds of years of continuous improvement, has become a kind of elegant and colorful arts and crafts. In ancient times, people use it to record the event, but now used mainly for decorative purposes. The knot means love, marriage and reunion in Chinese, knot is often used for jewelry as a gift exchange or pray for good luck and ward off evil spirits, This form of handicrafts from generation to generation, it has become increasingly popular in China and around the world.

真题 26

"Would you like tea or coffee?" Meals are frequently asked questions, many westerners will choose coffee, and the Chinese will choose tea, according to legend, a Chinese emperor discovered tea in five thousand years ago, and used to heal, in the Ming and qing dynasties, tea houses all over the country, tea drinking spread to Japan in the 6th century and spread to Europe and the United States, but it was not until the 18th century today, tea is one of the most popular beverage in the world, tea is the treasure of China. It is also an important part of Chinese tradition and culture.

真题 27

Many people like Chinese food. In China, cooking is not only regarded as a skill but also an art form. The well / carefully-prepared Chinese food is tasty and displayed beautifully. The way of cooking and selection of ingredients vary greatly across China. However, good cooking has one thing in common, that is, to always consider colors, smell, tastes and nutrition. As food is vital for our health, good cooks always make an effort to maintain balance between grains meats and vegetables. Thus, Chinese food is both delicious and healthy.

大学英语六级翻译历年真题及参考译文

真题 1

青海湖位于海拔 3205 米、青海省省会西宁以西约 100 千米处。是中国最大的咸水湖,面积 4317 平方千米,最深处 25.5 米,有 23 条河注入湖中,其中大部分是季节性的。80% 的湖水源于五条主要河流。青海湖位于跨越亚洲的几条候鸟迁徙路线的交叉处。许多鸟类把青海湖作为迁徙过程中的暂息地,湖的西侧是著名的"鸟岛",吸引着来自世界各地的观鸟者。每年夏天,游客们也来这里观看国际自行车比赛。

真题 2

洞庭湖位于湖南省东北部,面积很大,但湖水很浅。洞庭湖是长江的蓄洪池,湖的大小很大程度上取决于季节变化,湖北和湖南两省因其与湖的相对位置而得名,湖北意为"湖的北边",而湖南则为"湖的南边"。洞庭湖作为龙舟赛的发源地,在中国文化中享有盛名。据说龙舟赛始于洞庭湖东岸。为的是搜寻楚国爱国诗人屈原的遗体。龙舟赛与洞庭湖及周边的美景,每年都吸引着成千上万来自全国和世界各地的游客。

真题 3

太湖是中国东部的一个淡水湖,占地面积 2250 平方千米,是中国第三大淡水湖,仅次于鄱阳湖和洞庭湖。太湖约有 90 个岛屿,大小从几平方米到几平方千米不等。太湖以其独特的"太湖石"而闻名,太湖石常用于装饰中国传统园林。太湖也以高产的捕鱼业闻名。自 20 世纪 70 年代后期以来,捕捞鱼蟹对沿湖的居民来说极为重要,并对周边地区的经济做出了重大贡献。太湖地区是中国陶瓷(ceramics)业基地之一,其中宜兴的陶瓷厂家生产举世闻名的宜兴紫砂壶(clay teapot)。

真题 4

唐朝始于 618 年,终于 907 年,是中国历史上最灿烂的时期。经过近三百年的发展,唐代中国成为世界上最繁荣的强国,其首都长安是当时世界上最大的都市。这一时期,经济发达、商业繁荣、社会秩序稳定,甚至边境也对外开放。随着城市化和财富的增加,艺术和文学也繁荣起来。李白和杜甫是以作品简洁自然而著称的诗人。他们的诗歌打动了学者和普通人的心。即使在今天,他们的许多诗歌仍广为儿童及成人阅读背诵。

真题 5

宋朝始于960年,一直延续到1279年。这一时期,中国经济大幅增长,成为世界上最先进的经济体,科学、技术、哲学和数学蓬勃发展,宋代中国是世界历史上首先发行纸币的国家。宋朝还最早使用火药并发明了活字(movable-type)印刷。人口增长迅速,越来越多的人住进城市,那里有热门的娱乐场所。社会生活多种多样。人们聚焦在一起观看和交易珍贵艺术品。宋朝的政府体制在当时也是先进的。政府官员均通过竞争性考试选拔任用。

真题 6

明朝统治中国276年,被人们描绘成人类历史上治理有序、社会稳定的最伟大的时代之一。这一时期,手工业的发展促进了市场经济和城市化。大量商品,包括酒和丝绸,都在市场销售。同时,还进口许多外国商品,如时钟和烟草。北京、南京、扬州、苏州这样的大商业中心相继形成。也是在明代,由郑和率领的船队曾到印度洋进行了七次大规模探险航行。还值得一提的是,中国文学的四大经典名著中有三部写于明朝。

真题 7

随着生活水平的提高,度假在中国人生活中的作用越来越重要。过去,中国人的时间主要花在谋生上,很少有机会外出旅行。然而,近年来中国旅游业发展迅速。经济的繁荣和富裕中产阶级的出现,引发了一个前所未有的旅游热潮。中国人不仅在国内旅游,出国旅游也越来越普遍。2016年国庆节假日期间,旅游消费总计超过4 000亿元。据世界贸易组织估计,2020年中国将成为世界上最大的旅游国,在未来几年里将成为出境旅游支出增长最快的国家。

真题 8

随着中国经济的蓬勃发展,学汉语的人数迅速增加,使汉语成了世界上人们最爱学的语言之一。近年来,中国大学在国际上的排名也有了明显的提高。由于中国教育的巨大进步,中国成为最受海外学生欢迎的留学目的地之一就不足为奇了。2015年,近40万国际学生蜂拥来到中国市场。他们学习的科目不再限于中国语言和文化,而包括科学与工程。在全球教育市场上,美国和英国仍占主导地位,但中国正在迅速赶上。

真题 9

农业是中国的一个重要产业,从业者超过3亿。中国农业产量全球第一,主要生产水稻、小麦和豆类。虽然中国的农业用地仅占世界的百分之十,但为世界百分之二十的人提供了粮食。中国7700年前开始种植水稻。早在使用机械和化肥之前,勤劳和富有创造性的中国农民就已经采用各种各样的方法来增加农作物产量。中国农业最近的发展是推进有机农业。有机农业可以同时服务于多种目的,包括食品安全,大众健康和可持续发展。

真题 10

中国的创新正以前所未有的速度蓬勃发展。为了在科学技术上尽快赶超世界发达国家,中国近年来大幅度增加了研究开发资金。中国的大学和研究所正在积极开展创新研究,这些研究覆盖了从大数据到生物化学,从新能源到机器人等各类高科技领域。它们还与各地的科技园合作,使创新成果商业化。与此同时,无论在产品还是商业模式上,中国企业家也在努力争做创新的先锋,以适应国内外消费市场不断变化和增长的需求。

真题 11

深圳是中国广东省一座新开发的城市。在改革开放之前,深圳不过是一个渔村,仅有三万多人。20世纪80年代,中国政府创建了深圳经济特区,作为实施社会主义市场经济的试验田。如今,深圳的人口已超过1 000万,整个城市发生了巨大的变化。

到2014年,深圳的人均(per-capita) GDP已达25 000美元,相当于世界上一些发达国家的水平。就综合经济实力而言,深圳居于中国顶尖城市之列。由于其独特的地位,深圳也是国内外企业家创业的理想之地。

真题 12

旗袍(qipao)是一种雅致的中国服装,源于中国的满族(Manchu Nationality)。在清代,旗袍是王室女性穿着的宽松长袍。20世纪20年代,受西方服饰的影响,旗袍发生了一些变化。袖口(cuffs)变窄,袍身变短。这些变化使女性美得以充分展现。

如今,旗袍经常出现在世界级的时装秀上。中国女性出席重要社交聚会时,旗袍往往是她们的首选。很多中国新娘也会选择旗袍作为结婚礼服。一些有影响的人士甚至建议将旗袍作为中国女性的民族服饰。

真题 13

在中国,父母总是竭力帮助孩子,甚至为孩子做重要决定,而不管孩子想要什么,因为他们相信这样做是为孩子好。结果,孩子的成长和教育往往屈从于父母的意愿。如果父母决定为孩子报名参加一个课外班,以增加其被重点学校录取的机会,他们会坚持自己的决定,即使孩子根本不感兴趣。

然而在美国,父母可能会尊重孩子的意见,并在决策时更注重他们的意见。中国父母十分重视教育或许值得称赞。然而,他们应该向美国父母学习在涉及教育时如何平衡父母与子女间的关系。

真题 14

最近,中国政府决定将其工业升级,中国现在涉足建造高速列车、远洋船舶、机器人,甚至飞机。不久前,中国获得了在印度尼西亚(Indonesia)建造一条高铁的合同;中国还与马来西亚(Malaysia)签署了为其提供高速列车的合同。这证明人们信赖中国造产品。

中国造产品越来越受欢迎。中国为此付出了代价,但这确实有助于消除贫困,同时还为世界各地的人们提供了就业机会。这是一件好事,值得称赞。下次你去商店时,可能想看一看你所购商品的出产国名。很有可能这件商品是中国造的。

真题 15

在帮助国际社会于2030年前消除极端贫困过程中,中国正扮演着越来越重要的角色。自20世纪70年代末实施改革开放以来,中国已使多达4亿人摆脱了贫困。在未来五年中,中国将向其他发展中国家在减少贫困、发展教育、农业现代化、环境保护和医疗保健等方面提供援助。

中国在减少贫困方面取得了显著进步,并在促进经济增长方面做出了不懈努力,这将鼓励其他贫困国家应对自身发展中的挑战。在寻求具有自身特色的发展道路时,这些国家可以借鉴中国的经验。

真题 16

中国传统的待客之道要求饭菜丰富多样,让客人吃不完。中国宴席上典型的菜单包括开席的一套凉菜及其后的热菜,例如肉类、鸡鸭、蔬菜等。大多数宴席上,全鱼被认为是必不可少的,除非已经上过各式海鲜。如今,中国人喜欢把西方特色菜与传统中式菜肴融于一席,因此牛排上桌也不少见。沙拉也已流行起来,尽管传统上中国人一般不吃任何未经烹饪的菜肴。宴席通常至少有一道汤,可以最先上或最后上桌。甜点和水果通常标志宴席的结束。

真题 17

2011年是中国城市化(urbanization)进程中的历史性时刻,其城市人口首次超过农村人口。在未来20年里,预计有3.5亿农村人口将移居城市。如此规模的城市发展对城市交通来说既是挑战,也是机遇。中国政府一直提倡"以人为本"的发展理念,强调人们以公交而不是私家车出行。它还号召建设"资源节约和环境友好型"社会。有了这个明确的目标,中国城市就可以更好地规划其发展,并把大量投资转向安全、清洁和经济型交通系统的发展上。

真题 18

汉朝是中国历史上最重要的朝代之一,汉朝统治期间有很多显著的成就。它最先向其他文化敞开大门,对外贸易兴旺。汉朝开拓的丝绸之路通向了中西亚乃至罗马。各类艺术一派繁荣,涌现了很多文学历史哲学巨著。公元100年中国第一部字典编撰完成,收入9 000个字,提供释义并列举不同的写法。期间科技方面也取得很大进步。发明纸张水中日晷(sundials),以及测量地震的仪器。汉朝经历了四百年,但统治者的腐败导致了它的灭亡。

真题 19

反应在艺术和文学中的乡村生活理想是中国文明的重要特征。这在很大程度上归功于道家对自然的感情。传统中国画有两个最受青睐的主题,一个是家庭生活的各种幸福场景,画中往往有老人在下棋饮茶,男人在耕耘收割,妇女在织布缝衣,小孩在户外玩耍。另一个是乡村生活的种种乐趣,画有渔夫在湖上打鱼,农夫在山上砍柴采药,或是书生坐在松树下吟诗作画。这两个主题可以分别代表儒家和道家的生活理想。

真题 20

中国将努力确保到2015年就业者接受过平均13.3年的教育。如果这一目标得以实现,今后大部分进入劳动力市场的人都需获得大学文凭。在未来几年,中国将着力增加职业学院的招生人数;除了关注高等教育外,还将寻找新的突破以确保教育制度更加公平。中国正在努力最佳地利用教育资源,这样农村和欠发达地区将获得更多的支持。教育部还决定改善欠发达地区学生的营养,并为外来务工人员的子女提供在城市接受教育的同等机会。

真题 21

自从1978年启动改革以来,中国已从计划经济转为以市场为基础的经济,经历了经济和社会的快速发展。平均10%的GDP增长已使五亿多人脱贫。联合国的"千年(millennium)发展目标"在中国均已达到或即将达到。目前,中国的第十二个五年规划强调发展服务业和解决环境及社会不平衡的问题。政府已设定目标减少污染,提高能源效率,改善得到教育和医保的机会,并扩大社会保障。中国现在7%的经济年增长目标表明政府是在重视生活质量而不是增长速度。

真题22

中文热词通常反映社会变化和文化,有些在外国媒体上越来越流行。例如,土豪和大妈都是老词,但已获取了新的意义。

土豪以前指欺压佃户和仆人的乡村地主,现在用于指花钱如流水或喜欢炫耀财富的人,也就是说,土豪有钱,但是没有品位。大妈是对中年妇女的称呼,但是现在特指不久前金价大跌时大量购买黄金的中国妇女。

土豪和大妈可能会被收入新版的牛津(Oxford)英语词典,至今约有120中文加进了牛津英语词典,成了英语语言的一部分。

真题23

北京计划未来三年投资7 600亿元治理污染,从减少 $PM_{2.5}$ 排放入手。这一新公布的计划旨在减少四种主要污染源,包括500万辆机动车的尾气排放、周边地区燃煤、来自北方的沙尘暴和本地的建筑灰尘,另外850亿元用于新建或升级城市垃圾处理和污水处理设施,加上300亿元投资未来三年的植树造林。

市政府还计划建造一批水循环利用工厂,并制止违章建筑,以改善环境。另外,北京还将更严厉地处罚违反减排规定的行为。

真题24

最近中国科学院出版了关于其最新科学发展与未来一年展望的年度系列报告。该报告包括三部分:科学发展报告,高技术发展报告,中国可持续战略报告。第一份报告包含中国科学家的最新发现,诸如新粒子研究与H7N9病毒研究的突破。该报告还突出强调了未来几年需要关注的问题。第二份报告公布了一些应用科学研究的热门领域,如3D打印和人造器官研究。第三份报告呼吁加强顶层设计,以消除工业升级中的结构性障碍,并促进节能减排。

真题25

中国园林是经过三千多年演变而成的独具一格的园林景观。它既包括为皇室成员享乐而建造的大型花园,也包括学者、商人和卸任的政府官员为摆脱嘈杂的外部世界而建造的私家花园。这些花园构成了一种意在表达人与自然之间应有的和谐关系的微缩景观。典型的中国园林四周有围墙,园内有池塘、假山、树木、花草以及各种各样由蜿蜒的小路和走廊连接的建筑。漫步在花园中,人们可以看到一系列精心设计的景观犹如山水画卷一般展现在面前。

真题26

中国人自古以来就在中秋时节庆祝丰收,这与北美地区庆祝感恩节的习俗十分相似,过中秋节的习俗于唐代早期在中国各地开始流行,中秋节在农历八月十五,是人们拜月的节日,这天夜晚皓月当空,人们合家团聚,共赏明月。2006年,中秋节被列为中国的文化遗产,2008年又被定为公共假日,月饼被视为中秋节不可或缺的美食,人们将月饼作为礼物馈赠亲友或在家庭聚会上享用。传统的月饼上带有"寿"(longevity)、"福"或"和"等字样。

真题27

闻名于世的丝绸之路是一系列连接东西方的路线。丝绸之路延伸6 000多千米。得名于古代中国的丝绸贸易。丝绸之路上的贸易在中国、南亚、欧洲和中东文明发展中发挥了重要作用。正是通过丝绸之路,中国的造纸、火药、指南针、印刷等四大发明才被引介到世界各地。同样,中国的丝绸、茶叶和瓷器(porcelain)也传遍全球。物质文化的交流是双向的。欧洲也通过丝绸之路出口各种商品和植物,满足中国市场的需要。

参考译文

真题 1

3 205 meters above (the) sea level, Qinghai Lake is located about 100 kilometers west of Xining, capital of Qinghai province in western China. Qinghai Lake, the largest saline lake in the country, has a surface area of 4 317 square kilometers with a maximum depth of 25.5 meters. Most of the 23 rivers and streams that empty into Qinghai Lake are seasonal. Five major streams provide 80% of the lake's total influx. Located at the crossroads of several bird migration routes across Asia, Qinghai Lake offers many species an intermediate stop during their migration. On the western side of the lake are the well-known "Bird Islands", which attract birdwatchers from across the globe. Every summer sees numerous visitors come here to watch the Qinghai Lake International Cycling Race.

真题 2

Dongting Lake is a large, shallow lake in northeastern Hunan province, China. It is a flood basin of the Yangtze River. Hence, the lake's size depends on the season. The provinces of Hubei and Hunan are named after their location relative to the lake. Hubei means "North of the Lake" and Hunan, "South of the Lake". Dongting Lake is famous in Chinese culture as the birthplace of dragon boat racing, which is said to have begun on the eastern shores of Dongting Lake as a search for the body of Qu Yuan, the Chu poet (340—278 B.C.). Together with the lake and its surrounding beauty, the racing appeals to thousands of tourists from others parts of China and beyond each year.

真题 3

With an area of 2 250 square kilometers, Lake Tai or Lake Taihu is the third largest freshwater lake after Poyang Lake and Dongting Lake. The lake in eastern China houses about 90 islands, ranging in size from a few square meters to several square kilometers. The lake is renowned for its unique limestone formations or "Taihu stones", which are often prized as a decorating material for traditional Chinese gardens/are employed to decorate traditional Chinese gardens. The lake is also known for its productive fishing industry. Since the late 1970s, harvesting fish and crabs has been invaluable to people living along the lake and has contributed significantly to the economy of the surrounding area. The lake is home to an extensive ceramics industry, including the Yixing pottery factory, which produces the world-renowned Yixing clay teapots.

真题 4

The Tang dynasty, which began in 618 and ended in 907, is generally regarded as the most prosperous period in Chinese history. After three hundred years of development, the Tang Dynasty has become the most prosperous power around the world. Its capital Chang'an was the largest city in the world at that time. During this period, economy developed, commerce thrived, social order was stable, and even the border was open to the outside. Wealth increased due to urbanization, art and literature also flourished. Li Bai and Du Fu are poets who are renowned for their simple and natural writing style. Their poems touched the hearts of scholars and ordinary people; even today, many of their poems are still widely read and recited by children and adults.

真题 5

The Song dynasty began from 960 and ended in 1279. During the period, China had witnessed huge growth in the economy, making it the most advanced economy in the world. Science and technology, philosophy and mathematics also flourished at that time. In the Song dynasty, China was the first country in the world to issue paper money, use gunpowder and invent movable-type printing. With rapidly increasing population, more and more people moved into the city, in which entertainment venues were very busy. People could enjoy various social life, getting together to appreciate and trade precious artworks. The Song dynasty also enjoyed an advanced government system in the world. All of the government officials were selected and appointed through the competitive examination.

真题 6

The Ming Dynasty, which reigned China for 276 years, is described as one of the greatest epochs with orderly governance and social stability in human history. During this period, the development of handicraft industry promoted the development of market economy and urbanization. Large scale of commodities, including wine and silk, were sold in the market. Meanwhile, many foreign goods such as clocks and tobacco were imported. Business centers like Beijing, Nanjing, Yangzhou, Suzhou were taking shape in succession. It was also in Ming Dynasty that Zheng He led the seven large-scale expeditions to the Indian Ocean. Particularly worth mentioning is that three of the four great classics in Chinese literature are written during the Ming Dynasty.

真题 7

With the improvement of living standards, vacation is playing an increasingly important role in Chinese people's life. In the past, Chinese people mainly spent their time on earning a living and seldom did they have the opportunities to travel abroad. However, the recent years has witnessed a fast development of China's tourism industry. The boom of economy and emergence of the affluent middle class, has triggered an unprecedented tourism boom. Chinese people are not only traveling within China, but traveling abroad is also becoming more and more popular. During the National Day holiday of 2016, the consumption of tourism adds up to more than 400 billion. According to the estimate of the WTO, China will become the country with the largest tourism industry in the world in 2020, and it will become the country with the fastest consumption increase in traveling abroad in the next few years.

真题 8

As China's economy booms, there is a dramatic increase in the number of people learning Chinese, which makes it become one of the most popular languages. In recent years, international ranks of Chinese universities have apparently boosted. Owing to the progress of Chinese education, it is not odd that China has become one of the most favorite destinations for oversea students studying abroad. In 2015, around four hundred thousand international students piled into China to study. What they learn is no more limited to the subjects of Chinese and Chinese culture, they also learn science and engineering. In the global education market, America and Britain still play dominant roles, while China is catching up.

真题 9

Agriculture is one of the most important industries in China which embraces more than 300 million workers. China's agriculture output ranks the first all over the word, and it mainly produce rice, wheat and beans. China provides 20 percent of the world food, though its agriculture land only accounts for 10% of the world's total. China's history of planting rice dates back as early as 7 700 B. C. Long before the use of machinery and fertilizers, industrious and creative farmers had already used different kinds of methods to increase crop yields. The latest trend of the agriculture development in China is to promote organic agriculture. And the organic agriculture can serve a variety of purposes, which including food safety, public health and sustainable development.

真题 10

China's innovation is booming at an unprecedented speed. In order to catch up with the developed countries in the world in science and technology as soon as possible, China has increased dramatically in recent years. The research and development is extremely rapid. China's universities and research institutes are actively carrying out innovative researches. These studies cover from large data to biochemistry, new energy to the robot and other high-tech fields. They also work with the park, which is an innovation commercialization. At the same time, either in products or business models, Chinese entrepreneurs are also trying to be the pioneers of innovation, aiming at adapting to consumers' market, which has constantly changing and growing demand both at home and abroad.

真题 11

Shenzhen, a newly-developing country in Guangdong Province, China, was only a fishing village with about 30 000 population before the Reform and Opening up. In 1980s, Chinese government made Shenzhen the special economic zone as the experimental field of the market-oriented economy. Now, Shenzhen, with population of over 100 million, has witnessed its own radical changes.

In 2014, the per-capita GDP of Shenzhen has been 25 000 dollars, the level of some developed countries in the world. As for the comprehensive power, Shenzhen has been ranked the top among Chinese cities. Shenzhen's unique geographic position brings both domestic and overseas entrepreneurs an ideal place to start their career.

真题 12

Qipao, as an exquisite Chinese clothing, originates from China's Manchu Nationality. In the Qing Dynasty, it was a loose robe specially for the royal women. In the 1920s, influenced by Western clothing, it embraced many changes, for example, narrower the cuffs and shorter the dress. These changes enabled Qipao to fully express women's beauty. Nowadays, Qipao quite often appears on world-class fashion shows. It is usually the first choice for Chinese women as they attend social parties. Meanwhile, many Chinese brides will select it as their wedding dress. Some influential personalities even suggest making it as the national costume for Chinese women.

真题 13

Parents in China are always trying to help their children, even to make the most important decision for them, regardless of what the children really want, because parents believe it's all for the benefit of their children. This has led to the result that the children's growth and education tend to give way to their parents' wishes. Once the parents decide to sign up an afterschool class for their children in order to increase their chance of being admitted to a good school, they will stick on their decision, even their children have no interest in it at all. In America, however, parents tend to respect their children, especially when making decisions. Perhaps it is commendable that Chinese parents lay much importance on education, but Chinese parents still need to keep the balance between the parents and children in the perspective of education as the American parents do.

真题 14

Recently, the Chinese government decided to upgrade its industry. China is now involved in the construction of high-speed trains, ocean ships, robots, and even aircraft. Not long ago, China signed a contract to build a high-speed rail in Indonesia. China also signed a contract with Malaysia to provide high-speed trains. These facts prove that people rely on Chinese-made products.

Products made in China are becoming more and more popular. China has paid a price for it, but it does help to eliminate poverty. At the same time, it provides employment opportunities for people all over the world. This is a good thing to be praised. The next time you go to the store, you may want to take a look at the home of your purchase. Chances is made in China.

真题 15

In the process of helping global communities to terminate extreme poverty by 2030, the role China plays enjoys an increasing level of significance. 400 million people have already gotten rid of poverty since the 1970s, when the reforming and opening up policy started. In the five years to come, China is going to provide the other developing countries with the help in terms of the elimination of poverty, the development of education, the modernization of agriculture, environmental protection as well as medical care.

The progress made by China in the elimination of poverty is obviously great and China has been making persistent efforts in promoting the economic growth, which serves as an example to inspire other developing countries to confront with challenges in their own development. The Chinese experience could help a lot in the search of the development patterns with their own characters.

真题 16

The traditional Chinese hospitality requires food diversity, so that guests will be full before eating up all the dishes. A typical Chinese banquet menu includes cold dishes served at the beginning, followed by hot dishes, such as meat, poultry, vegetables, etc. At most banquets, the whole fish is considered to be essential, unless various kinds of seafood have been served already. Today, Chinese people would like to combine Western specialties with traditional Chinese dishes. Therefore, it is not rare to see steak being served as well. Salad is gaining popularity, although traditionally the Chinese people generally do not eat any food without cooking. There is usually at least a bowl of soup, served at the beginning or in the end of the dinner party. Desserts and fruit usually mark the end of the feast.

真题 17

The 2011 is a historic moment in Chinese urbanization process, when the urban population surpassed the rural population for the first time. During the next 20 years, it is estimated that about 350 million rural population will move to cities. Such large-scale of urbanization is both a challenge and an opportunity to the urban traffic. The Chinese government has always been advocating "people-oriented" developing concept, emphasizing that people should travel by buses instead of by private cars. It also calls for the construction of "resource saving and environment friendly" society. With this explicit goal, China can have a better-planned urbanization process, and therefore divert more investment to the development of safe, clean and economical transportation system.

真题 18

The Han Dynasty is one of the most significant dynasties in the history of China and it attained lots of remarkable achievements during the reign. The Han Dynasty is the first in opening its door to other cultures, with the foreign trade prosperous. The Silk Road exploited in Han Dynasty lead to the central and west part of Asia, even Rome. The schools of art also present a state of flourish, springing up lots of monumental works in literature, history and philosophy. The first dictionary in China was compiled and finished in 100 A. D., which not only contains nine thousand Chinese characters, but also offers paraphrases and examples of different writing skills. Science and technology also made much progress during this period. People invented water clock, sundials and the instruments that can predict the earthquake. The Han Dynasty witnessed four hundred years and went to doom because of governors' decadent.

真题 19

The ideal of country life reflected by the art and literature is the important feature of Chinese culture, which is, to a large degree, attributed to the feelings to the nature from Taoist. There are two most popular topics in the traditional Chinese painting. One is the various scenes of happiness about family life, in which the old man often plays chess and drinks tea, with the man in the harvest, woman in weaving, children playing out of doors. The other scene is all kinds of pleasures about country life, in which the fisherman is fishing on the lake, with the farmer cutting wood and gathering herbs in the mountains and the scholar chanting poetry and painting pictures. sitting under the pine trees. The two themes can represent the life ideal of Confucianism and Taoism.

真题 20

China will endeavor to ensure every employee to have average 13. 3 years of education. If the goal is achieved, a majority of people entering the labor market will be having Bachelor's degree. In the next few years, China will increase the number of people in vocational college. Except focusing on the higher education, the government will find a breakthrough point to ensure the justice of education. China is trying to optimize education resources and, accordingly, the countryside as well as the less developed areas will receive more support. In addition, the education ministry decides to improve the nutrition of students in less developed areas and provides equal opportunities for the children of workers from out of town to receive education in the city.

真题 21

Since the reform in 1978, with the rapid development of economy and society, Chinese economy has transferred into market economy from command economy. The average 10% growth of GDP has lifted more than 500 million people out of poverty. The Millennium Goal of the U. N. has been fully or partially achieved throughout China. At present, the 12th Five-year Plan in China emphasizes the development of service industry and the solution of imbalance of environment and society. The government has set goals to reduce pollution, enhance energy efficiency, improve educational opportunities and medical insurance and expand social security. The 7% growth annual goal demonstrates that the government is concentrating on the quality of life rather than the speed of growth.

真题 22

Chinese hot words are usually been regarded as a reflection of the social change and a reflection of some certain culture phenomena, some of which are quite popular in the foreign media. Tuhao and dama, for example, are both old words, but in nowadays, they have gained the new meanings.

Tuhao was used to refer to Local tyrants or village landlords who oppressed tenants and servants before, but now, the word is used to refer the people who spend money like water or the people who like to show off their wealth. It means that Tuhaos are rich, but they have no taste. Dama is the appellation for middle-aged woman, but now it is used to describe the Chinese women who rushed to purchase gold when the gold priced plunged sharply not long ago.

Tuhao and dama are likely to be included into the new edition of Oxford Dictionary. Up to now, about 120 Chinese words have been included into Oxford Dictionary, and these words have woven themselves into the texture of the English language.

真题 23

Beijing is going to invest 760 billion yuan to curb environmental pollution in the next three years, starting from reducing the emissions of PM 2.5 emissions. The newly announced plan is intended to reduce the four major sources of pollution, including emissions of 5 million motor vehicles, coal-burning in surrounding areas, sandstorms from the north and construction dust in the locality. Another 85 billion yuan is used for establishing or upgrading the facilities of municipal waste treatment and sewage treatment. Besides, 30 billion yuan invests to the afforestation program in the next three years.

In order to improve the environment, the municipal government also plans to build a good number of plants which can use recycled water and to stop illegal construction. In addition, Beijing will punish those people who violate the regulations of emission-reduction more severely.

真题 24

Recently Chinese Academy of Science published annual report on the latest scientific development and the expectations for the coming year in a series. The report is composed of three parts: scientific development report, high-tech development report and Chinese sustainable strategy report. The first report includes Chinese scientists' recent discoveries, such as the breakthrough in the research field of new particle and H7N9 virus. It also emphasizes the issues we need to pay attention in the next years. The second report announces some hot areas in applied scientific study, like 3D printing and artificial organ. The third report appeals to strengthen the top-level design so as to eliminate structural obstacle in industrial upgrading and promote energy-saving and emission-reduction.

真题 25

After 3 000 years of evolvement, Chinese gardens have become a unique landscape. This includes both large gardens built as entertainment venues for royal family, and private gardens built as secluded retreats for scholars, merchants and retired government officials. These gardens have constituted a miniature that is designed in praise of the harmony between man and nature. A typical Chinese garden is surrounded by walls and consists of various buildings linked by winding trails and corridors, with ponds, rockeries, trees, and flowers scattered in it. Wandering in such a well-designed garden, people may feel that they are walking in a landscape painting.

真题 26

Since ancient times, the Chinese people usually celebrate harvest in the Mid-Autumn, which is similar to the custom of celebrating Thanksgiving in the North America. The tradition of celebrating Mid-Autumn festival became popular throughout China in the early Tang dynasty. The lunar August 15 is a day for people worshiping the moon. On this day, under the dazzling bright moon, families reunite and enjoy the moon's beauty. In 2006, Mid-Autumn festival was listed as one of China's cultural heritage, and in 2008, it was classified as a public holiday. Moon cakes, as indispensable delicious food of the festival, were gifts people sent to families and friends during the festival and usually eaten on family gatherings. There are characters of "longevity" "good fortune" and "harmony" on the Traditional moon cakes.

真题 27

The world-renowned Silk Road is a series of routes connecting the East and the West. It extended more than 6 000 kilometers. The Silk Road was named after ancient China's silk trade which played an important role in the civilization development of China, South Asia, Europe and the Middle East. It was through the Silk Road that papermaking, gunpowder, compass and printing of the four great inventions of ancient China were introduced around the world. Similarly, Chinese silk, tea and porcelain spread all over the world. Europe also exported various goods and plants through the Silk Road to meet the needs of the Chinese market.

参考文献

[1] Halliday M. A. K., Hasan R. Cohesion in English[M]. London：Longman，1976.
[2] Newmark P. Approaches to Translation[M]. Shanghai：Shanghai Foreign Language Education Press，2001.
[3] Nida, Eugene A. Towards Science of Translation[M]. Holland：Brill Academic Publishers，2003.
[4] 包彩霞. 动态与静态——谈汉译英中汉语动词的处理[J]. 北京第二外国语学院学报，2006（6）：17-32.
[5] 蔡基刚. 英汉汉英段落翻译与实践[M]. 上海：复旦大学出版社，2001.
[6] 崔永禄. 文学翻译佳作对比赏析[M]. 天津：南开大学出版社，2000.
[7] 丁大刚. 旅游英语的语言特点与翻译[M]. 上海：上海交通大学出版社，2008.
[8] 丁衡祁. 汉英翻译实践是再创作的过程[J]. 中国翻译，2005(5)：25-29.
[9] 董晓波，陈钟梅. 商务翻译概论[M]. 北京：对外经济贸易大学出版社，2014.
[10] 丰国钦. 汉英词汇对比[M]. 北京：清华大学出版社，2016.
[11] 方梦之. 译学词典[C]. 上海：上海外语教育出版社，2004.
[12] 方梦之，毛忠明. 英汉—汉英应用翻译教程[M]. 上海：上海外语教育出版社，2004.
[13] 冯庆华. 文体翻译论[M]. 上海：上海外语教育出版社，2002.
[14] 冯庆华. 实用翻译教程（英汉互译）[M]. 上海：上海教育出版社，2010.
[15] 冯庆华，陈科芳. 汉英翻译基础教程[M]. 北京：高等教育出版社，2008.
[16] 郭富强. 意合与形合的汉英对比研究[D]. 上海：华东师范大学，2006.
[17] 郭建中. 翻译中的文化因素：异化与归化[J]. 外国语（上海外国语大学学报），1998(2)：13-20.
[18] 葛瑞红. 例谈中文科技论文摘要的翻译[J]. 湖北工业大学学报，2012(6)：94-98.
[19] 何家弘. 法律英语[M]. 北京：法律出版社，2004.
[20] 何善芬. 英汉语言对比研究[M]. 上海：上海外语教育出版社，2002.
[21] 黄国文. 从《天净沙·秋思》的英译文看"形式对等"的重要性[J]. 中国翻译，2003(2)：21-23.
[22] 何青芳，陆琪青. 中外科技报告的检索方法与获取途径[J]. 现代情报，2005(9)：116-118.
[23] 胡壮麟. 语篇的衔接与连贯[M]. 上海：上海外语教育出版社，1994.
[24] 贾文波. 文本类型的翻译策略导向——"异化""归化"讨论后的思考[J]. 上海科技翻

译,2004(3):6-11.
[25] 李长栓. 非文学翻译理论与实践[M]. 北京:中国对外翻译出版公司,2004.
[26] 李静,钱晗颖. 实用商务英语翻译[M]. 南京:东南大学出版社,2014.
[27] 李克兴,张新红. 法律文本与法律翻译[M]. 北京:中国对外翻译出版公司,2006.
[28] 刘宓庆. 翻译教学:实务与理论[M]. 北京:中国对外翻译出版公司,2003.
[29] 刘宓庆. 文化翻译论纲[M]. 修订本. 北京:中国对外翻译出版公司,2007.
[30] 刘宓庆. 新编汉英对比与翻译[M]. 北京:中国对外翻译出版公司,2006.
[31] 刘士聪. 英汉·汉英美文翻译与鉴赏:英汉对照[M]. 南京:译林出版社,2010.
[32] 连淑能. 论中西思维方式[J]. 外语与外语教学,2002(2):40-46.
[33] 连淑能. 英汉对比研究[M]. 北京:高等教育出版社,2006.
[34] 骆世平. 英语习语研究[M]. 上海:上海外语教育出版社,2006.
[35] 李运兴. 语篇翻译引论[M]. 北京:中国外翻译出版公司,2000.
[36] 王东风. 归化与异化:矛与盾的交锋[J]. 中国翻译,2002(5):24-26.
[37] 魏羽,高宝萍. 汉英科技翻译教程[M]. 西安:西北工业大学出版社,2010.
[38] 许峰. 实用文体翻译理论与实践[M]. 郑州:河南大学出版社,2015.
[39] 许卉艳. 科技英汉互译教程[M]. 北京:知识产权出版社,2015.
[40] 许钧. 文学翻译的理论与实践:翻译对话录(增订本)[M]. 南京:译林出版社,2010.
[41] 许明武. 新闻英语与翻译[M]. 北京:中国对外翻译出版公司,2003.
[42] 苑春鸣,姜丽. 商务英语翻译[M]. 北京:外语教学与研究出版社,2013.
[43] 杨全红. 汉英翻译词语初探[M]. 上海:汉语大辞典出版社,2003.
[44] 杨永林. 标志翻译1000例(理论篇)[M]. 北京:高等教育出版社,2013.
[45] 张德禄. 汉英语篇连贯机制对比研究[J]. 中国海洋大学学报(社会科学版),2008(4):31-35.
[46] 张美芳. 文本类型理论及其对翻译研究的启示[J]. 中国翻译,2009(5):53-60.
[47] 张培基. 英汉翻译教程[M]. 上海:上海外语教育出版社,2009.
[48] 朱植德. 专利说明书的英译策略[J]. 中国翻译,2008(2):66-70.